$25⁰⁰

Terrorism in America

SUNY Series in
New Directions in Crime and Justice Studies

Austin T. Turk, Editor

Terrorism in America

Pipe Bombs and Pipe Dreams

Brent L. Smith

Foreword by
Austin T. Turk

STATE UNIVERSITY OF NEW YORK PRESS

Production by Ruth Fisher
Marketing by Fran Keneston

Published by
State University of New York Press, Albany

For information, address the State University of New York Press,
State University Plaza, Albany, NY 12246

Library of Congress Cataloging-in-Publication Data

Smith, Brent L.
    Terrorism in America : pipe bombs and pipe dreams / Brent L. Smith.
        p.   cm. — (SUNY series in new directions in crime and justice
studies)
    Includes bibliographical references and index.
    ISBN 0-7914-1759-X (acid free). — ISBN 0-7914-1760-3 (pbk. : acid
free)
    1. Terrorists—United States.   2. Terrorists—United States—
Psychology.   3. Terrorism—United States.   I. Title.   II. Series.
HV6432.S63   1994
303.6'25'0973—dc20   93-6941
                                                                          CIP

10 9 8 7 6 5 4 3 2 1

In Memory of
Johnie Virgil Smith
1926–1990

Contents

Foreword

Austin T. Turk

This is an important work. Previous studies of terrorism have been driven mainly by operational and ideological concerns, and accordingly have contributed little to the development of criminological theory—i.e., predictively useful causal generalizations about the contexts, causation, and consequences of illegal behavior. Even specialists in research on political violence have had surprisingly little to offer specifically to our understanding of terrorism (with the notable exception of Ted Robert Gurr's work on "oppositional terrorism"), while the few criminologists especially interested in political criminality have tended to deal only tangentially and selectively with aspects of terrorism instead of systematically investigating terrorism as such.

Brent Smith offers here not only the most systematic empirical analysis yet of terrorism in modern America but also a suggestive effort to link his findings to theoretical propositions about criminal behavior, societal reaction (labeling), social conflict, and social change. In a refreshing departure from the usual practice of attempting yet another abstract definition of terrorism, he accepts the FBI's definition—which focuses his study on unlawful acts by persons associated with organizations identified as using violence "to intimidate or coerce" for political reasons. While this precludes examining the use of terror by state agents and isolated individuals, it does facilitate analysis of the data obtained from the FBI's Terrorist Research and Analytical Center and federal court records.

The considerable effort which was required to locate and access the records on persons indicted during the 1980s has paid off in our now having available the most comprehensive report ever generated on the characteristics of terrorists active in the United States. Moreover, we have here an informative case study detailing the impact of political and legal developments on counterterrorist policies and operations.

Several bits of conventional wisdom about terrorists are refuted by the evidence. For example, political extremist violence is not youthful excess but the considered tactic of older "thirty-something" activists. This is especially true for rightists, who typically do not begin their political violence until in their thirties. Rightist domestic terrorism is a greater threat than leftist terrorism, and is increasing, while leftist terrorism is decreasing. The notion that domestic terrorists are mostly either "over-educated" higher class students or nonwhite militants is contradicted by the finding that rightist terrorists come mainly from the less educated and lower end of the white social ladder. Although women are prominent in leftist terrorist groups, they are virtually nonexistent in rightist organizations despite concerns voiced by some commentators about violence promulgated or encouraged by "KKK mothers."

Similarly, some widely held beliefs about counterterrorist operations are inconsistent with the evidence. Perhaps the biggest surprises to some readers will be the findings that the constitutional rights of defendants are not violated and that sentence severity was unrelated to ideology, gender, or race. Being a leader in a terrorist group was the primary determinant of severity, but the political element was not introduced until the sentencing stage after conviction for a traditional crime. Not as surprising will be findings that known terrorists were repeatedly arrested to "get them off the streets," that terrorists received longer sentences than did conventional offenders, and that terrorists were far less likely to be given probation instead of prison. And few will be surprised to learn just how much counterterrorist policies and operations were influenced by shifts in the political climate and resulting legal changes.

Most importantly, in my view, Smith demonstrates how inapplicable to terrorists are many standard explanations of criminal behavior and how intractible are the problems encountered when governments use criminal laws and procedures to deal with political conflicts. The evidence is overwhelmingly against theoretical expectations that violent offenders will "mature" to nonviolence and strongly suggests that there are fundamental differences between the processes leading to conventional criminality and those through which individuals become terrorists. As for the strategy of "conventionalizing" political crimes, while it is understandable and ostensibly effective in the short term, it fails to deal with the conflicts and grievances generating such crimes. The most sobering message of this study is that despite the decline of leftist terrorism (associated more with the decline of communism than the success of governmental control efforts), the United States faces the growing menace of rightist and environmental terrorism.

Acknowledgments

Without the help of numerous persons, this study of American terrorism could not have been possible. In completing it, I have been encouraged and reassured by the assistance provided by the Federal Bureau of Investigation, the Administrative Office of the United States Courts, the U.S. Sentencing Commission, and countless federal district courts and federal records centers throughout the United States. Financial support for the project was provided by a grant from the University of Alabama at Birmingham. In particular, I would like to thank Neil Gallagher, Walter Mangiacotti, Bill Hart, and Patricia Bryan of the FBI's Terrorist Research and Analytical Center; Jim Hopson of the Department of Justice; and David Cook, Rick Ransom, and Garcia Allen of the Administrative Office of the U.S. Courts for assistance in providing data for the study. In addition, Mark Wolfson of Stanford University and Dena Olson of the University of Washington took time from their busy graduate student schedules to visit federal courts and national archives on the West Coast to complete data collection on federal cases involving members of the Aryan Nations and the Order.

I owe particular gratitude to Charles Lindquist, John Sloan, Austin Turk, Ron Huff, Peter Flemming, and Jeff Ross for their encouragement, comments, and suggestions during the project. Special thanks to Davietta McDole for her unfailing typing support and to Margaret Armbrester for her astute editorial vision. Finally, I am especially grateful to my wife, Sherylyn, who with wisdom and love provided an environment conducive to completing a project such as this.

Taylor and Francis, Inc. has kindly allowed me to reprint, with alterations, portions of Chapter 7, which first appeared in "Anti-terrorism Legislation in the United States," 1985, Vol. 7(2): 213–231, *Terrorism: An International Journal* (New York: Crane Russak).

Introduction

Terrorism was alive and well in America during the 1980s. Although international terrorism received the bulk of media attention, the 1980s witnessed the growth of a variety of home-grown terrorist organizations. The emergence of right-wing terror in the United States challenged our assumptions about terrorism as the exclusive tool of violent leftists and forced us to reevaluate previous notions regarding the motivations of terrorists. The decade also provided a social laboratory for governmental intervention. It was a period when the federal government solidified its position on appropriate responses to terror, developed new strategies for law enforcement, and implemented new prosecutorial approaches. The events of the 1980s—including the actions of the law enforcers as well as the law violaters—will shape American terrorism for years to come.

This book is about the varied philosophies and events associated with terrorism and terrorist motives including bombings, assassinations, Marxism, Christianity, airline hijackings, and governmental authority—including the power to collect taxes. It investigates people who became terrorists, their motivations, and their violent acts. Within this study we will define terrorism, look at when and how the federal government intervenes, and at what happens to those who are labeled as terrorists. These fundamental issues are important ones to address.

In late April 1985, as spring brought renewed life to the Ozark Mountains of north Arkansas, FBI agents swept into the encampment of the Covenant, Sword, and Arm of the Lord (CSA), ending a three-day seige with members of the isolated commune. This group, which began over fifteen years before as a fundamentalist church with beliefs common to many Americans, had turned into an armed enclave resentful of those with different beliefs or physical traits, deeply suspicious of the federal government, and

1

despising federal authority. Since 1977 the group had engaged in paramilitary training, teaching its members how to survive the apocalypse they believed was imminent. They committed thefts, manufactured weapons, and burned buildings and churches. But it was not until 1984 that the group came under the watchful eye of federal agents. Why did CSA turn to violence to achieve its so-called Christian objectives? Why did it take so long for the FBI to become involved? Why did the FBI become involved at all? Why not let local authorities deal with the group?

For seven years CSA conducted weapons training and engaged in the illegal manufacture of silencers and automatic weapons, yet they were not labeled "terrorists" until 1984 or 1985. From 1975 until 1983, a left-wing, violent Marxist group calling itself the United Freedom Front (UFF) bombed corporate and government buildings on the East Coast. But not until 1983 did the federal government embark on an intensive campaign to capture Raymond Luc Levasseur and his UFF followers. Had these groups finally committed some act that qualified as terrorism, or had the definition of terrorism changed? What unleashed the FBI's assault on terrorism in the 1980s? These answers have rarely been addressed empirically. An examination of these governmental decisions and their impact on terrorism in America is a primary purpose of this work.

This book looks at the process of becoming a terrorist. It follows the lives of men and women who have committed themselves to their view of a utopian way of life. Terrorists in America come from many philosophical, ideological, and religious backgrounds. They are neo-Nazis, Marxist revolutionaries, Puerto Rican nationalists, and anti-Castro Cubans. Yet the terrorists who come from these diverse backgrounds share an important commonality: they all have been willing to use indiscriminate violence to further their political or social dreams. How they came to the decision to employ violence is one part of the process of becoming a terrorist that this work investigates.

Secondly, this process is as much about governmental reaction as it is about the actions of terrorists. Unlike traditional criminal offenses, there is no specific crime of terrorism. Consequently, the terrorist label is applied in ways and for reasons that reflect more than the mere criminality of the act. The behavior of the terrorist is expressly political, and the government's response, try as it might, cannot avoid the political ramifications of the behavior or the process that results in some people being called "terrorists." During the course of this book, I frequently refer to governmental reaction to terrorist activity as "labeling." In many ways, one could not select a better concept: the entire process is reminiscent of Frank Tannenbaum's notion of 'the dramatization of evil'[1] and Howard Becker's definition of 'deviance'.[2] It is not my intent, however, to reduce this process (as some labeling theorists have) to one of blaming society for the actions of terrorists. While it is a noble task to examine the societal causes that may lead someone to bomb airliners or crowded waiting rooms, such violence is always unjustifiable. Therefore, the term *labeling* in this work is used merely to imply the circumstances—the interactions that take place as a result of the commission of 'terrorist' behaviors and the application of an elaborate set of guidelines that determine intervention strategies—under which the polity decides to define someone's behavior or some group's actions as terroristic. The application of these guidelines has not always remained the same: it has been easier at some times to label terrorism than at others. While variations in the labeling process make the study of terrorism more fascinating, they also make it more frustrating. For if the definition of what we identify as terrorism one day is changed the next, our statistics will be flawed. Despite these difficulties, my examination of terrorism addresses three major questions: (1) How is terrorism defined by the American political system, and how much terrorism does that system quantify as occurring in this country? (2) What types of behavior do terrorists commit, and why do they engage in these activities? (3) What happens to terrorists after they are apprehended by the justice system?

This study examines only the groups and individuals who came to the attention of the FBI's counterterrorism program and whose behaviors were 'officially designated' as acts of terror. This approach has strengths as well as weaknesses. Since terrorism is, by definition, a political offense, a study of officially designated terrorism is an appropriate method to examine the way in which the polity defines and applies the concept. In limiting the study to persons or groups investigated for official acts of terrorism, one avoids the tendency to adopt a definition or to include groups within that definition that reflect the ideological beliefs of the researcher. More importantly, the restriction of the study to officially designated acts allows the researcher, for the first time, to see if persons labeled as "terrorists" are handled differently from "traditional" criminals by the criminal justice system. From initial FBI investigation to indictment, from the development of a prosecutorial strategy to ultimate conviction and sentencing, this study suggests that different standards, strategies, and sanctions *are* applied.

Finally, we have limited our examination of American terrorism to the decade of the 1980s. The 1980s saw the rise of some of the most spectacular and dangerous groups in American history. It was a time when left-wing and right-wing terrorists prospered only to see the pipe dream burst, when the American judiciary increasingly responded to international terrorism, and when environmental terrorists appeared. It was a period during which the federal bureaucracy looked for the best approaches to deal with terrorists and then tested its strategies.

In summary, this work suggests that what is ultimately defined as terrorism reflects not only the illegal acts of some people, but a number of other social phenomena as well. Chapters 1 and 2 focus upon the official process that results in someone being labeled a "terrorist." This part of the study includes an investigation of the development of the FBI's definition of terrorism, how the designation affects investigative strategies, and how these definitions have changed over the years. The behavior of the terrorists as well as variations in the application of the guidelines defining terrorism are reflected in official statistics on American terrorism. Chapters 3–7 provide detailed information on the types of people being called "terrorists," their motives and ideologies, and the criminal acts they committed that ultimately resulted in that designation. Chapters 8 and 9 are concerned with governmental response: the strategies federal prosecutors use to prosecute terrorists, the outcomes of criminal cases involving terrorists, and the level of severity with which terrorists are punished. Chapter 10 concludes our study by summarizing the data and discussing the future of terrorism in America.

Chapter 1

Terrorists in the Criminal Justice System: Political and Conceptual Problems

The criminalization of no other behavior evokes as much debate as terrorism and terrorists. Although the focus of this work is an examination of 'officially designated acts of terrorism' and the criminal investigations of groups resulting from those acts, it would be naive to accept governmental definitions of terrorism without comment. The debate about terrorism and how it should be studied reflects a common problem in criminology. While many criminologists accept the government's legal definitions of crimes (as well as the statistics generated by such definitions), others contend that the study of crime must include, for example, violations of 'human rights,' racism, and other behaviors not explicitly defined as criminal in the legal codes.[1]

Students of terrorism grapple with the same issues. While some accept governmental figures and statistics on terrorism at face value,[2] others contend that governmental definitions of the subject render official statistics meaningless. Consequently, scholars have defined, refined, and redefined terrorism to accommodate personal preferences regarding what should or should not be labeled "terroristic." Each published work on terrorism seems to compound the vagueness of the concept rather than provide conceptual clarity to the subject.[3] Unfortunately, the variations in definitions of terrorism have given some legitimacy to the aphorism "One man's terrorist is another man's freedom fighter." In the current study, the acceptance of the FBI's official definition of terrorism is somewhat restrictive. It eliminates any examination of state-sponsored terror and, as we shall see, it largely eliminates consideration of acts of terrorism committed by isolated individuals. Nonetheless, the history of the American government's official definition of terrorism and its subsequent response to terrorism provides useful insights into the polity's own difficulty in coming to grips with the conceptual problems associated with defining and criminalizing terrorism. To the casual observer terrorists appear to be treated no differently than other criminals. And, as we shall see, the polity usually makes every effort to perpetuate that view. In reality, the Federal Bureau of Investigation's definition of terrorism and the guidelines used to investigate these offenders set in motion intervention strategies that clearly separate terrorists from traditional criminals throughout the judicial process—from investigation to prosecution and eventual sentencing.

The FBI's Definition of Terrorism

While some claim that the American political system vacillates over who is labeled a "terrorist," depending on current public opinion, the official definition of terrorism used by the FBI has remained unchanged for many years.[4] Terrorism is officially defined by the bureau as:

> the unlawful use of force or violence against persons or property to intimidate or coerce a government, the civilian population, or any segment thereof, in furtherance of political or social goals.[5]

The definition itself is not unlike that used by many academicians. There are, however, at least two characteristics of this definition worthy of note.

First, the use of the term *unlawful* restricts the application to criminal conduct. The FBI has resisted demands by some members of Congress to expand its application of the concept to *potentially* politically subversive groups. FBI Director William Webster told a congressional subcommittee in 1987 that the most important characteristic of the FBI's definition of terrorism "is emphasizing the criminal aspect of it. . . . I have some resistance to reinjecting into the equation political motivation unnecessarily."[6] Second, while FBI officials focus on a criminal's conduct during the course of an investigation, it is the *motivation* of the perpetrator that determines the intensity of that investigation. Terrorism, as most would agree, involves some effort to invoke "political or social change." However, this salient feature of terrorism—political motivation—overshadows all efforts to criminalize terroristic behavior. Unlike most alleged offenders investigated by the FBI, those identified as terrorists have committed, or are suspected of having committed, crimes for political reasons. While motive is not normally recognized as an intrinsic element of any criminal offense, it is the *motivation* of the terrorist that allows the FBI to elevate investigation of his or her crimes to the highest governmental priority.

The persons eventually arrested and indicted for acts of terror are not formally charged with "terrorism." While some states have created "terroristic threatening" statutes,[7] no federal crime called "terrorism" exists. The inclusion of the motive of the offender as an essential part of the crime precludes a legally acceptable definition. Consequently, indicted terrorists are charged with a plethora of traditional and, occasionally, exotic criminal offenses. Given the ambiguity of any definition of terrorism (including the government's), one of the most intriguing aspects of the government's response to terror involves an examination of the decision-making process by which some persons are labeled as terrorists, while others who commit similar crimes avoid that label.

The FBI and the Politics of Terrorism

The FBI has the responsibility to investigate ongoing or suspected acts of terrorism.[8] In addition, the agency itself has the onerous task of deciding which incidents merit this designation. How those decisions are made reflect the tremendous political pressure put on the FBI to combat politically subversive groups. During the heyday of the Hoover era of the FBI, the bureau enjoyed an untarnished, almost glorified image as America's elite crime-fighting organization. During the late 1960s and early 1970s, however, the FBI experienced a dramatic reversal of reputation. The Senate Watergate hearings in 1973 revealed extensive FBI misconduct from the 1940s through the late 1960s.[9]

Changes in the FBI during the 1970s and early 1980s as a result of the Watergate hearings dramatically affected the investigation and capture of known terrorists in the United States as well as having an impact on subsequent levels of terrorist activity. The collection of intelligence information on U. S. citizens was severely limited as the FBI dismantled its domestic intelligence units in the wake of post-Watergate reaction.[10] The number of domestic security investigations declined from more than 20,000 in 1973 to less than 300 by the end of 1976.[11] That decline mirrored Congressional and public dissatisfaction with the role of the FBI as a 'political police' agency. Congressional inquiries during that period led to the adoption of the Levi Guidelines on April 5, 1976. Named after Attorney General Edward Levi, the new guidelines identified the standards by which an internal security investigation could be initiated as well as the length of the investigation. Furthermore, the guidelines divided investigations into three levels (preliminary, limited, and full) and specified the type of investigative techniques appropriate to each level.[12]

In August 1976, FBI Director Clarence Kelley further pacified congressional critics by moving investigations of terrorist organizations from the Intelligence Division to the General Investigative Division.[13] Previously, the investigation of domestic terrorism cases fell under the Intelligence Division, where norms regarding the rule of law "had been nonexistent."[14] The effect of this move was to limit the types of techniques that could be used to investigate terrorism cases to the standards used for traditional criminal cases. Although some of these changes were modified in the 1980s, the decision to treat terrorism cases as traditional crimes signaled the transition to a clearly defined strategy in the prosecution of terrorists. To further distance the agency from public criticism, succeeding FBI Director William Webster changed the title of these investigations from "domestic security" to "terrorism". While these semantic alterations clearly indicated an effort to improve public perceptions of the FBI, the changes were not merely cosmetic.

With the election of Ronald Reagan to the presidency in 1980, congressional criticism of FBI abuses of due process diminished. Instead of being critical of the extensive nature of FBI investigations of dissident political groups, congressional subcommittees lamented the lack of FBI resources expended on domestic security.[15] In particular, Congressman Joseph Early of Massachusetts and Senator Jeremiah Denton of Alabama were harshly critical of the low priority given to terrorism and domestic security by Director Webster. Fearing that the FBI might once again become embroiled in the issue of political policing, Webster resisted the new Republican leadership's efforts to increase spending for domestic terrorism investigations and to relax the Levi Guidelines. He eventually lost on both counts.

Although FBI resources committed to domestic security/terrorism account for only a small fraction of the investigations conducted by the FBI, the publicity surrounding such cases leaves the impression that these investigations represent the bulk of FBI work. With the image of the FBI beginning to improve after the ravages of Watergate, Webster resisted congressional efforts to allocate more resources to the counterterrorism program for fear it would undermine the reforms of the mid-1970s. In the late 1970s, in fact, Webster routinely returned appropriations for this function to Congress.[16] Pressure from the administration and conservative congressional leaders continued, but Webster remained committed to decreasing the role of the FBI in domestic security/terrorism—until the fall of 1981.

At the appropriations hearings for fiscal year 1982, the FBI proposed that the counterterrorism program be decreased by over $250,000 and that twenty-one positions be either reallocated or eliminated.[17] While Webster argued before a Senate subcommittee on security and terrorism that "there is no known coalescing of an ideological synthesis among (domestic terrorist) groups, nor do we have any sense that they have become effective,"[18] other events were taking shape that would undo his efforts to restrict FBI involvement in domestic security.

In October 1981, long-forgotten members of the Weather Underground (WU), the Black Liberation Army (BLA) and the Black Panther party emerged as the newly formed May 19th Communist Organization (M19CO). The robbery of a Brinks armored truck in Nyack, New York, that left two police officers and a security guard dead renewed concern about terrorism. Evidence obtained during the ensuing investigation revealed an even broader coalescence. By Thanksgiving 1981, investigators learned that not only had these groups merged for specific missions but that they had also provided assistance to the Armed Forces of National Liberation (FALN), a violent Puerto Rican extremist group. These revelations, which cast doubt on Webster's previous comments, encouraged further administration and congressional demands for expansion of domestic security programs. Webster was embarrassed further when on December 21, 1981 members of the United Freedom Front (UFF), a left-wing terrorist group that had operated with impunity since 1976, killed New Jersey state trooper Philip Lamonaco along a rural stretch of interstate highway during a routine traffic stop.[19]

The public response was predictable: the news media talked of the reemergence of the radicalism of the late 1960s, and public support for FBI intervention increased. Only one year after recommending a reduction in program allocations for terrorism investigations, the FBI elevated its counterterrorism program from a Priority 3 program to the highest investigative priority—Priority 1.[20] To further the government's new goals, Attorney General William French Smith, in a memorandum to William Webster on March 7, 1983, issued new guidelines for domestic security/terrorism investigations.[21] Contending that the old Levi Guidelines were too restrictive, Smith streamlined the investigative process and gave greater flexibility to FBI field offices with the new guidelines.

The impact of these changes on the FBI cannot be overstated. Within three years after the elevation of the FBI's counterterrorism program to Priority 1 and the issuance of the new investigative guidelines, the FBI scored dramatic successes against terrorists in the United States. A law enforcement task force consisting of local, state, and federal agencies sharing intelligence information was created in February 1983 to snare members of the UFF. Most of the members, who had been on the FBI's Ten Most Wanted list since 1976, were captured in November 1984. Two remaining members, Thomas and Carol Ann Manning, were arrested in April 1985.[22] By May 1985 the leader of M19CO, Marilyn Buck, and nearly twenty others involved in the Nyack, New York, armored truck robbery and murders had been arrested. Two years after the Levi Guidelines were revised, almost all members of the major left-wing terrorist groups had been captured and were awaiting trial.

By sheer coincidence, about the time the counterterrorism program was elevated to Priority 1 and the Smith Guidelines issued, right-wing extremists also turned violent. On June 3, 1983, just three months after Attorney General Smith issued his guidelines, Gordon Kahl was killed in a firefight with state and federal agents in northwest Arkansas. The death of Kahl, a staunch member of the Sheriff's Posse Comitatus (SPC)—a violent, anti-tax group—signaled the beginning of a move toward violence among right-wing groups. Declaring "War in '84," Robert Mathews formed the Order in September 1983. During the next two years, the Order, the Aryan Nations, SPC, the Arizona Patriots, the White Patriot party (WPP), and the CSA became household words. For adherents of the extreme right, right-wing terrorism could not have picked a worse time to rear its head. The violent fringe of the Christian Identity Movement, to which most of these groups were related, was crushed in a wave of federal indictments and successful prosecutions that lasted until 1987. Richard Butler, head of the Aryan Nations, commenting on the failure of the Order, said: "Mathews made his move too soon."[23] In view of the changes in federal policy just discussed, perhaps Butler should have said: "he

made his move too late." Mathews, James Ellison, the leader of
CSA and Frazier Glenn Miller, leader of the White Patriot Party,
and other leaders of extreme right terrorist groups never knew
what hit them. The reemphasis on domestic security caused a
wholesale housecleaning of American terrorist groups—Left and
Right—during the mid-1980s.

The Attorney General's Guidelines

In many ways procedures to determine who the FBI could investigate and under what circumstances are as important as its definition of terrorism in determining who was ultimately labeled "terrorists." Two sets of guidelines provide authority and direction to
the FBI in its investigation of terrorism. Investigation of international terrorism is provided by the "Attorney General's Guidelines
for FBI Foreign Intelligence Collection and Foreign Counterin-
telligence Investigations."[24] These guidelines are classified, however, and not available for public dissemination. It is known that
the FBI is authorized under these guidelines to investigate acts
that involve "terrorist activity committed by groups or individuals
who are foreign-based and/or directed by countries or groups outside the United States or whose activities transcend national
boundaries."[25] Generally, these guidelines allow the FBI greater
latitude in investigative techniques and in the length and scope of
such investigations than do the guidelines that direct domestic security investigations.

Domestic terrorism investigations are conducted under the
provisions of the "Attorney General's Guidelines on General
Crimes, Racketeering Enterprise and Domestic Security/Terrorism
Investigations."[26] These guidelines provide insight into the manner
in which the FBI ultimately categorizes some offenses as terroristic. A number of characteristics that determine the groups and
types of behaviors investigated emerge within the guidelines:

1. *Use of violence*—The guidelines specify that the group en-
    dorses and utilizes "activities that involve force or vio-
    lence."[27] Within this framework, the behaviors of non-
    violent political dissident groups would not qualify for
    investigation as terrorism. However, as the second charac-
    teristic demonstrates, violence does not have to actually
    occur, nor does it have to be recent.

2. *Political motivation*—The 1983 Smith Guidelines incorpo-
    rate criminal enterprises and terrorism under a single set

of directives. Consequently, identification of a political motive is not necessary to initiate a criminal investigation.
Identification of a political motive allows investigation under the domestic security/terrorism subsection rather than
the racketeering subsection. The distinction is important.
Terrorism investigations may remain open even though a
group "has not engaged in recent acts of violence, nor is
there any immediate threat of harm—yet the composition,
goals and prior history of the group suggests the need for
continuing federal interest."[28]

3. *Focus on groups rather than individuals*—While the activities of individual citizens acting alone may result in a
   criminal investigation, they will seldom be designated as
   an act of terror. The guidelines are specific: terrorism investigations are "concerned with the investigation of *entire
   enterprises, rather than individual participants.*"[29] In addition, terrorism investigations may not even be initiated
   unless "circumstances indicate that two or more persons
   are engaged in an enterprise for the purpose of furthering
   political or social goals . . . that involve force or violence
   and a violation of the criminal laws of the United States."[30]

4. *Claimed responsibility*—In recent years the FBI has tended
   not to include bombings as acts of terrorism unless a claim
   of responsibility by a terrorist group was made or the FBI
   could positively identify such a group as responsible.

Consequently, crimes like the assassination of federal judge
Robert Vance in December 1989 were not labeled "terroristic." Although an anonymous caller claimed to have committed the bombing for a group calling itself "Citizens for a Competent Judicial
System," the assassin, Walter Moody, apparently acted indepen-
dently of the influence of any organizations. This particular crime
is not even mentioned as a possible suspected terrorist incident in
FBI annual reports. Other bombings, including those of abortion
clinics, appear to fit the same pattern—they are the result of decisions made by individuals without the conspiratorial support of
others. These characteristics emphasize the FBI approach to countering terrorism—the 'decapitation' of the leadership of terrorist
organizations in an effort to gain 'early interdiction of unlawful
violent activity.'[31] The arrest and conviction of persons actually
committing officially designated acts of terror are viewed as a less

effective strategy than destroying the organization that spawned the violence.

Needles in the Haystack: Terrorists in the Justice System

The study of terrorism presents unique problems to those who try to empirically examine the phenomenon. Selective enforcement, higher priorities, greater allocations of resources, the use of non-legal criteria, and the lack of a specific crime of terrorism confound efforts to adequately study the extent of terrorism in America. For example, if a researcher wants to study people who commit robbery, offenders are easily identified as those who have been charged with a specific offense in the criminal code appropriate to the jurisdiction. By contrast, since there is no specific crime of terrorism, terrorists are charged with scores of different violations of federal law. Unless the persons who have been labeled as terrorists can be identified, finding terrorists in the criminal justice system becomes an almost impossible task. To further complicate the work of researchers, some terrorists have a history of criminal behavior that predates or coincides with their lives as terrorists. Should all of the criminal acts committed by terrorists be considered terroristic? Obviously not. How, then, can one distinguish between the terroristic behaviors and non-terroristic crimes committed by persons alleged to be terrorists? The question is not easily answered. Consequently, this study examines the behaviors of persons indicted, as a result of FBI investigations, of officially designated acts or suspected acts of terror. It is apparent that most of the crimes for which terrorists are indicted as a result of these investigations are not terroristic in themselves. Instead, they tend to be crimes committed in support of the group's survival or in efforts to procure materials for the commission of terrorist acts.

After extensive discussions with the FBI's Terrorist Research and Analytical Center, an analyst was assigned to identify the names of persons indicted since 1980 as a result of FBI terrorism investigations. All of the persons eventually identified were indicted in federal court. The list included the names of persons indicted under the counterterrorism program from 1980–1989, as well as the specific offenses for which the persons were charged, and the date and place of indictment. This original list included the names of approximately 170 persons.

The list on page 14 (table 1.1), was supplemented with the names of persons identified from the FBI's annual report on terror-

Table 1.1 Indictments from the FBI's Counterterrorism Program: 1980–1989 (Compared with Sample Cases)

TERRORIST ORGANIZATION	TOTAL NUMBER OF PERSONS	NUMBER INCLUDED IN SAMPLE
Domestic		
1. Aryan Nations	4	3
2. Arizona Patriots	10	10
3. Covenant, Sword, and Arm of the Lord	22	22
4. Ku Klux Klan	1	1
5. The Order	48	48
6. The Order II	5	5
7. Sheriff's Posse Comitatus	5	5
8. White Patriot Party	9	9
9. El Rukns	10	7
10. Macheteros	20	20
11. FALN	6	5
12. May 19 Communist Organization	20	11
13. United Freedom Front	11	9
14. Republic of New Africa	1	0
15. New African Freedom Fighters	9	9
16. Provisional Party of Communists	1	1
17. Jewish Defense League	4	0
18. Earth First	5	5
19. Individual Act[a]/Group Unknown	4	3
Subtotal	195	173
International		
1. Armenian Secret Army for the Liberation of Armenia	4	0

Table 1.1 *Continued*

TERRORIST ORGANIZATION	TOTAL NUMBER OF PERSONS	NUMBER INCLUDED IN SAMPLE
2. Justice Commandos of the Armenian Genocide	5	0
3. Ejercito Revolucionario Del Pueblo	8	0
4. Indian Sikhs	2	0
5. Irish National Liberation Army	1	0
6. Japanese Red Army	1	1
7. Libyans	10	7
8. Omega 7	9	7
9. Palestinian/Syrian	4	4
10. Provisional Irish Republican Army	26	21
11. Individual Act[a]/Group Unknown	23	0
Subtotal	93	40
TOTALS	288	213

a. For years 1983 and prior, the acts of some individuals were classified as terrorism. In subsequent years, in accordance with the new guidelines, only persons affiliated with terrorist groups were listed.

ism in the United States. Most of the investigations are mentioned in these annual reports, and the persons involved are identified. The names and places of indictment, where omitted, were then obtained from the Terrorist Research and Analytical Center. The final list included the names of 213 persons indicted for nearly 1,400 different violations of federal law. They represented twenty–one different terrorist organizations: sixteen domestic groups and five groups that had committed acts of international terrorism.

This list should not be taken as complete, however.[32] To check the validity of the list, annual reports of the FBI's counterterrorism program were used to identify other persons who had been indicted but not included in the original list. An examination of these reports revealed an additional seventy–five names for which data could not be collected. The complete list was compared with the list for which information regarding indictment was available (table 1.1). Case files were examined for approximately 90 percent of the known indictments against domestic terrorists from 1980–1989. The data set includes virtually all of the indicted right-wing terrorists, as well as the vast majority of the most famous left-wing group members from the 1970s and 1980s. Among domestic groups, criminal case histories were not located for four members of the Jewish Defense League indicted in 1987.

Locating the criminal case files of persons indicted for acts of international terrorism was more difficult. Many of the cases were several years old and had already been removed from local federal district courts. Fewer than half of the international cases were examined. In particular, no information was gathered on members of Armenian or Turkish independence groups who committed bombings on the West Coast in the early 1980s. Nor was information gathered on international terrorists whom the FBI designated as belonging to an "unknown group." Of international terrorists belonging to a known group, nearly three-fifths (57 percent) of the case files were examined. Cases against Armenian terrorists and members of Ejercito Revolucionario del Pueblo (ERP) represent the only major cases omitted from the analysis. Overall, nearly three-fourths (74 percent) of the persons indicted under the FBI's counterterrorism program from 1980–1989 are included in the sample. The completed data set contains information about the type of terrorist group in addition to demographic, case outcome, and sentencing information on the 213 indicted terrorists.[33]

Chapter 2

The Extent of Terrorism in America

From 1980 to 1989 the FBI designated 219 different crimes as official acts of terrorism.[1] During this same period it identified scores of additional acts as 'suspected acts of terrorism,' many of which were later confirmed as terrorist actions. In 1982, the FBI also began to maintain records on 'prevented acts of terrorism.' From 1982–1989, sixty-five terrorist acts were believed to have been prevented due to local and federal law enforcement intervention. While a detailed discussion of the acts of many of these terrorists is provided in chapters 4–6, what follows is a brief discussion of the patterns of terroristic behavior during the 1980s. Of particular importance is the impact that arrests and indictments have had on terroristic groups and their behaviors.

General Trends in American Terrorism

Terrorist acts steadily increased in America during the early part of the 1980s. The number of incidents grew from twenty-nine in 1980 to forty-two the following year and eventually peaked at fifty-one in 1982. These increases were due primarily to international and Puerto Rican terrorists (fig. 2.1). 1982 also saw the largest number of Americans killed or injured by terrorist acts on American soil. During that year seven persons were killed, and an additional twenty-six were injured due to terrorist bombings and assassinations in the United States (fig. 2.2).[2]

The increase in terrorism on American soil during the early 1980s was the primary catalyst for the escalation of the FBI's coun-

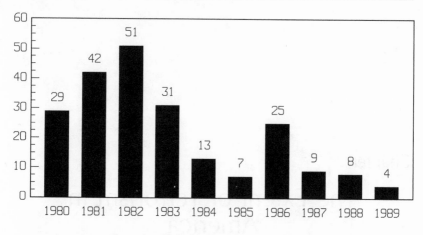

Source: F.B.I. Terrorist Research
and Analytical Center

Figure 2.1 Terrorist Incidents in the United States 1980–1989

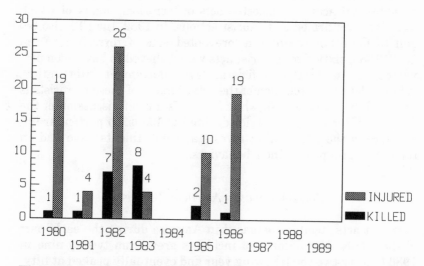

Figure 2.2 Number of Persons Killed and Injured Due to Terrorism 1980–1989

terterrorism program to a Priority 1 program in late 1982 and the
relaxation of the Levi Guidelines in March 1983. Whether or not
these changes had a major impact on future levels of American
terrorism is hard to assess. The deterrent effect of most law enforcement initiatives is extremely difficult to measure empirically.

In this instance, however, strong circumstantial evidence exists that the hardened governmental attitude had a profound impact on the level of American terrorism for the remainder of the decade. The number of terrorist incidents dropped approximately forty percent in 1983 from that of the previous year. Although the number of terrorist victims killed during 1983 reached an all-time high, decreases in subsequent years suggest that increased FBI expenditures on counterterrorism and the expansion of domestic security investigations begun that year had a substantial adverse effect on terrorism in this country. In a three-year period, the number of acts of terrorism fell from a record fifty-one in 1982 to only seven in 1985.[3]

Although leftist terrorists on the East Coast, right-wing affiliates of the Christian Identity Movement, and Puerto Rican extremists all suffered major blows during 1984 and 1985, by 1986 several of the organizations had regrouped and embarked on a renewed campaign of terror. Twenty-five acts of terrorism were committed during 1986, most of which were carried out by Puerto Rican nationalists. Neo-Nazis finally made their mark on the terrorist scorecard, registering five bombings in the Coeur d'Alene, Idaho area. The most violent and successful of the terrorists during 1986 were, oddly enough, Jewish extremists. Although only committing two of the twenty-five incidents, they were responsible for seventeen of the nineteen injuries that occurred that year from terrorist bombings and assassination attempts.[4]

By 1987 federal indictments began to have a major effect on the leadership and organizational management of domestic terrorist groups in America. The leaders of right-wing terrorist groups were either in prison or awaiting trial. The Aryan Nations, the CSA, the White Patriot party, and the Order were all in states of disarray as a result of FBI operations and federal indictments. Similarly, members of the major leftist terrorist groups, the UFF and M19CO, were awaiting trials in Boston and in Washington, DC. Even the previously immune leaders of the Macheteros in Puerto Rico found themselves under federal indictment in Hartford.[5]

With terrorist groups scrambling to reorganize and recruit to replace lost personnel, acts of terrorism waned during the late 1980s. The number of incidents dropped from twenty-five in 1986 to only nine in 1987 and eventually to a decade low of four in 1989. Had it not been for the emergence of the environmental terrorists during the closing years of the decade, terrorism in America would have been virtually non-existent during the late 1980s. The num-

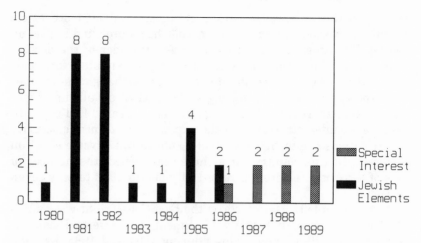

Figure 2.3   Terrorist Incidents by Group Type 1980–1989 Jewish and Special Interest Groups

ber of persons killed or injured as a result of terrorism also reflects this trend. The last three years of the decade witnessed no injuries or deaths due to terrorist bombs or assassins.[6] Although the number of terrorist incidents increased to seven in 1990 (not shown in Figure), that was the fourth consecutive year in which America experienced no deaths or injuries due to terrorism.[7]

Terrorism Trends by Type of Group

In most of its annual reports, the FBI's Terrorist Research and Analytical Center identified the number and types of terrorist acts committed by different groups. Of the 219 officially designated acts that occurred from 1980 to 1990, 209 were attributed to specific groups; the ten remaining acts were committed by either an unknown group or by individuals believed to be acting entirely on their own. The perpetrators of these crimes can be divided into six major categories: left-wing or right-wing terrorists, Puerto Rican nationalists, international terrorists, Jewish extremists, and special interest terrorists primarily concerned with environmental issues. Figures 2.3–2.5 reveal the trends in terroristic activity among these groups during the 1980s. Each figure shows the activities of two of the group types.

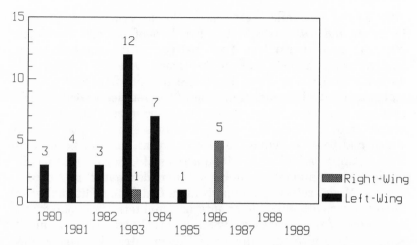

Figure 2.4 Terrorist Incidents by Group Type 1980–1989 Left-Wing and Right-Wing Groups

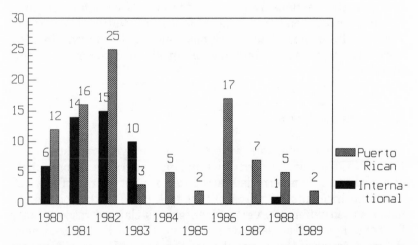

Figure 2.5 Terrorist Incidents by Group Type 1980–1989 Puerto Rican and International Groups

International Terrorism

The early part of the decade was dominated by the activities of international terrorists, extreme Jewish elements, and Puerto Rican nationalists. Armenian terrorists struck targets repeatedly in

1982 on the East and West coasts. Not to be outdone, Croatian terrorists and anti-Castro Cuban members of Omega 7 committed numerous bombings in New York that year as international terrorism reached its highest levels of the decade. Omega 7 members and an unknown Haitian group dominated the international terrorism statistics in 1983, committing nine of the ten acknowledged acts. However, one year later international terrorism virtually disappeared from the American scene. The mysterious Haitian group, which had been so active the previous year, has not been heard from again. In addition, the 1983 arrests of Omega 7 founder Eduardo Arocena and several of his followers decimated the New Jersey and Miami cells of his organization. Only one additional act of terrorism was attributed to an international terrorist group for the remainder of the decade. In 1988, an anti-Castro group calling itself the "Organization Alliance of Cuban Intransigence" bombed the residence of the executive director of the Institute of Cuban Studies in Coral Gables, Florida. While other international terrorists have attempted to commit acts of terrorism in this country since the mid-1980s, they have been thwarted before being able to carry out their actions. Libyan agents in the Washington, DC area in 1987,[8] three members of the Syrian Social Nationalist party in 1987,[9] and Japanese Red Army member Yu Kikumura[10] in 1988 were each captured before carrying out planned bombings in this country.

Puerto Rican Terrorism

Puerto Rican nationalists were the most active terrorists in the United States and its territories during the 1980s. From 1980–1982 Puerto Rican terrorists accounted for fifty-three of the 122 terrorism incidents (43 percent) that took place in that period. As many as ten different Puerto Rican groups claimed responsibility for bombings and assassinations during the early 1980s. Among the most active of these groups were the Armed Forces of National Liberation (FALN), the Armed Forces of Popular Resistance (FARP), and Ejercito Popular Boricua—Macheteros (EPB–Macheteros). Of these three, the FALN operated primarily in the continental United States, while the other two committed most of their acts on the island of Puerto Rico. The arrests of numerous members of the FALN in 1982 and 1983, however, seriously eroded the ability of this American-based organization to carry out planned bombings. Although FALN leader and fugitive William

Morales continued to run FALN operations from Mexico during this time, the organization was largely ineffective.[11]

By the mid-1980s, the Macheteros ("the Machete Wielders") and the Organization of Volunteers for the Puerto Rican Revolution (OVRP) arose as the major replacements for the FALN. In September 1983, Victor Gerena Ortiz, a member of the Macheteros and a part-time employee of Wells Fargo, stole $7 million from the Wells Fargo depot in Hartford. The money quickly made its way to the Macheteros by way of Mexico and, eventually, Cuba. The robbery, however, proved to be of greater harm than value to the Macheteros. In August 1985, federal agents in Puerto Rico arrested the leading figures in the organization for conspiracy and brought them back to Hartford for trial. In response to the arrests, the Macheteros, in cooperation with OVRP, escalated the violence in 1986, committing seventeen bombings, attempted bombings, or assassinations. Despite these increases in 1986, terrorist activities by the island's nationalist extremists declined annually from 1986–1989. These groups rebounded with five bombings in 1990, but recent efforts in the U.S. Congress to allow Puerto Ricans to vote on the future political status of the island may have had an adverse effect on violent nationalists' recruitment efforts.

Jewish Terrorism

Pro-Israeli terrorists in the United States have generally been members of either the Jewish Defense League (JDL) or the United Jewish Underground (UJU). Of the two, the JDL has been the most active. Started in 1968 by Rabbi Meir D. Kahane, the JDL is composed primarily of young Jewish-American extremists fighting to "protect" the rights of Jews and in support of the state of Israel.[12] Jewish terrorists were most active during 1981 and 1982; during that time sixteen terrorist acts were committed by the JDL or the UJU. Eighteen of the twenty-five acts committed by Jewish extremist groups during the 1980s were attributed to the JDL.

The majority of JDL bombings took place in New York City, JDL headquarters. Highly proficient, their bombings have been among the most lethal of those by American terrorists. Jewish extremists were responsible for several deaths and numerous injuries during the 1980s, as they primarily targeted Soviet interests in the United States to protest the poor treatment of Jews in the Soviet Union. JDL members apparently were responsible for the 1986 release of a tear gas grenade at the Metropolitan Opera House in

New York City that injured seventeen persons. The incident forced the evacuation of more than 4,000 spectators, including the Soviet ambassador to the United States.[13]

An intensified federal investigation into the activities of the JDL led to the 1987 arrests of four of its members who were linked to numerous bombings between 1984 and 1986. In August 1987, all four pled guilty, but one of them, Jay Cohen, committed suicide prior to being sentenced. The remaining members—Sharon Katz, Victor Vancier, and Murray Young—received prison sentences ranging from 'house arrest' to ten years imprisonment. Since their arrests, no terrorist acts have been attributed to Jewish extremists in this country.[14]

Left-Wing Terrorism

Leftist terror in America in the 1980s in many ways reflects the growth, dissolution, and reemergence of leftist extremism since the 1960s. Leftist terrorists who operated in the United States during the past decade were primarily holdovers from the leftist student movement and the radical prison reform and prison unionization efforts of the late 1960s and early 1970s. Although other leftist groups committed some terrorist-related crimes during the 1980s, M19CO and the UFF were the only leftist groups to which officially designated acts of terrorism were attributed.[15] M19CO was composed primarily of remnants of the Weather Underground, the Black Panther party, and other extremists from the defunct Students for a Democratic Society (SDS). In contrast, the UFF was formed by a small, highly cohesive group of former prison inmates and SDS members engaged in prison reform at institutions in New England. Both groups were strongly committed to the destruction of American imperialism and capitalism.

Formed in 1975, the UFF never had more than eight members despite its relatively long existence. By the time the 1980s began, the UFF had established itself as a worthy adversary of law enforcement officials; the small size of the group, its cellular structure, and its minimal efforts to recruit additional members made it an impenetrable organization. The group's bombings were highly coordinated, logically timed to allow adequate planning, and evenly distributed among states in the Northeast. During its decade of terror, its members committed nearly twenty-five terrorist acts, in addition to a number of bank robberies committed to fund its operations. Their efforts peaked in 1983 and 1984, coinciding with the height of M19CO activities. The UFF was responsible for nine bombings during that two-year period. With the escalation of the FBI's counterterrorism program to Priority One and the relaxation of the Levi Guidelines, the UFF became the target of a massive federal, state, and local task force created specifically to snare Raymond Luc Levasseur and his followers. Most of the members were captured in late 1984. The remaining members were arrested in early 1985, when the terrorist activities of the UFF ceased.

Like the UFF, M19CO met a similar fate. The group began with a flourish in 1979, freeing BLA leader JoAnne Chesimard from a New Jersey prison and arranging the escape of imprisoned FALN leader William Morales from a New York hospital.

Following their infamous Nyack, New York armored truck robbery, M19CO committed numerous bombings over a three-year period ending in 1985. Claiming responsibility for its crimes using its aliases, "Revolutionary Fighting Group," "Armed Resistance Unit," and "Red Guerrilla Resistance," M19CO confounded law enforcement officials until the arrest of members Timothy Blunk and Susan Rosenberg in November 1984. M19CO committed its last bombing three months later. The lone terrorist act committed by left-wing terrorists in the United States in 1985 occurred when remaining M19CO members bombed the Patrolmen's Benevolent Association in New York City. By May 1985, almost all of the active members of M19CO were behind bars awaiting trial. The leftist terror spawned by the student movement of the late 1960s and early 1970s appears to have been silenced with the dismantling of M19CO and the UFF. No confirmed terrorist acts have been committed by similar groups since 1985.

Right-Wing Terrorism

Statistics on right-wing terrorism in America are a confusing enigma. Although more than seventy-five right-wing extremists were prosecuted for terrorist-related offenses during the 1980s, members of right-wing groups accounted for only six of the 219 terrorist acts during that decade. The reason for the disparity is clear, however. Right-wing extremist groups did not turn violent until the summer of 1983, just eight months after the FBI increased its expenditures for counterterrorism and only four months after the Levi Guidelines were revised. Therefore, FBI resources and procedures were in place to intervene before right-wing terrorists had an opportunity to commit acts of terrorism. While members of the Order, CSA, the Aryan Nations, and SPC were busy trying to procure funding for their terrorist campaigns, the FBI began to close in. Following a shootout with SPC activist Gordon Kahl in Medina, North Dakota in February 1983 in which two United States marshals were killed, federal agents began to intensify their investigations of the extreme right. When Kahl was killed by federal agents on June 3, 1983 at Imboden, Arkansas, extremist members of the Christian Identity Movement created the Order and turned to terrorism—using the directives of *The Turner Diaries*[16] as a guide.

The Order existed for only a year after its creation, and it is obvious that the alterations in federal law enforcement policy that took effect during 1983 shortened the life span of the Order and its affiliated groups. While these groups prepared for the coming terrorist "War in '84" by accumulating cash and weapons through robberies and theft, federal agents arrested the overwhelming majority of their members before actual acts of terrorism could be committed. Between 1985 and 1987, numerous members of the Aryan Nations, the White Patriot party, CSA, SPC, the Order, and the Arizona Patriots were standing trial for crimes committed in preparation for the coming "race war." The infrastructures of these organizations were decimated by the convictions of their leading figures. But typical of many within terrorist organizations, remaining members attempted to reorganize and engage in a quick campaign of terror as a way of showing support for the arrested members of the original group. Such was the case with the Order. The Bruder Schweigen Task Force II (Order II) was credited with all five of the bombings committed by right-wing terrorists in 1986. Following these bombings at Coeur d'Alene, Idaho, however, right-wing terrorist groups were silent for the remainder of the decade.

Special Interest or Single-Issue Terrorism

Although special interest or single-issue terrorists can be a very diverse lot, in the 1980s only one type of special interest terrorism made its way into the FBI's official statistics—the environmental terrorist. Environmental terrorism stands in stark contrast to the other types of terror that occurred in the United States during the 1980s. Not only are the motives of environmental extremists different from those of other terrorist groups, these environmental terrorists also cut across the trends exhibited by other terrorist groups. While almost all types of terrorism declined during the latter half of the 1980s, it was during this period that environmental extremists made their way into the official statistics on terrorism. Although environmental extremists have sabotaged or 'monkey-wrenched' construction and development projects around the country for many years, it was not until the late 1980s that they began committing acts of sufficient severity to attract federal attention.

Extremist members of Earth First, founded by David Foreman, and the Animal Liberation Front (ALF) accounted for all seven acts of terrorism attributed to environmental groups in the United States. They committed their first officially designated acts of terror in 1986 and 1987. It was not until 1988, however, that the FBI officially recognized these crimes as terrorist incidents and reclassified them as such.[17] So little was known about the Evan Mecham Eco-Terrorist International Conspiracy (EMETIC) that it took two years for the 1986 sabotage at the Palo Verde Nuclear Generating Station, near Phoenix, and the 1987 vandalism of the Fairfield Ski Bowl, near Flagstaff, Arizona, to be recognized as acts of an organized group planning additional sabotage to nuclear facilities in the Southwest. Similarly, the 1987 arson of a veterinary research facility at the University of California at Davis by members of the ALF was not officially designated until its pattern of destruction continued over the next three years.

Although activities of EMETIC ceased after the arrest of five members of Earth First in 1989, members of the ALF have evaded detection and arrest. ALF members committed two of the four acts of terrorism that occurred in 1989, and a new environmental group, calling itself the "Earth Night Action Group," made its way into the statistics in 1990 with the destruction of power poles in Santa Cruz, California that caused a power outage affecting approximately 95 percent of that area's residents. The similarity between the act of sabotage carried out by the Earth Night Action Group and the activities of EMETIC suggest that, although EMETIC has now been dismantled, other members of the Earth First movement remain willing to carry the banner of environmental issues to violent excess. Environmental extremism may become a common fixture in American terrorism during the next decade.

General Conclusions about 1980s Trends

Four distinct patterns of American terrorism and counterterrorism emerged during the 1980s (figs. 2.6 and 2.7). First, the decade be-

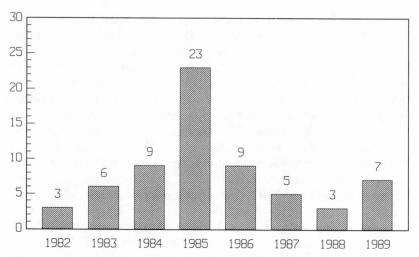

Figure 2.6 Terrorist Incident Preventions 1982–1989

gan with terrorism at an all-time high, followed by intense federal initiatives to combat the problem. Third, by the mid-1980s, as successful federal prosecutions decimated terrorist organizations in the United States, some groups tried to rebound from the devastation of arrests and indictments by staging retaliatory strikes. These efforts generally were short-lived and represented short-term increases in the decade's statistics. Finally, the decade closed on an ominous note with the arrival of environmental terrorism.

Unlike many types of crimes, terrorism occurs rather infrequently and is committed by relatively few persons. Terrorist organizations typically are not as large nor as well entrenched in legitimate business activities as most organized crime groups. Consequently, the effect of intense federal intervention efforts is felt more critically by terrorist groups than by traditional organized crime elements. Federal criminal investigations into some organized crime groups occasionally net the leaders of these organizations incidental to law enforcement efforts. Unfortunately, many of these underworld organized crime groups are so large that their leaders are quickly replaced by aspiring, younger proteges. The organizational structure of the group remains intact despite the loss of its leadership, and the group's criminal enterprises continue unabated. Terrorist groups generally are not so fortunate. The arrests and indictments of the leaders of relatively few terrorist organizations can have a dramatic impact on terrorism statistics.

Figure 2.7 shows the patterns of terrorist activity in the

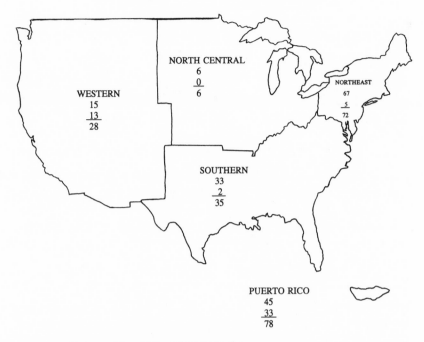

a. First row of figures under each region heading.
b. Second row of figures under each region heading.
c. Totals for each region provided; total number of incidents, 219.

SOURCE: Compiled from data provided by the FBI Terrorist Research and Analytical Center

Figure 2.7   Terrorist Incidents by Region 1980–1984,[a] 1985–1989,[b] 1980–1989[c]

United States during the 1980s. Only in the Western region and in Puerto Rico did terrorism levels remain moderately high in the latter half of the decade. The reasons for the continuation of terrorism in these areas are vastly different, however. In Puerto Rico, the rather large infrastructure and support groups of extreme nationalist groups account for the ability of Puerto Rican terrorist groups to continue operations. On the other hand, levels of terrorism in the western United States remained high due to changes in the types of groups that operated in that area. While international terrorists (primarily Armenians) dominated the statistics during the early 1980s in the western region, the latter half of the decade witnessed the growth of environmental (single-issue) terrorism in Arizona, California, and Oregon.

Chapter 3

Extremists Right and Left

Profiles and typologies of terrorist groups have become common-place. Since Charles Russell and Bowman Miller first published "Profile of a Terrorist" in 1977,[1] attention has been focused repeatedly upon the demographic and psychological characteristics of the men and women who turn to terroristic violence.[2] We have been told, for example, that they tend to be young, generally between eighteen and thirty-five years old; that they are primarily male, although a larger percentage of women are involved than in traditional criminality; and that they are better educated than others in their age group.[3] We have also been informed that, contrary to Marxist expectations, these men and women generally are from middle or upper income families whose parents were predominantly professional or white-collar workers.[4]

However, almost all of these findings are based upon studies of international terrorism. With terroristic activity occurring infrequently within the United States and with international terrorism dominating the news, the American revolutionary has been an ignored and frequently forgotten source of violence. Most people assume that the extremists in America who are willing to use terrorism as a political or social lever are closely related to their European cousins—politically leftist with anarchist overtones.[5]

This view of the terrorist as universally leftist and Marxist permeates not only the news media but has left its mark upon academic studies of terrorism. The typologies developed to create some order from the numerous terrorist groups reveal researchers' fascination and preoccupation with leftist violence.[6] Ever since Russell and Miller categorized the three major varieties of the 'urban guerilla' as 'anarchist,' 'Marxist-Leninist,' and 'nationalist,' re-

31

search in terrorism has focused upon leftist political violence. We have accepted, with few reservations, that "it is the combination of these three in specific contexts which produces the variant left extremist philosophies espoused by most terrorists today."[7]

In contrast to these notions, we find that terrorism in the United States during the 1980s was not overwhelmingly leftist. The American view of terrorists as ideologically Marxist and supported by Cuba or some other communist third-world country is largely due to our memory of Castro's support of the leftist student movement in the 1960s through the guise of the Vinceremos Brigades.[8] The annual sugar cane harvests were routinely turned into an indoctrination for American students who migrated to Cuba to assist in the harvest. They subsequently returned with well-read copies of Carlos Marighella's "The Urban Guerilla."[9] While persons advocating Marxist revolution have done their share of terrorism in America, a substantial number of those involved in terroristic violence in this country during the past decade have been members of or associated with right-wing groups (table 3.1).

Of the 170 individuals in our study who were named in indictments for domestic terrorism or terrorism-related activities during the 1980s, 103 were members of or associated with a loose coalition of right-wing groups frequently referred to as being part of the Christian Identity Movement. In actuality, not all of the groups involved in right-wing terrorism in the 1980s adhered to that philosophy; neither have all those who advocate these religious beliefs turned to violence to further their goals.

Others indicted for terrorism-related activities in the United States have been members of a variety of violent political movements: celebrated revolutionary groups such as M19CO and the United Freedom Front; nationalist/separatist groups like the FALN and the Macheteros; and the El Rukns, a violent Chicago street gang that became party to terrorism as a result of its ties to Libya. The 1980s also witnessed the first indictments and trials of environmental terrorists. Environmental extremists added monkey-wrenching to the repertoire of terrorist tactics.

The remaining indictments were issued against persons categorized by the FBI as having been involved in international terrorism. The Provisional Irish Republican Army (Provos) was the largest group within this category. Most of its activities involved gun-smuggling rather than targeting American persons or property for destruction. Likewise, Omega 7 primarily targeted Cuban diplomats at the United Nations, although in later years it became less discriminating. Only the Japanese Red Army, Libyan representatives, and Syrians were positively identified as being actively in-

Table 3.1 Sample Characteristics of Persons and Groups
Indicted for Terrorism/Terrorist Related Activities: 1980–1989

NAME OF GROUP	NUMBER OF PERSONS INDICTED	TOTAL NUMBER OF INDICTEES[a]
Domestic Terrorism		
Right-Wing		
1. Aryan Nations	3	3
2. Arizona Patriots	10	10
3. Covenant, Sword, and Arm of the Lord	17	22
4. Ku Klux Klan	1	1
5. The Order	28	48
6. The Order II	5	5
7. Sheriff's Posse Comitatus	4	5
8. White Patriot Party	7	9
Left-Wing		
9. El Rukns	7	7
10. Macheteros	19	20
11. FALN	5	5
12. May 19 Communist Organization	7	11
13. United Freedom Front	8	9
14. New African Freedom Front	9	9
15. Provisional Party of Communists	1	1
Single-Issue		
16. EMETIC	5	5
Subtotal	136	170
International Terrorism		
1. Japanese Red Army	1	1
2. Provisional Irish Republican Army	16	21
3. Omega 7	4	7
4. Libyans	7	7
5. Palestinian/Syrian	4	4
Subtotal	32	40
TOTALS	168	210

[a]"Indictees" refers to the total number of individuals indicted. In 42 cases the same persons were named in more than one indictment. Consequently, the number of indictees may exceed the number of persons for each group. The three indictees for whom group information was not known were excluded from analysis.

volved in international terrorism in America during the 1980s. The one remaining case, which involved Palestinian Fawaz Yonis, actually took place overseas. He was arrested and brought to the United States for trial after changes in federal law granted jurisdiction to American courts for crimes against American citizens that took place outside the territorial limits of the United States.[10]

Typologies of American Terrorists

In an effort to understand and simplify our world, people use every device imaginable to discriminate, categorize, and pigeonhole other people, objects, and places. The same is true of the study of terrorism. Typologies of terrorists and terrorist groups abound. Peter Flemming, Michael Stohl, and Alex Schmid have identified nearly fifty different typologies that attempt to categorize the varieties of terrorism.[11] They further reduce these typologies to four major types: (1) those based on terrorist groups; (2) those based on the motivation of the terrorist; (3) those that discriminate on the basis of the method of operation or types of targets selected by the terrorist group; and (4) those that use the historical origins of a terrorist group to distinguish it from other groups.[12]

According to Flemming and his colleagues, the best typologies are mutually exclusive, are valid and reliable, and have a high degree of functional utility. In other words, one should be able to assign a terrorist group to one, and only one, category in any typology; different persons should be able to correctly label the category in which the terrorist group fits within the typology; and finally, the categories within the typology should be able to help us predict different behaviors or actions by terrorist groups assigned to those categories.[13]

Unfortunately, most typologies fail to meet one or more of these criteria. Efforts to create typologies that are mutually exclusive usually result in categories that are too specific and fit only single terrorist groups. On the other hand, a typology that reduces terrorist groups to two or three categories may conceal or mask important ideological differences—differences that could affect the prediction of terrorist targets.

Due to the relatively small number of persons identified as having been involved in terrorism in America, a typology with a large number of categories limits any efforts to make statistical comparisons. Consequently, a relatively simple approach to analyzing persons involved in violent extremist behavior is necessary at this stage in the study of American terrorism. The FBI has categorically divided these persons' activities into 'domestic' and 'international' terrorism. For the purpose of this study, 'domestic terrorism' will be divided further into: (1) left-wing, (2) right-wing, and (3) single-issue terrorism. Single-issue terrorists in the United States have focused primarily upon environmental issues. However, due to the small number of persons who have been indicted for these acts, no statistical comparisons can be made. The activities of environmental terrorists are discussed in detail in Chapter 6. These distinctions are very similar to one of Paul Wilkinson's typologies, which identified four categories of extremism: Left, Right, ethnoreligious, and single-issue extremist movements.[14]

While some may consider these categories too simplistic to be of any utility, in actuality the terrorist groups that were active in the United States during the 1980s closely fit the descriptions. Left- and right-wing extremists involved in terrorism in America, for example, differ significantly in certain characteristics and traits. Yet the similarities within the categories are sufficient to allow generalizations to be made about groups falling within one or the other categories. Unlike the concerns raised by Flemming, Schmid, and Stohl, these categories are unlikely to result in different observers assigning groups to inappropriate categories; in other words, they are generally reliable. As we shall see, the characteristics used to distinguish various terrorist groups are mutually exclusive and of functional utility for predicting terrorist activities. The contrasting ideological traits of left- and right-wing groups in America produce interesting demographic distinctions between the two categories, as well as differences in target selection.

Characteristics of Left-Wing and Right-Wing American Terrorists

Wilkinson wrote that the 'extreme Left' is characterized by extreme egalitarianism, an extreme hatred of racism and capitalism, and an overt opposition to militarism. He described those within the 'extreme Right' as having "a belief in the instrinsic superiority of their own race or national group and the need to make their own race or national group supreme over other groups . . . and a belief in the necessity and desirability of war as a means of realising national or racial destiny."[15] With the exception of the single-issue terrorist (e.g., animal rights activists), Americans indicted for terrorism or terrorist related activities fall readily into one of these two categories. The right-wing groups are easiest to label since most are tied together by the Christian Identity Movement. The Aryan Nations; Arizona Patriots; CSA; various factions of the Ku Klux Klan; the Order and Order II; SPC; and the White Patriot Party fit this category. But simply labeling the remaining groups as leftist presents some problems. The El Rukns, Macheteros, FALN, M19CO, UFF, New African Freedom Front (also known as the New African Freedom Fighters or NAFF), and the Provisional Party of Communists are different from each other in many ways. For example, one might think that the El Rukns street gang would have little in common with Puerto Rican independence groups like the FALN and the Macheteros. Yet on a number of major identifying characteristics all of these groups bear striking resemblances. In particular, left-wing terrorists in America are bound together by at least five major similarities: 1) their ideology and beliefs about human nature; 2) their views on economics and the distribution of wealth; 3) their bases of operations; 4) their tactical approach; and 5) the targets they select. American right-wing terrorists can be distinguished from their leftist counterparts by using the same characteristics (table 3.2).

Ideology

While left-wing terrorist groups in America have adopted primarily a political focus, most right-wing terrorists are ideologically bound by religious beliefs. The Christian Identity Movement provides the link that has tied rightist groups in America together. Frequently referred to as the "British Theory," the Christian Identity Movement is based on the belief that Aryans, not Jews, are God's chosen people—a conviction widely held by many fundamentalist churches in America. Sheldon Emry, pastor of the Lord's Covenant Church in Phoenix, Arizona, is one of the movement's chief spokesmen. His radio program "America's Promise" was broadcast widely throughout the United States during the 1970s and 1980s. Members and leaders of SPC, the Aryan Nations, and CSA have come from among those sharing that belief. The movement, which is anti-Semitic and anti-black, argues that America is the promised land, reserved for the Aryan people of God. Similar to Shiite terrorism in its justification of violence, right-wing religous extremists in America advocate the use of terrorism as a prelude to war—the Armageddon, which will establish Christ's kingdom.[16]

Left-wing extremists traditionally have been sympathetic to,

Table 3.2 Characteristics of Left-Wing and Right-Wing
Terrorist Groups in America

	TYPE OF GROUP	
Characteristic	Left-Wing	Right-Wing
Ideology	Political focus; primarily Marxism	Religious focus; ties to Christian Identity Movement
Economic Views	Pro-communist/socialist; belief in Marxist maxim "receive according to one's need"	Strongly anti-communist; belief in Protestant work ethic, distributive justice
Base of Operations	Urban areas	Rural areas
Tactical Approach	Cellular structure; use of safehouses	National networking; camps and compounds
Targets	For funding: armored trucks preferred	For funding: armored trucks preferred
	Terrorist targets: seats of capitalism/government buildings	Terrorist targets: federal law enforcement agencies/opposing racial or religious groups

if not ardent advocates of, Marxism and, unlike religious right-wing groups in the United States, are apt to view religion, as Marx did, as 'the opiate of the masses.' Advocating the overthrow of capitalism as an economic and political system, Marx maintained the necessity of a 'worker' revolution before a classless society could be installed.[17] Religion, which has prevented the development of a proletariat collective consciousness necessary for revolutionary action, slows that process. While some left-wing extremist groups in America may not explicitly espouse Marxism, they share one major ideological similarity—a disdain for U.S. capitalism and its 'imperialialism' and 'colonialism.' That commonality has led leftist groups to seek funding from similar sources. For example, while the El Rukns were seeking Libyan funds to bomb buildings in Chicago,[18] Moammar Kaddafi was simultaneously funding the travels of such diverse extremists as Vernon Bellecourt, Bill Means, and Kwame Ture (a.k.a. Stokely Carmichael).[19]

It is ironic that the so-called Marxist basis of much left-wing terrorist ideology runs counter to the original teachings of Karl Marx. Believing that a socialist revolution could only be successful if large masses of the populace participated, Marx helped to expel anarchist Mikhail Bakunin from the International Workingmen's Association in 1872 because of Bakunin's advocacy of small guerilla forces using terrorist tactics to elicit political change.[20] As long as socialist revolution loomed on the horizon, terrorism lay dormant as a leftist strategy. However, as leftist communicators became frustrated "in their ability to affect the audience using non-violent language," they turned to terrorism to awaken the passive masses.[21] Leftist terrorists, therefore, are willing to use indiscriminate violence not only against the symbols of capitalism, but also against the working class itself. Members of the working class may be killed or maimed, but this sacrifice is viewed as acceptable if blame can be transferred to capitalist governments, thereby inciting the masses to revolt.

Views on Human Nature and Economic Structure

Underlying both left- and right-wing terrorist group ideologies are their views on human nature and human motivation. The basic beliefs on these issues provide the framework by which extremists of either type view the world, American government, and social programs funded by tax money. The groups categorized in this work as right-wing repeatedly write of their belief that people should be rewarded on the basis of the value of their labor. Described by George Homans as 'distributive justice,'[22] the concept suggests the commonly held belief that humans are motivated by rewards and punishments. When combined with the religious influence of the Christian Identity Movement, most right-wing terrorists express a strong belief in the 'protestant ethic.'[23] Logically expanded, these basic views are central to the right-wing terrorists' opposition to affirmative action, welfare, and educational programs for the economically disadvantaged that exclude non-minorities.

With their strong belief in the righteousness of capitalism and a disdain for communism, terrorists of the right have little sympathy for the wayward and dispossessed. While many Americans harbor the same attitudes, the violent extremists of the Right see as futile any attempts to rectify the perceived injustices of affirmative action or welfare fraud through legislative change. Common to many Americans who retain a strong belief in state's rights, right-wing extremists desire to maintain control over public funds at the local level. Consequently, the anti-tax beliefs of SPC permeate most of the groups of the extreme Right. With the Zionist Occupation Government (ZOG) firmly in control, the seemingly disparate extremists of the Christian Identity Movement turned to militant action under the guise of preparing for Christ's Second Coming.[24]

Leftist ideology holds basically to Marx's maxim "From each according to his abilities, to each according to his need."[25] While not all of the groups categorized in our study are purely Marxist, all share Marx's views on human nature. Believing that capitalist societies unleash and encourage a manipulative greed in humans, leftist terrorist groups in America today typically aspire to create a social system devoid of the greed they maintain characterizes American society.

Consequently, such disparate groups as the FALN and the Macheteros, the UFF, and the NAFF held similar views regarding the United States. All of these groups were allied ideologically by their opposition to capitalism's presumed exploitation of blacks, Hispanics, and the working class.[26] They perceived welfare and affirmative action programs as inadequate efforts to reform post-industrial capitalist society while maintaining the corrupt status quo. Such efforts were viewed as attempts to pacify the dissatisfied masses and prevent the development of the collective consciousness necessary for revolutionary action. Having given up on their ability to change the system without violent action, these left-wing extremists turned to Leon Trotsky's views on 'heroic terrorism' out of frustration and despair.[27]

Base of Operations

The FALN was active in the New York and Chicago areas; the Macheteros in the Hartford, Connecticut area; M19CO in New York, New Jersey, and Washington, D.C.; the New African Freedom Fighters in New York City; the El Rukns in Chicago. In contrast, the Aryan Nations and its violent offshoots, the Order and Order II, were based in the rural resort area of Hayden Lakes, Idaho, and the mountains of Montana. CSA lived out its existence in the mountains of northwest Arkansas. Members of the Arizona

Patriots wanted to create a camp in the desert mountains near Flagstaff. Leftist groups found urban areas more to their liking, while right-wing extremists have preferred the countryside. Merely coincidence? Possibly. After all, many members of leftist groups are blacks or Hispanics, and large concentrations of Puerto Ricans live in Chicago and Hartford. Blacks also disproportionately live in urban areas. But there is more to this dramatic difference between where left-wing and right-wing terrorist groups are concentrated than merely residential patterns. Much of the explanation has to do with the ideological and tactical differences between the two.

The Christian Identity Movement spawned its radical terrorists during the past decade only. In contrast, violent left-wing extremists in America have been in the business of terrorism at least since the 1960s. During that time, leftist radicals learned to focus their attention on urban areas in America and, to some extent, developed a fear of basing their operations in the countryside. Part of that fear grew as a result of revolutionary failures in the 1960s.

When Fidel Castro defeated the Batista regime in Cuba in 1959, he became the darling of the oppressed masses. By mounting a campaign of extortion, terror, and conventional guerilla warfare, Castro first concentrated on taking the rural countryside of Cuba. Since the export of sugar was the economic base of the island, Castro gradually strangled Havana by capturing and controlling the plantations of rural Cuba.

With Che Guevara at his side, Castro became the leading spokesperson for revolution in the Americas. At the Tricontinental Conference in 1966, Guevara presented the idea of exporting Castro's revolution to Bolivia. By mounting a rural revolutionary campaign, he believed the Bolivian government could be overthrown and the base created there could be used to further export revolution to neighboring countries, particularly to his homeland of Argentina.[28] However, Guevara's capture and death in October of 1967 had a chilling effect on the advocates of rural revolution. The failure of the National Liberation Army (ELN) to wage a successful rural campaign in Bolivia was carefully scrutinized by leftist strategists in Latin and North America. They turned to a more radical approach, one brought forward by despair and frustration at being unable to mount a successful conventional guerilla campaign or to develop the collective consciousness of the masses. The urban strategies of Carlos Marighella and Abraham Guillen became the logical alternative to rural revolution.[29] The urban setting was described by Marighella in the *Mini-manual of the Urban Guerilla* as the ideal location for terrorist operations. Originally published in 1967, the *Mini-manual* has been found among the possessions of almost every leftist terrorist group in America, perhaps due to Castro's distribution of it to the Venceremos Brigades, the leftist students who came to Cuba in the late 1960s to help with sugar cane harvests. The manual advocated an urban location for two reasons. Theoretically, it provided the opportunity to strike at the very seat of capitalism; tactically, it offered the anonymity of the crowd as a safe haven for its revolutionary members.

Right-wing terrorist groups in America could learn a lot from their leftist counterparts. Almost exclusively based in rural America, violent extremists of the right have met with much the same fate as Guevara's army. With their fixed bunker-style camps, they have been identified with ease, and were arrested and prosecuted in large numbers during the 1980s. Despite these weaknesses, groups like CSA had specific reasons for choosing to locate in the hinterlands of America. With the purported imminence of Armegeddon, these groups viewed their survivalist camps as necessary and required by God. They interpret biblical passages that speak of end-time events as being addressed directly to and for them. Numerous scriptures are interpreted by the militant Right as commands by God to prepare for Armegeddon.[30]

But the camps of the Christian Identity extremists were more than just a tactical choice; they represented an effort to escape the pollutants of urban life—large concentrations of ethnic minorities, a tolerance for homosexual rights, and a liberal press.[31] These camps frequently housed entire families, with a church as the center of social life. CSA, for example, at one time housed upwards of one hundred persons. Most of the camp's inhabitants never became involved in terrorist activity. Unfortunately, however, some did.

Tactical Approach

Extremist groups that engage in violent action to overthrow established governments are faced with a paradox. On the one hand the criminal nature of much of their activities requires that they maintain a clandestine existence. On the other hand the organization must engage in political and propagandistic activity to elicit public support for the movement.[32] All violent extremists, whether leftist or rightist, are faced with the dilemma of needing both secrecy and publicity.

Inspired by the writings of noted South American revolutionary theorists Abraham Guillen and Carlos Marighela, leftist revolutionaries in the United States adopted the use of cellular structures: safe houses, "mail drops" as a means of communication, and a variety of other clandestine tactics that have been successful in maintaining the anonymity of group members. The best example is provided by members of the UFF, the leftist revolutionary band headed by Levasseur. Members of the group successfully evaded capture for nearly a decade before their arrests in 1984. The leader of the UFF, Raymond Levasseur, had been on the FBI's Ten Most Wanted list since 1977. As James Greenleaf, an FBI special agent involved in the manhunt, explained, "UFF members have an ability to blend in with the community as average citizens . . . . If you are willing to cut your ties with the past, it's pretty easy to disappear in this country."[33] In adopting a clandestine cellular approach, however, their ability to recruit and to engage in legitimate political propagandizing is severely restricted.

Extremists on the Right, particularly those of the Christian Identity Movement, have not had the benefit of exposure to the writings and experience of leftist revolutionaries from the 1960s. Consequently, they struggled in the 1980s with the same questions that perplexed Guillen and Marighela in the 1960s: How does a revolutionary movement achieve popular support while remaining clandestine? At what point should the movement progress beyond terrorist cells to create a conventional guerilla army?

Christian Identity extremists chose to build popular support by creating 'survivalist' camps. Such camps also allowed male members to bring their families to live on the compound. Unfortunately, from the terrorist's point of view, such permanent sites are easily located and observed by law enforcement personnel. Abraham Guillen made the same observations regarding the failures of the Tupamaros in Uruguay: the establishment of 'fixed fronts' for supplies, support, and propaganda were easy targets for governmental responses.[34]

In addition, the right-wing terrorist groups chose to link their organizations nationally rather than develop distinct clandestine cells. Apparently, this issue was debated extensively by the members of various Identity groups. Tom Hoover, a member of the Arizona Patriots, was recorded discussing this issue with an undercover FBI agent in May of 1985: Although his fears went unheeded the conversation is, nonetheless, instructive.

> HOOVER: Again, you know, I encourage you to have everybody set up by cells. Because we don't all need to know each other. It's nice and there's camaraderie there, you know, but what . . .

SOURCE: Visual support. We don't need that.

HOOVER: We're not, you know, we're not going to ever get
to be a field army like you put a field army out.

SOURCE: And like Ty was talking about last night. You
know, having companies of this and doing that.

HOOVER: Bull———— . . . Yeah, forget it. I don't, I don't
even like the idea of one centrally located supply
point. I'd like to see it scattered out in caches.[35]

Within two years the major leaders of right-wing terrorist groups
from around the country were on trial for conspiring to overthrow
the U.S. government.[36] Major pieces of evidence introduced during
their trials included verbal and written communications to almost
every known leader in the movement, newsletters, and evidence of
a computerized national telephone network. The violent extremists
of the Right had learned the same lesson the Tupamaros learned
twenty years before.

Targets

Almost all violent extremist movements select two basic types of
targets: those that help to fund their operations and those that
help to further the political or social causes advocated by the organization. Marighela referred to the first of these targets as "the
appropriation of government resources."[37] Both left- and right-wing
extremists in America have found robbery necessary for funding
the revolution. Few have found sufficient external support to make
ends meet otherwise. Others, like the El Rukns, have solicited
funds from outside sources. Unfortunately for El Rukns leaders,
the U.S. Attorney's Office viewed with little humor their efforts to
obtain $2.5 million from Kadaffi in exchange for the bombing of
planes and government buildings in Chicago.[38]

Consequently, most violent extremist groups, Left and Right,
are forced to stoop to "ordinary" criminality to support their
causes. In fact, some of the biggest armored car robberies in American history have involved American terrorists (table 3.3). It is one
of the few similarities between the two polar types.

Beyond the issue of funding, however, leftist and rightist
groups bear marked differences in target selection. Since terrorism
is, in many ways, a staged media event, the symbolic nature of the
target frequently is as important to the terrorist as the extent of

Table 3.3 Noted Examples of Extremist Group Involvement in Armed Robbery to Fund Terrorist Activities

NAME OF GROUP	DESCRIPTION OF ROBBERY
Left-Wing	
May 19 Communist Organization	October 20, 1981; Nyack, New York. Brinks armored car robbery of $1.6 million.
Macheteros	September 12, 1983; West Hartford, Connecticut. Wells Fargo depot robbery of $7.1 million.
United Freedom Front	1974–1984; primarily East Coast region. Robbed banks of approximately $900,000.
New African Freedom Front	January 1984–October 1984; New York, New York. Conspired to rob Brinks armored car following tradition of 1981 Nyack, New York robbery.
Right-Wing	
The Order	April 23, 1984; Seattle, Washington. Continental Armored Transport Company robbery of approximately $535,000.
	July 20, 1984; Ukiah, California. Brinks armored car robbery of approximately $3.6 million.
Arizona Patriots	January–December, 1986; conspired to rob Wells Fargo armored car to support building of survivalist camp.

damage the incident causes. For both, the targets ultimately selected bear the mark of their respective ideologies.

Militant members of the Christian Identity movement have frequently spoken of striking out against ZOG. In reality their activities have been limited primarily to strikes against Jewish persons and property or against groups supportive of activities considered immoral by Identity members, such as adult theaters and organizations allegedly promoting homosexual rights. Order members were indicted for firebombing the Embassy theater in Seattle, Washington; attempting to burn the Congregation Ahavath Israel Synagogue in Boise, Idaho; and for machine-gunning Jewish talk show host Alan Berg outside his home in Denver, Colorado. Similarly, two Aryan Nations members were arrested in Seattle in May 1990 for conspiring to bomb black bars in Tacoma, Korean businesses in south Tacoma, and a Jewish synagogue in Seattle, Washington.[39] CSA member Richard Wayne Snell was convicted of the 1984 shooting death of a black Arkansas state trooper and is now on death row for the slaying of a Jewish Texarkana, Arkansas pawn shop owner. Another CSA member, Willam Thomas, was linked with the August 1983 firebombing of the Jewish Community Center in Bloomington, Indiana.[40]

Although the violent acts of right-wing extremists have been limited primarily to racial and religious "enemies," there have been ominous and foreboding exceptions that indicated the leaders of the extreme Right intended to expand their terrorist activities. James Ellison, CSA leader turned prosecution witness, testified at the 1988 national trial of right-wing extremist leaders that Robert Miles, former KKK leader, gave him a thirty-gallon barrel of cyanide and declared: "The ones who would be killed would not really matter. It would be a good cleansing."[41] Ellison claimed the Washington, D.C., water system was suggested as a possible target. Although Miles was acquitted of the charges, more recent threats have been received that suggested the release of dangerous chemicals in densely populated areas. The evidence suggests a move toward more indiscriminate violence by right-wing terrorists.[42]

Extremists of the Left have been much more politically oriented in their selection of targets. Rather than churches, synagogues, homosexual bars, and non-governmental individuals, leftist terrorists have focused upon (1) representatives of government—civil and military personnel, buildings, and equipment; and (2) large corporations—symbols of capitalism. For example, the 1986 federal indictments of eight members of the UFF listed the bombings of two county courthouses in Massachusetts; twelve bombings of major corporations such as IBM, Honeywell, Mobil Oil and Union Carbide; one bank; and four Army and Navy reserve centers or recruiting offices. They financed their operations from 1976 to 1984 by robbing eight banks in Maine, Connecticut, Vermont, New York, and Virginia.[43] M19CO was responsible for a series of similar bombings from 1983–1985. During that period the group bombed five federal and military installations, including the U.S. Capitol, and three other targets: the South African Consulate, the Patrolmen's Benevolent Association, and the Israeli Aircraft Industries Building. FALN bombings in Chicago followed similar patterns. The 1983 indictment of four FALN leaders cited the bombings of four banks, thirteen corporate buildings, five military installations or buildings, as well as the headquarters of the Chicago Police Department, the Cook County Building, and a U.S. Post Office building.[44]

Profiling the American Terrorist

As stated earlier, most descriptions of terrorists suggest that they tend to be young and are mostly male, that they are better educated than most people their age, and that they come primarily from the middle and upper classes. However, these descriptions are drawn largely from studies focusing on international terrorism. It has been assumed that such traits are also common to violent extremists in America. Most of these studies of international terrorism also concentrate on leftist groups, and it may be that leftist American terrorists fit this mold. But are those characteristics also true of America's violent Right? Do they, too, tend to be young, educated, and privileged? Our study concludes that violent leftists in America resemble closely the traditional view of the terrorist. Right-wing extremists differ significantly, however (table 3.4).

Age

Virtually all studies of the personal traits of terrorists conclude (or assume) that the average terrorist is young, usually between twenty to twenty-five years old.[45] A National Governors Association publication listed the average age of domestic terrorists as twenty.[46] Our review of the characteristics of persons indicted for terrorism or terrorist-related activities in the United States during the 1980s reveals, however, that the average age at indictment was considerably older—thirty-five. While some of the crimes for which these persons were indicted took place when the individuals were much younger, the vast majority of offenses occurred during the year or two prior to indictment. A conservative estimate of the average age of the American terrorist would place him at no younger than thirty-two or thirty-three, again considerably older than

Table 3.4 Demographic Characteristics of Left-Wing and
Right-Wing Terrorist Groups in America

Demographic Characteristic	TYPE OF GROUP*	
	Left-Wing	Right-Wing
Age	Average age at indictment: 35. Only 18% over age 40.	Average age at indictment: 39. 36% over age 40.
Sex	73% male 27% female	93% male 7% female
Race	29% white 71% minority	97% white 3% American Indian
Education	54% have college degrees. 12% have GED equivalent or less.	12% have college degrees. 33% have GED equivalent or less.
Occupation	Mixed, but many professional workers: physisian, attorney, teacher, social worker, etc.	Also mixed, but a large number of unemployed or impoverished self-employed workers.
Place of Residence	Urban	Rural

*Left-wing domestic terrorists included members from the following groups: El Rukns, Macheteros, FALN, May 19 Communist Organization, United Freedom Front, New African Freedom Front, and the Provisional Party of Communists.
Right-wing domestic terrorists included members of the Aryan Nations; Arizona Patriots; Covenant, Sword, and Arm of the Lord; the Ku Klux Klan, the Order, the Order II, Sheriff's Posse Commitatus, and the White Patriot party.

previous estimates. Part of the discrepancy may be that most prior studies included not only those involved in terrorism itself but also the remaining members of extremist groups. It may be that older, more experienced members are more likely to be involved in the actual terrorist incidents committed by a particular group. Another possible explanation, at least among leftist extremists in

America, is that many of the leftist terrorists indicted in the 1980s have been involved in terrorism for many years. Many of the leftist extremists finally apprehended in the 1980s had been involved with the "revolution" for a decade or more.

The ages of left- and right-wing terrorists differ significantly. The average age of right-wing terrorists in America was thirty-nine, higher than either the average age of domestic left-wing group members or of international terrorists. Over one-third of the right-wing terrorists were over forty. In contrast, less than 20 percent of the leftist terrorists were over forty. Much of this difference is found in the leadership of the Christian Identity Movement. Four of those acquitted at the national trial of white supremacists in 1988 were over sixty years old. Aryan Nations leader Richard Butler, Order member Artie McBrearty, KKK leader Robert Miles, and CSA member William Wade were sixty-plus, while the most active of the white supremacists, Richard Scutari, was only thirty-nine at the 1988 trial. Members of the UFF were all under forty at their indictment in 1986. Yet even the violent extremists of the Left depict the greying of terrorists. Levasseur, leader of the UFF, was thirty-nine at his indictment in 1986; Marilyn Buck of Weather Underground and M19CO fame was forty at her indictment in 1987. Even examination of the Puerto Rican separatist groups, the FALN and the Macheteros, as well as members of the El Rukns, the NAFF, and other leftists indicted for terrorist activities reveals a membership averaging in their thirties. Fifty percent of the leftist extremists indicted for terrorist-related activities during the 1980s were between thirty-one and forty years old.

Gender

While terrorism remains a predominantly male phenomenon, the proportion of females involved in extremist violence is far greater than in traditional crime. Aprroximately 5 percent of America's prison population are females, while slightly over 12 percent of the persons indicted for terrorist-related activities in America are females. If international terrorists are excluded, the percentage is even greater. Of 131 persons indicted for domestic terrorism, twenty (15 percent) were females.

As one might suspect, substantial differences exist between leftist and rightist groups regarding female involvement. The role of women in terroristic violence in America is directly related to the ideological foundations of the groups to which they belong.[47] Of fifty-six leftist extremists indicted, slightly over one-fourth (27 percent) were females. Extremists of the Left have a long history of advocating egalitarianism. Some groups like M19CO are predominantly female: Marilyn Jean Buck, Susan Lisa Rosenberg, Laura Whitehorn, Linda Sue Evans, and Elizabeth Duke all have played major roles in the activities of that group. Similarly, almost half of the members of the UFF and the NAFF were females. Female participation within Puerto Rican separatist groups is substantially lower, just over 10 percent, but is still higher than levels of female participation within rightist groups.

Among right-wing terrorists females present an interesting dilemma. Although many right-wing extremists moved their wives and children to remote survivalist camps, it does not appear that these women became involved in actual terrorist or criminal acts with nearly the same frequency as those among leftist groups. Only five of the seventy-five (7%) right-wing extremists indicted for terrorist-related activities were females. In almost all of these cases, the women were married to active members of violent elements of the extreme right. Only two played major roles in terroristic violence: Margaret Jean Craig performed the surveillance on Allen Berg prior to his assassination, and Deborah Dorr, along with her husband, was a leader of the Order II.

Ethnicity

Members of minority groups are more likely than whites of English heritage to believe that they have been exploited by American expansionism and colonialism. This belief permeates the violent left in America. Consequently, these groups have been able to attract a large following of minority group members. Nearly three-fourths (71 percent) of the leftists indicted for terrorist-related activities were minorities. The NAFF and the El Rukns are all-black groups; the Macheteros and FALN are overwhlemingly comprised of white Hispanics; even the violent members of the M19CO, the UFF, and the Provisional Party of Communists are racially mixed.

In contrast, the violent extremists of the Right, with their religiously based beliefs in the superiority of the Aryan race, are virtually all white. Of seventy-five members of the extreme right indicted for terrorist-related activities, only two claimed to be of other than Aryan extraction. William Wade and his son, Ivan, both affiliated with the CSA and the SPC, listed their ethnic background at their 1987 trial as American Indian. The Wades claimed

to be descendants of the Wade clan of tribal Indians who came into
the Oklahoma territory in the 1800s. Consistent with the beliefs of
SPC members, they maintained that the federal court at Fort
Smith had no jurisdiction over their activities. With an abiding
hatred for blacks and Jews and a disdain for federal policies allowing the immigration of Mexicans, Vietnamese, and other Asians,
the extremists of the far Right leave little room for minority participation in their activities.

Education and Occupation

Most studies of terrorism conclude that terrorists are university
educated, middle or upper class, and professionally trained. Government publications in particular are apt to portray terrorists in
this light. One such document described the characteristics of the
American terrorist as:

> an average age of 20; male and female; single or separated;
> middle or upper class; urbanites; university graduates; Marx-
> ist and anarchist in ideology; recruited at universities; and
> (composed of) students, lawyers, doctors, government employ-
> ees, sociologists, and psychologists.[48]

While leftist terrorists in America closely resemble this description, violent extremists of the Right are significantly different. Although over half of the leftists indicted during the 1980s for terrorist activities were college or university graduates, only 12 percent
of the right-wing terrorists held college degrees. A third of the violent extremists of the Right had not graduated from high school.

These educational differences resulted in significant differences in the occupations and incomes of the leftist and rightist
group members. Violent leftist groups were more likely to have
members who were physicians, attorneys, teachers, and even government workers. For example, the eighteen members of the Macheteros indicted in 1986 for the 1983 robbery of the Wells Fargo
depot in West Hartford, Connecticut included Jorge Farinacci Garcia, Roberto Maldonero Rivera, and Paul Weinberg—all attorneys.
Most of the remaining indictees in this case have university degrees in political science, sociology, and anthropology and are employed as teachers, occupational therapists, and independent arti-
sans.

M19CO and the NAFF reveal similar educational and occupational backgrounds. M19CO member Alan Berkman is trained as a physician, while his associate, Susan Lisa Rosenberg, is the daughter of a prominent physician. NAFF leader Coltrane Chimurenga, previously known as Randolph Simms, pursued his doctorate at Harvard University, while other members of the group, most of whom have college degrees, were employed in government service.

By contrast, violent extremists associated with the Christian Identity Movement are much less likely to be college educated. Although some of the leaders of the various groups are well educated, many cadre members lack even minimal educational and job skills. The better educated members of these groups have evolved, of course, as leaders of the extreme right—Richard Butler, head of the Aryan Nations, is an engineer as is Wilhelm Schmitt of the SPC. Perhaps the presiding judge at Schmitt's sentencing described it best:

> you have a high IQ and are well-educated with college degrees and extensive training in mathematics, physics, and religious studies. You have been gainfully employed as a research engineer for Lockheed Missile and Space Company, and as a consulting engineer for other reputable companies. You are a successful inventor and have been honored for your part in the development of Polaris missiles. You furnished the leadership and very substantial financial support to maintain your co-defendants and to effect the illegal conduct for which you and they have been convicted. It is quite likely that absent your direction and support, these co-defendants, a truck driver, an appliance repairman, and a carpenter, would not and could not have committed these crimes.[49]

The generally lower educational and job skills of the extreme right required group members to rely more heavily on petty theft and robbery to finance their operations. After several successful robberies in the Northwest, members of the Order, for example, discussed sending money to the CSA camp in north Arkansas citing the extreme poverty of group members.[50] In fact, many of the members of these groups were drawn to these organizations by the lure of a place to stay and a modest monthly salary in exchange for work at the compounds.

At first glance the characteristics and activities of violent American extremists are concealed by the diversity of the groups involved. In attempting to understand the phenomenon, we are tempted to accept the commonly held view of terrorists as ideologi-

cally leftist, predominantly Marxist, and typically young, egalitarian, well-educated recruits from the middle and upper strata of society. Unfortunately, such a description only characterizes about
half of those who have been indicted for terrorist-related activities
in the United States during the past decade. Unless we contrast
right- and left-wing terrorists in America in an analysis of this
phenomenona, any differences we might find are attenuated and
lost in the averaging of dissimilarities between the two. Thus a
separate and complete examination of both left- and right-wing
terrorism during the 1980s is necessary to our understanding of
the bizarre, occasionally farcical, but always deadly serious activities of terrorists in the United States.

Chapter 4

The Righteous and the Extremists of the Right

When Americans think of right-wing terrorism, the Ku Klux Klan often comes immediately to mind.[1] Yet right-wing terrorists in America during the 1980s were more closely allied with the Christian Identity Movement than with the Klan. Apparently developed by Englishman Richard Brothers in the late eighteenth century, the Identity Movement had its origins in what is now known as "Anglo-Israelism." Believing that Christ was of Aryan ancestry, the British theory contends that the ten lost tribes of Israel migrated to the European continent and later to Great Britain. Identity historians maintain, for example, that even the word "British" was derived from the Hebrew *berit-ish*, meaning "man of the covenant."[2] The "Israel of God" subsequently migrated to the United States, the promised land where Christ would eventually return and set up his kingdom. Members of the two southern tribes, the Jews, were portrayed as the killers of Christ and the offspring of Satan.

Although this theory has been widely debated since its inception, it has rarely attracted large numbers of converts. However, in the mid-twentieth century Anglo-Israelism experienced a resurgence through the teachings of a Methodist minister named Wesley Swift. By maintaining that Jews are the descendants of Cain brought about by an illicit sexual relationship with Eve, Swift contended that Jews, in confederation with Satan, have been battling God and his righteous people for control of the world since the fall of Adam.[3] Swift found support for his views from his good friend Gerald L. K. Smith, publisher of Henry Ford's *The International Jew*.[4] Ford's book, which suggested an international conspir-

53

acy on the part of Jews to control the world's economy, is widely read and cited by Identity believers.

Before Swift's death in 1970, he managed to attract a sizable following to his congregation in southern California. A friend and close associate of Swift's was William Potter Gale, pastor of an Identity church in Mariposa, California, and later founder of the violent anti-tax groups the SPC and the Committee of the States. It was Gale who introduced a youthful Lockheed aeronautical engineer by the name of Richard Girnt Butler to Wesley Swift. In 1973, Butler moved Swift's church, the Church of Jesus Christ Christian, to Hayden Lakes, Idaho. Butler maintains that he is the direct successor to Swift's Lancaster, California legacy.

Although a number of church groups adhere to the teachings of the Christian Identity Movement, only a few turned violent in the 1970s and 1980s. The SPC, the Aryan Nations and its violent offshoots the Order and the Order II, the CSA, and the Arizona Patriots played major roles in the outbreak of right-wing terrorism in the United States during the 1980s. Of the seventy-five persons indicted for right-wing terrorism in America during that period, all were closely allied with the Christian Identity Movement. While some groups, like Glen Miller's White Patriot Party, may not have adhered completely to identity theology, right-wing terrorist groups all became well-known to each other through annual National Alliance conventions. Identity groups routinely invited members of other right-wing organizations to speak at rallies, provided them with specialized paramilitary training, and established and maintained contacts with them for the coming revolution. Such contacts sometimes resulted in financial support from one organization being diverted to another. For example, the Order supposedly gave $300,000 of its stolen money to support Miller's White Patriot Party.[5]

The Ku Klux Klan

Although right-wing terrorists in the 1980s were affiliated primarily with the Identity Movement, many of the movements' recruits and some of its leaders did, in fact, come from the Ku Klux Klan. Most notable were Louis Beam, former Grand Dragon of the Texas Knights of the KKK, and Robert Miles, former Grand Dragon of the Michigan Realm, United Klans of America.[6] Although the Klan is notorious for its violent, terroristic efforts to restore white supremacy in the South, the overwhelming majority of its members have not committed criminal acts that would be labeled by federal authorities as terroristic. This does not mean that some KKK members have not been involved in American terrorism. Generally, however, these individuals became involved with smaller, more radical right-wing groups as an outgrowth of their Klan affiliation. The Klan was merely a first stop on the long road to extremism. The only officially designated act of suspected terrorism attributed to a Klan member not affiliated with one of the smaller, more violent groups involved Walter Wolfgang Droege.[7]

Despite the KKK's relative absence from FBI records as the group directly responsible for acts of terrorism in the 1980s, it exerted tremendous influence on the Christian Identity Movement through Miles, Beam, and Miller. Miles left his job as an insurance company branch manager in 1970 at age forty-five to devote himself full-time to his Identity-affiliated Mountain Church of Jesus Christ. At the time he also served as Grand Dragon of the Michigan Realm of the KKK. In 1971 Miles' activities came to a screeching halt. A staunch opponent of busing to achieve racial balance, Miles and four others were arrested and convicted of bombing ten school buses in Pontiac, Michigan and for his participation in the tarring and feathering of a school principal.[8] Sentenced to nine years in prison, he was released in 1979.

As part of his parole agreement, Miles resigned from the Klan. However, he stepped up his supremacist rhetoric immediately upon release. Through regular contacts with other leaders of the Identity movement, the Aryan Nations prison ministry, and the National Alliance, Miles quickly became a leader of the extreme Right, operating from his seventy-acre farm near Lansing, Michigan.[9] Although active as the leading spokesperson for the extreme Right, Miles steered clear of any direct involvement in criminal violence. However, when James Ellison, leader of the CSA, turned state's evidence in 1987, Miles was identified as the leader of a national conspiracy by the extreme Right to overthrow the United States government. Ellison testified, for example, that it was Miles who gave him a thirty-gallon barrel of cyanide to pollute Washington, D.C.'s water system.[10] The conspiracy charges against Miles and other leaders of the movement fell apart, however, and Miles was acquitted of the charges in 1988.[11] Miles, now in his late sixties, has maintained a much lower profile since his acquittal.

While Miles played the role of patriarch for the extreme Right, Beam became its most ardent recruiter. By the time he turned thirty in 1977, Beam was already the Grand Titan of David Duke's newly formed Knights of the Ku Klux Klan. By 1980 Beam had become the Grand Dragon of the Texas KKK. He led Klan rallies in the Galveston area in opposition to Vietnamese shrimpers in Galveston Bay. The harassment continued until a federal civil suit was filed by the Vietnamese Fishermen's Association and the court prohibited further Klan intimidation. They were also barred from operating paramilitary camps in Texas. One year later Beam was convicted of using government land near Fort Worth for paramilitary training. Given six months probation, Beam resigned as Grand Dragon of the Texas KKK and moved to Hayden Lakes, Idaho.

There, he assumed the role of ambassador-at-large for Butler's Aryan Nations. It was Beam who developed the national computerized network that created a point system for assassinations and other terrorist acts. According to James Ellison, Beam, Butler, and Miles developed an elaborate conspiracy to overthrow the U.S. government at a meeting of the Aryan Nations Congress in 1983. The three leaders envisioned the terrorist activities of CSA and the Order as the catalysts that would start the revolution.[12]

When the crackdown on the Order began in December 1984, Beam fled to Mexico, where he wrote a lengthy essay entitled (not accidentally) "Common Sense." He advocated that white Americans move to the Northwest, where they could create a racially pure republic. By this time Butler had been arrested and was scheduled for trial in Fort Smith. Beam concluded his essay with the following macabre comments:

> Several requests have been made of me for an autographed copy of my wanted poster. Anyone who donates fifty or more dollars to the defense of Pastor Butler or Robert Miles after December 1, 1987 will receive one.[13]

Beam remained on the FBI's Ten Most Wanted list until his capture in November 1987. Beam's wife critically wounded a Mexican federal judicial police officer during the shootout at his residence in Guadalajara. The national trial involving the leaders of the extreme Right was delayed pending Beam's return to the United States. Finally, on April 7, Beam and the other co-conspirators, including Butler and Miles, were acquitted of all charges. Bowing before a memorial to Confederate soldiers in Fort Smith, Beam declared: "the Zionist Occupation Government has suffered a terrible blow."[14] Beam returned to his small business, in Hayden Lakes, which specializes in camping and survival gear. He continues to speak at rallies for white supremacy around the nation.[15]

As a result of prior convictions, both Beam and Miles had officially resigned their positions within the KKK as part of sentencing agreements that required them to disassociate themselves with its activities. Unlike these men, Miller, the noted founder of the Carolina Knights of the Ku Klux Klan, did not leave the Klan under pressure. Instead, he found that public opinion against the white-robed Klan had a severely adverse effect on recruiting. He subsequently changed the name of the Carolina Knights to Confederate Knights of the Ku Klux Klan and eventually to the White Patriot Party.

Miller sought to modernize Klan appearance by exchanging the white robes and hoods for combat battle dress uniforms. In transforming the group to a paramilitary unit, Miller attracted new members into the organization. Well over 300 uniformed participants marched with Miller in North Carolina cities throughout the mid-1980s. With strong connections nationally to other neo-Nazi groups, Miller funneled members from his organization into other violent extremist groups. In return he received funding from such noted extremists as Robert Jay Mathews and his illegally obtained coffers of the Order.[16] Despite the activities of these former Klansmen, the KKK took a back seat to SPC, CSA, and the Order during the early 1980s.

Sheriff's Posse Comitatus

Sheriff's Posse Comitatus was formed in 1969 by Henry Beach and William Potter Gale. After its inception in Portland, Oregon, SPC spread quickly into thirteen states during the early 1970s. By the early 1980s new leaders emerged in SPC, including James P. Wickstrom, pastor of an Identity church in Wisconsin known as the Life Science Church. He quickly arose as a prominent spokesperson for the organization from his compound in rural Tigerton.[17]

Like other Identity groups, SPC believes in the superiority of the Aryan race and has a distinct anti-Jewish, anti-black philosophy. Contending that the federal government is controlled by Jews, Beach and Gale chose a name for the group that reflected their disdain for federal authority. In 1878 Congress passed the Posse Comitatus Act,[18] which was intended to prohibit military involvement in local law enforcement. In place of the military, the act granted the county sheriff the authority to deputize citizens for this purpose. Gale, Wickstrom, and other leaders of the movement recognize no governmental authority higher than the county. Consequently, they refuse to recognize the federal government's right to collect taxes.

SPC attracted many converts during its early years. It acted as a clearinghouse for "information relating to the procedures and methods of protecting property and/or evading state and federal taxation."[19] Over the years the movement became increasingly violent. Beach wrote:

> In some instances of record the law provides for the following prosecution of officials of government who commit criminal acts or who violate their oath of office . . . He shall be removed by the posse to the most populated intersection of streets in the township and, at high noon, be hung by the neck, the body remaining until sundown as an example to those who would subvert the law.[20]

In keeping with the tradition of the rural revolutionary, SPC literature demanded: "Get Out of the Cities!! Prepare to Defend in Rural Areas!!"[21]

In 1974, Gordon Wendell Kahl, an active member of the SPC and the Identity-affiliated Gospel Doctrine Church of Jesus Christ in Texas, refused to pay his income tax. To further demonstrate his disdain for state authority, he refused to renew his driver's license. Kahl was subsequently arrested, and in 1977 he was convicted of income tax evasion. Released on five years probation, Kahl returned to his home state of North Dakota but failed to report to his Bismarck-assigned probation officer. In February 1983, with arrest warrant in hand, United States marshals and local authorities attempted to arrest Kahl in Medina, North Dakota. Kahl killed two marshals and wounded three others during the firefight that ensued. He escaped and for four months was hidden by others in the Identity movement. During this period he wrote to Wickstrom detailing the events of the shooting and proclaiming "We are a conquered and occupied nation—conquered and occupied by the Jews."[22]

Kahl made his way to northern Arkansas, where he hid in a secluded farmhouse owned by 63-year-old William Wade, an associate of the CSA, a then relatively unknown religious-paramilitary group.[23] After authorities were alerted by an informant, 63-year-old Kahl was killed in a gun battle with state and federal authorities on June 3, 1983. Kahl quickly became a martyr for the extreme right and a catalyst for the revolution espoused by the Order, CSA, and the White Patriot Party.

After Kahl's death other SPC members began making more

intense preparations for the coming "war" with federal authorities. One of them was Wilhelm Ernst Schmitt, a former employee of Lockheed Missile and Space Company and an award-winning engineer for his work in the development of Polaris missiles.[24] A leader in the anti-tax movement in Minnesota, Schmitt had been convicted in federal court in Illinois of threatening an IRS agent in 1969.[25] Several years after his release from prison Schmitt settled in Bemidji, Minnesota, earning his living as an inventor (he holds several patents) and as a consulting engineer. By the early 1980s he had become the leader of an SPC chapter in the Bemidji area. Meetings of this local group had a decidedly religious flavor, held each Sunday morning at Schmitt's home, where discussions of tax protest methods mingled with Identity views on the coming Armageddon.

Aided by Harry Mott, the married 44-year-old owner of an appliance repair business and father of four; Roger Luther, a 46-year-old carpenter; and Ernest Foust, a 57-year-old divorced truck driver; Schmitt began stockpiling weapons and preparing for all-out war on the IRS and other federal agents. To fund these preparations, Schmitt considered bank robbery and sent Mott to gather information about four banks in North Dakota and Minnesota.[26]

By mid-1984 federal authorities were monitoring closely the activities of suspected SPC members. Suspecting that IRS agent Peter Gandrud was conducting surveillance on the group, Schmitt vowed to have him killed. With Foust, Schmitt experimented with a remote-control instrument capable of detonating an explosive device.[27] Before Schmitt could carry out his plans, on October 31, 1984 federal agents raided his home, finding several illegally owned handguns, machine guns and fragmentation hand grenades. The same day agents raided the bunker-style home of Luther located on eighty acres in rural Hubbard County, Minnesota. There they found underground tunnels leading to caches of arms and supplies. Military trip flares, a grenade launcher, and three fully loaded machine guns complete with instructions on test-firing the weapon on "the nearest judge or IRS agent"[28] were among the weapons discovered. Luther drove up just in time to find his home being searched. He was arrested while trying to obtain access to a fully loaded machine gun in the trunk of his car.

In January 1985 in federal court a jury found Schmitt, Foust, and Luther guilty of conspiracy to injure and impede Peter Gandrud in the performance of his duties as an IRS agent. Schmitt and Luther were also convicted on seven additional weapons charges. Schmitt was sentenced to twenty-six years in the federal penitentiary, while Luther and Foust each received eight years for their part in the plot. Schmitt and Mott received additional five-year sentences for their conspiracy to commit bank robbery.[29]

1985 was a turning point for SPC nationwide. When Wickstrom and Donald Minniecheske illegally created the new "township" of Tigerton Dells in Wisconsin, local and federal authorities closed in. Wickstrom was arrested and served thirteen months during 1984 and 1985 for impersonating a public official. (Wickstrom had declared himself the municipal judge of Tigerton Dells.) Law enforcement authorities swept down on the paramilitary camp in 1985, confiscating property and removing trailers that violated local zoning laws. Minniecheske, 56, who provided the land for the survivalist camp, was sentenced to nine years for possession of stolen property and other related violations. In what was supposed to have been a final chapter in SPC activities, James Wickstrom's sentence was commuted with the stipulation that he not become involved in other anti-tax or paramilitary movements. He moved to Pennsylvania, where he was again arrested, and was sentenced on August 7, 1990 to thirty-eight months in prison for conspiring to distribute $100,000 in counterfeit money.[30] The SPC camp near Tigerton, Wisconsin now stands empty; its owners and leaders are in prison,[31] and the government is seeking to foreclose on the remaining thirty to forty families who were members of the Tigerton group for failure to pay back taxes.[32]

The Aryan Nations

The Aryan Nations is estimated to have approximately 1,000 supporting members nationwide.[33] Having attended Swift's Identity church in Los Angeles regularly during the 1960s, Butler became its acknowledged leader after Swift's death in 1970. Three years later he moved the operation to Hayden Lakes.

In Hayden Lakes, Butler constructed a church building on his property that drew a small congregation. He called it "the Church of Jesus Christ Christian." His theology is typical of Identity preachers: a strong belief that the Aryan race was the "chosen seed" of Israel, a conviction that Jewish people had conspired to control the economic systems of the world in an effort to suppress God's chosen seed, and a commitment to readiness when the "inevitable" race war began. Upon his accepting that the federal government was controlled by the Zionist Occupation Government, other logical elements followed: a belief that federal taxes were illegitimate, that the FBI and the IRS were conspiring with Jewish elements to seek and destroy the chosen seed, and that efforts to combat these enemies pleased God. The apparent logic of Identity theology appealed to a wide range of extreme rightists. The anti-tax movement, fueled by SPC, found refuge in the theology's justifications for defiance of federal tax laws. KKK members were drawn to it as well as white prison inmates, who found a scapegoat for their misdeeds through prison "ministries" led by Butler and his Identity teachings.[34]

In addition to those he guided spiritually, Butler created a secular following in the Aryan Nations. His property in Hayden Lakes began to look more and more like the traditional Identity survivalist camp, complete with guard towers, defensive emplacements, and a print shop and crowded with followers from across the United States. In the late 1970s, Butler established a prison ministry in correctional institutions throughout the United States. One inmate attending such sessions led by Butler's followers in an Arizona prison was Gary Lee Yarbrough. Shortly after his release from prison in 1979, Yarbrough moved to Hayden Lakes, took a job as a dishwasher at a local restaurant, and became Butler's chief of security. Butler's ties to the neo-Nazi National Alliance also convinced Beam to move to Hayden Lakes, where he assumed the role of recruiter for the Aryan Nations.

The death of SPC member Kahl in June 1983 was the topic of conversation at the July 1983 Aryan Nations Congress, sponsored by Butler at Hayden Lakes. Throughout the convention, as CSA leader Ellison testified, secret meetings were held during which strategy for the overthrow of ZOG was plotted. Attending those meetings were Aryan Nation leaders Butler and Beam; ex-Michigan KKK leader Miles; Ellison; and a young representative of the National Alliance, Robert Mathews. Also attending the convention were the nine founding members of the Order.[35] Three months later Mathews met with his co-founders at his home in Metaline Falls, Washington, where they formed the Order (also known as "the Bruder Schweigen" or Silent Brotherhood).[36]

When first organized, the Order was as destitute financially as other Identity groups. Although later they would generate an abundance of operating funds from armored car robberies, initially the Order turned to counterfeiting to obtain funds to buy weapons and supplies. Within one month of organizing the Order, Mathews and other Order members used the Aryan Nations headquarters print shop to produce their first batch of counterfeit fifty-dollar bills.[37] (It is unknown whether Butler was aware that Aryan Nations equipment was being used for this purpose.)

Although Butler's role in the violence that emanated from

Hayden Lakes may have been limited to providing "spiritual" and ideological guidance, that was not the case with those who worked for him at the Aryan Nations. One by one, members of Butler's security force were indicted and convicted for crimes associated with the Order. In 1985, Yarbrough, the first of Butler's security chiefs during this period, was convicted for possession of explosive materials and for violations of Racketeering Influenced and Corrupt Organizations (RICO) statutes. Tate, frequently seen in Nazi uniform standing with Yarbrough at Butler's side as he addressed crowds of local believers, was convicted of murdering a Missouri state police officer while trying to escape to the CSA encampment in northern Arkansas.

Eldon "Bud" Cutler took Yarbrough's place as chief of security. An amiable, heavy-set, balding farmer, Cutler did not seem to fit the description of a man who could commit murder. One of the last members of Mathews' Order to be detected, Cutler was outraged at the death of Mathews and the capture of Order members during the six months following Mathews' death in December 1984. Believing Tom Martinez, an Order associate, to be responsible for the Order's demise,[38] Cutler ordered that Martinez be found and decapitated. When the FBI learned of the plot, undercover agents infiltrated the group and, ironically, were assigned the task of executing Martinez. The FBI arrested Cutler after he provided payment to an FBI undercover agent when shown staged pictures of Martinez's supposedly dead body.[39] In all of these events, however, Butler remained unimplicated, at least from a prosecutorial perspective. When FBI agents tried to include Butler in a conversation about wanting to kill Martinez, Cutler maintained that "the pastor actually knows nothing about this."[40] Since his acquittal in 1988, Butler avoids using words or phrases in his speeches that might suggest his group is at "war" with the federal government. Although in failing health, he remains active as a leader of the Aryan Nations. To learn of the violent potential of Aryan Nations rhetoric one need only examine the effect of Butler's beliefs on CSA and the Order.

Covenant, Sword, and Arm of the Lord

In 1971 thirty-one-year-old James Ellison moved from San Antonio, Texas to northwest Arkansas. A fundamentalist preacher with a bent for Identity doctrine, Ellison purchased 224 acres of remote timberland in Marion County from Campus Crusade for

Christ, an organization with which he once had been affiliated.[41] Over the next few years, Ellison converted his farm into a safe haven for the wayward and dispossessed, drug addicts, and ex-convicts. As Ellison explained to a grand jury in 1985, "God directed me to come to this part of the country, and acquire land, and establish a place of refuge for people that needed a place to live. . . . We have a religious society so to speak, a community."[42] Naming the camp "Zarephaph-Horeb" after a Biblical purging place, Ellison estimated that over 400 people passed through its gates seeking assistance.

Throughout its existence, CSA was led by Ellison. There was no disputing his leadership. Ellison made most important decisions alone—from the procurement of work for camp residents to the assignment of housing on the compound. Beneath Ellison in the camp hierarchy were five to six "elders." Most of the adult residents were young, age 25–35, and married with children. Most were impoverished. Many were ex-convicts, recently released from prison. The camp supported itself primarily by buying and selling guns at gun shows and selling handcrafts and survivalist equipment at flea markets. The camp was situated in thick timberland, and Ellison, who had worked as a logger, ran a logging business and a sawmill at the camp. Some of the residents held regular jobs, while others placed ads in local newspapers for jobs as carpenters or laborers. The organization paid some of the members $200 per month for services rendered at the camp. Although opposed to government welfare, ironically many of the members received Aid to Dependent Children checks monthly.

During its heyday in the mid-1980s, the camp housed more than 100 men, women, and children in three separate compounds. The main compound consisted of approximately twenty-five buildings, five of which were strictly organized as bunker-style fighting positions. The church, six residences, and assorted storage buildings were also located at the first compound. The other two, smaller compounds were referred to as the "plateau compound" and the "valley compound." When the seige with FBI agents began in April 1985, residents retreated to the main compound, abandoning the less defensible outer compounds. At least one land mine located on the main road near the main gate could be detonated by remote control from the radio room at the main compound. Numerous claymore-type homemade mines were positioned along the camp's property.[43]

The camp and its occupants maintained good relations with its neighbors during the first years of its existence, attracting little attention from local law enforcement authorities. But in 1977 Kerry Noble and another couple from Dallas, Texas visited the camp, liked what they saw, and stayed on. Within three weeks, Noble was named an elder by Ellison. That fall Randal Rader moved in and was also quickly appointed as an elder. Within six months Rader began military training sessions for members at the encampment. Believing that a collapse of the American economic system was at hand, the group prepared for the Armageddon. A mock-up training facility for urban fighting called "Silhouette City" was erected. The group began conducting the "Endtime Overcomer Survival Training School" for local Identity members and groups affiliated with the Identity movement.[44]

In 1979 Ellison left the compound to look for work. During his absence, Rader became increasingly militant and violence became a familiar topic at church services. The group began stockpiling weapons, mostly bought by Ellison and Rader at gun shows and flea markets in Missouri. Kent Yates and Rodney Carrington, two members close to Rader, were assigned the tasks of converting semi-automatic rifles to automatics and constructing silencers and hand grenades. During this time the group was frequently visited by Robert Smalley, who was later indicted for illegally obtaining weapons for the Order. Although evidence of conflict between Rader and Ellison is apparent from FBI interviews with indicted members, Ellison was not averse to the militant direction the group began taking in 1978.[45] Yet with the exception of a few non-terrorism related offenses, criminal activities of CSA members remained fairly limited until 1983. However, as early as 1982, links with the Aryan Nations were being solidified. In October, the compound was visited by Butler on a recruiting trip for the Aryan Nations. Within a few weeks Rader, Smalley, and several others left the organization. Rader and Smalley resurfaced two years later when the FBI began closing in on the Order.

When SPC member Kahl was killed in June 1983, the extreme Right moved into action. Within days of Kahl's death, Butler contacted Ellison and requested his attendance at the upcoming Aryan Nations Congress. Ellison arrived at the Aryan Nations headquarters in Hayden Lakes on July 6. During the next four days, according to testimony given by Ellison and others, the leaders of the movement plotted their strategy.[46] Butler, Ellison, Miles, Beam, and Mathews met privately to discuss the particulars of the campaign. The CSA compound was to be "an arms depot and paramilitary training ground for Aryan Warriors."[47]

Apparently whipped into a frenzy by the rhetoric of the Aryan

Nations Congress speakers, members of CSA immediately went into action. On August 9, 1983, Ellison and "elder" Bill Thomas, a thirty-four year old husband and father of three, burned the Metropolitan Community Church in Springfield, Missouri, for its support of gay rights. The following week Thomas and other CSA warriors burned the Jewish Community Center in Bloomington, Indiana.[48] With the formation of the Order in October 1983, at least five CSA members left for the Northwest. Remaining members of the CSA struck again on November 2, 1983. Thomas, Snell, and Stephen Scott detonated an explosive device along a natural gas pipeline where it crossed the Red River near Fulton, Arkansas. This pipeline is a major source of natural gas for the Midwest, running from the Gulf of Mexico to Chicago, Illinois. Although minimal damage occurred, the effort to disrupt the activities of large population centers represented a major expansion in the nature of the attacks. While in south Arkansas, Snell and Thomas robbed a pawn shop in Texarkana, killing the Jewish owner in the process.[49] In December 1983, Ellison became the first of the right-wing terrorists to issue a declaration of war, proclaiming "War in '84" as the motto of the white supremacists.

Their first "official" action against ZOG took place less than three weeks later when CSA members plotted to avenge the death of Kahl. Ellison had been contacted shortly after Kahl's death in June, 1983 by William Wade, 68, and his thirty-five year old son, Ivan, the owners of the house in which Kahl was killed. Believing that FBI Special Agent Jack Knox and U.S. District Judge H. Franklin Waters of Fort Smith were responsible for Kahl's death, plans were made to assassinate the two men. Although later acquitted of the charges in federal court, Ellison and five other CSA members supposedly left the CSA compound the day after Christmas 1983 on their assassination mission. An automobile accident prevented the group from reaching their assigned targets. The accident, which prevented the deaths of Judge Waters and Special Agent Knox, also left prosecutors with insufficient evidence to verify the existence of the plot.[50]

During 1984, while the Order was busy carrying out a series of spectacular armed robberies, CSA members remained ominously quiet. In October and November of that year a thirty-year-old gun dealer and member of CSA named Robert Smalley began buying AR-15s, a semi-automatic sporting version of the military's M-16 rifle. The guns were illegally transferred through a gun shop owned by William Brugle in Berryville, Arkansas. Brugle, a law enforcement officer with eleven years service, was paid thirty dol-

lars per weapon to fraudulently alter the records. Smalley ultimately provided the weapons to Rader, who had gone underground
with the Order.[51]

When Mathews was killed by FBI agents on Whidbey Island,
Washington in December 1984, remaining Order members scat-
tered to safehouses throughout the country. Several fled to the
CSA compound. By early April 1985, the links between CSA and
the Order had become apparent. As FBI agents closed in on the
encampment, at least two Order members, David Tate and Frank
Silva, tried to make it to the CSA compound near Three Brothers,
Arkansas. In mid-April 1985 Tate and Silva were stopped by two
Missouri state policemen in a routine traffic check. Tate opened
fire, killing one and seriously wounding the other officer. Silva was
arrested a few days later on April 15 at a rural campground in
Benton County, Arkansas. Tate abandoned his van filled with machine guns, nitrogylcerine, and hand grenades two days later and
fled on foot. The FBI laid siege to the CSA encampment later that
week. Tate was captured on April 20, 1985 without incident in For-
syth, Missouri, just north of the Arkansas state line.[52] The three-
day siege at the CSA encampment ended on April 22 when Ellison
and his remaining followers surrendered.

Several indictments against CSA members immediately followed. Ellison and five other CSA members were named in a
twenty-count indictment charging conspiracy to possess fully automatic weapons, making silencers and grenades, and a variety of
other weapons charges. All six men pled guilty in August 1985.
Three lesser defendants each received two-year suspended sentences, but Kerry Noble and Ellison were each sentenced to five
years in the federal penitentiary.[53] Robert Smalley and Bill Brugle
were convicted for their parts in providing weapons to the Order.
Brugle pled guilty, received an eighteen-month sentence, seventeen of which were suspended, and was fined $3,000. A jury found
Smalley guilty on both counts of the indictment, and he was sentenced to one year imprisonment.[54] As a result of additional indictments, CSA members were convicted of bombing the natural gas
pipeline, of arsons in Springfield, Missouri and Bloomington, Indiana, of the interstate transportation of stolen vehicles,[55] and of the
manufacture of silencers and automatic weapons.[56]

The Order

The Order represented the violent culmination of years of anti-
Semitic and anti-black rhetoric flowing from the Ku Klux Klan,

the Aryan Nations, the Christian Identity Movement, and the National Alliance. More than any other extremist group involved in American terrorism, the Order demonstrates the impact ideology has in shaping the deeds of people. Order members were heavily influenced by the teachings of William Pierce, a one-time physics professor at Oregon State University and founder of the National Alliance. Organized in 1970 in Arlington, Virginia, the National Alliance moved to rural Mill Point, West Virginia in 1985. A former editor for George Lincoln Rockwell's *National Socialist World*, Pierce drew most of the alliance's members from Rockwell's American Nazi party.

In 1978, under the pseudonym Andrew McDonald, Pierce published *The Turner Diaries*. The novel describes an America controlled by Jews who primarily use blacks to do their bidding. Eventually a resistance movement known as "the Order" is formed to combat the "evil, Jewish anti-christs" who seek to eradicate the "true seed of Christ." The diaries became the blueprint for Mathews' group, who literally followed the precepts of *The Turner Diaries* while committing terrorism by the book.

Mathews epitomized everything the National Alliance advocated. He was young, intelligent, white, and already at odds with the federal government when he joined the National Alliance. Born in 1953 in Marfa, Texas, Mathews joined the Sons of Liberty in 1974 at the age of twenty-one. The Sons of Liberty was one of a number of small anti-tax groups that sprang up in Phoenix, Arizona about the time that the SPC was having its greatest impact. In practicing his beliefs he ran afoul of the IRS. To avoid the watchful eye of IRS agents, in 1975 he moved to rural Metaline Falls in the far northeastern corner of Washington, not far from Canada and the Idaho border. He bought and cleared some land, moved two house trailers onto the property, and set up housekeeping for himself, his family, and his parents.[57] By 1978, when Pierce published *The Turner Diaries*, Mathews had become a member of the National Alliance. He was viewed with favor by the elder statesmen of the extreme Right as a convincing speaker and potential leader of the Christian Identity Movement. He addressed the September 1983 National Alliance convention in Arlington, Virginia just a few weeks before forming the Order. In his speech he enthusiastically informed the crowd that "the time for war has come."[58] Within a few months, federal authorities learned that Mathews was a man of his word.

Mathews faced two major problems in creating a clandestine army of Aryan warriors: 1) selecting reliable recruits with a common purpose, and 2) funding the army's activities once it was formed. The Aryan Nations Congress provided the fertile ground Mathews needed to recruit his army. All nine of the original Order members were present at the 1983 Congress in July that year.[59] Three months later, in a building on Mathews's property in Metaline Falls, these men gathered and in a ritualistic ceremony gave birth to the Order. In addition to Mathews, the original members included Mathews's chief lieutenants: Bruce Carroll Pierce (no relation to William Pierce) of Hayden Lakes, a member of the Aryan Nations; Gary Lee Yarbrough, an ex-convict from Arizona who also acted as Richard Butler's chief of security; and Randolph Duey, who screened new members.[60] Other original members included David Eden Lane, a Denver, Colorado organizer of the Knights of the Ku Klux Klan; Joseph Richard Scutari, a building contractor from Seattle, Washington; Andrew Virgil Barnhill of Florida; Ardie McBrearty from Gentry, Arkansas; Los Angeles native Frank Silva; Bob Mathews's close friend and neighbor, Kenneth Loff; the youthful Richard Kemp; and Denver Daw Parmenter, who eventually became the primary witness against the Order. Scutari and McBrearty used voice-stress analysis techniques to screen additional prospects, and within the next few months Mathews added more than a dozen new members to the secret organization, including CSA affiliates Randall Rader, David Tate, and Jean Craig, the mother of Mathews's girlfriend.[61]

All terrorist groups face financial difficulties. Once a group goes underground, monetary support can seldom be maintained by routine employment; criminal activity becomes essential if a group is to survive. The Order was no exception. Funding efforts for the Order began in earnest just two weeks after its formation. On October 28, 1983 members of the group traveled to Duey's hometown of Spokane, Washington and robbed the World Wide Video Store of $369.[62]

Realizing that funding a revolution on such meager assets was impractical, the group sought to make its own money. In November, Mathews and four of his confederates began using the Hayden Lakes printing press for their counterfeiting operations. The fifty-dollar bills were of such poor quality that Pierce was arrested almost immediately upon trying to pass them.[63] He was replaced by Robert Merki, an aircraft engineer who also provided group members with false identification cards and papers. Merki eventually moved the operation from Hayden Lakes and switched to counterfeiting ten-dollar bills, believing they would be less conspicuous. Impatient with the speed and success of the counterfeiting operations, Mathews launched the first of the group's highly successful robberies in December 1983 by robbing the Innis Arden branch of the City Bank of Seattle of nearly $26,000.

The following month Mathews and his Silent Brotherhood stepped up their criminal activities. The War in '84 had begun. On January 30, 1984 Pierce and Yarbrough robbed the Valley branch of the Washington Mutual Savings Bank of $3,600.[64] Selected members also began conducting surveillance on armored car routes and schedules. On April 22, 1984 Yarbrough planted a bomb at the Embassy Theatre, a pornographic movie house in Seattle. The next day, while police were busy cordoning off the area near the theatre, seven members of the Order robbed an armored truck belonging to the Continental Armored Transport Service while it was parked at the Northgate Shopping Mall. With Richard Kemp holding up the infamous sign that read "Get Out or You Die," remaining members relieved the drivers of $534,000 in cash and checks.[65] Confident of their success, Pierce and Kemp drove to Boise, Idaho the following week and burned the Congregation Ahavath Israel Synagogue.[66] During the next few weeks, the group celebrated its success by distributing the money from the Continental robbery to various members and sympathizers across the country.

With the exception of Robert Mathews and a small cadre of individuals committed to neo-Nazi, Identity ideology, about half of the Order members were a ragtag band of ex-convicts and alcoholics searching for some sense of direction in life. The Order provided that direction, at least for a while. Despite elaborate screening procedures by Scutari, Duey, and McBrearty, many of the Order members were not only uncommitted, but incompetent.

One such member was Walter West, a forty-five-year-old alcoholic who blamed his failures in life on blacks and Jews. Fearing that West was "running his mouth about Gary's (Yarbrough) army," Mathews ordered that West be executed.[67] The cold, calculated manner in which West was killed revealed the polarity within the group—a central core of deadly serious terrorists surrounded by a periphery of members only marginally committed to a life underground. After West was lured to an isolated spot in the mountains by Duey, his closest friend, West was hit over the head with a sledgehammer, leaving him stunned but conscious. Duey finished the job by shooting him in the head with a rifle.[68] West's murder was the first killing for the group. They did not wait long to kill again.

The target this time was the Jewish host of a radio talk show, Alan Berg. A long-time nemesis of the Aryan Nations and Tom Metgzer's White Aryan Resistance, Berg frequently berated Identity beliefs on the air. One of those who listened to his show in Denver and frequently called in to defend Identity theology was David Lane. In the late 1970s Lane was well known to locals in the Denver area as a long-time Klansman and racial activist. However, in 1982, with his financial status in a downward spiral, Lane left Denver and moved to Hayden Lakes, where he was welcomed with open arms into Butler's Aryan Nations. Rejuvenated, he returned to Denver a year later to assume charge of the Colorado branch of Metzger's White American Political Association.[69] As a result of his efforts to recruit members for Metzger's neo-Nazi group, he became the frequent subject of Berg's commentaries.

In mid-1983 Lane was working as a security guard for Roderick Elliott, publisher of an independent local newspaper in Denver that Berg claimed was anti-Semitic. As a result of publicity created by Berg, subscriptions to the paper declined and it subsequently folded. Lane found himself out of a job. Lane again left Denver and headed to the Northwest—this time to join the Order. In early 1984, Berg openly castigated the pastor of an Identity church in Laporte, Colorado during his radio broadcast. Both Lane and Mathews, occasional visitors to this church, were offended at Berg's attack. Not one to forget, four months later Mathews sent Jean Craig to conduct surveillance on Berg. On June 18, 1984, Bruce Carroll Pierce and two others machine-gunned Berg to death outside his home in Denver, Colorado. Lane drove the getaway car.[70] It was nearly six months later before the FBI linked the Berg killing to the Order.

In the meantime, Mathews resumed efforts to fund his Aryan army. Through connections with the National Alliance, he became friendly with Charles Ostrout, a neo-Nazi sympathizer who worked as a money room supervisor for Brinks Armored Car Company in San Francisco. Ostrout enlisted the aid of Brinks Operations Supervisor Ronald King to help provide useful information to the Order.[71] In June 1984 Ostrout told the group about the shipment in a Brinks armored truck of a large amount of money from northern California to the Federal Reserve Bank.

After a final planning meeting with Ostrout and King in Santa Rosa, California on July 16, approximately a dozen Order members stopped the Brinks truck as it turned onto Highway 20 near Ukiah, California. While some members calmly directed traffic around the stopped vehicles, others transferred $3.6 million into the getaway cars.[72] Unaware of the existence of the Order until this event, FBI agents linked the robbery to a weapon left at the scene by Bob Mathews—a weapon registered to Order member Andrew Barnhill.

As a reward for their participation in the scheme and as an enticement for future cooperation, Order members met with the two Brinks employees at the Holiday Inn near the San Francisco International Airport. There, King and Ostrout were given voice stress analysis tests and officially inducted into the Order.[73] During the meeting King gave Pierce the drawings for what was to be their next big theft: a diagram of the Brinks offices and cash vault on 12th Street in downtown San Francisco. However, they now had more money than they knew what to do with, and the cash vault robbery never took place.

Initially the $3.6 million from the Ukiah robbery was taken to a house in Boise, Idaho occupied by Jean Craig and Robert Merki's wife, Sharon. There the money was distributed to Order members: some as payment for their participation, some to be delivered to other extremist groups. Kenneth Loff took about half of the money ($1.5 million) and hid it on his farm. A portion of the money was used to procure weapons and paramilitary equipment through a front business, the Mountain Man Supply Company. With their share of the take, members of the group went on a buying spree. During the next three months, they bought vehicles, guns, hundreds of acres of property to establish training camps, explosives, motor homes, and computers.

Most disturbing was the distribution of money to other groups. Within a week of the robbery, money began pouring into the coffers of extremist leaders. Mathews generously provided financial support to numerous Identity preachers[74] and neo-Nazi[75] and KKK leaders.[76] The good times did not last long, however, as two events hastened the demise of the Order. The first occurred when Mathews's gun was traced to Barnhill. A subsequent search led to the discovery of a cache of Aryan Nations literature, the first clue police had that they were not dealing with just another gang of bank robbers. The second was the arrest of Thomas Martinez, who eventually provided useful information to the FBI. The Philadelphia native had a long history of Klan activities and had become an active member of the National Alliance. The Philadelphia area was home to several Order members and sympathizers who with Martinez had assisted in laundering much of the counterfeit money produced once Merki took over the operation. Martinez's decision to turn informant proved fatal to the organization.

With FBI guidance, Martinez arranged a meeting with Mathews in Portland, Oregon in late November 1984. As an unexpected bonus, Yarbrough, who had escaped after shooting it out with FBI agents near Sandpoint, Idaho a month before, attended the meeting. When FBI agents raided the motel where the men were staying, Mathews was wounded but escaped. Yarbrough was captured. Mathews sought refuge in a series of safehouses that members of the Order had rented in the Mount Hood area in Washington. He eventually made it to three safehouses on Whidbey Island, a small, relatively inaccessible island in Puget Sound. From there, almost a year after James Ellison declared War in '84, thirteen Order members including Mathews, the Merkis, Pierce, Duey, Silva, Richard Evans, Richard Scutari, Mark Franklin Jones (alias Fred Johnson), and Michael Stanley Norris (alias Andrew C. Stewart)[77] issued their own declaration of war. The document reflects the fatalistic mood that befell the group after Martinez's betrayal. It begins:

> It is a dark and dismal time in the history of our race. All about us lie the green graves of our sires, yet, in a land once ours, we have become a people dispossessed.[78]

Found with the declaration of war were an open letter to Congress and "Principles of War and Rules of Engagement." Angered that members of Congress had secured their elections by appeasing blacks and other minorities through affirmative action, the letter derides congressional fence-straddling and concludes with the following statement:

> When the day comes, we will not ask whether you swung to the right or whether you swung to the left; we will simply swing you by the neck.[79]

The FBI was aware of the presence of Order members on Whidbey Island as early as November 26, 1984. During the next ten days members came and went at will. Those who left and thus avoided capture included: Pierce and Scutari, the suspected killers of Alan Berg; Tate, who later killed a Missouri state policeman;[80] and Silva, Norris, and Jones, all of whom signed the declaration of war. The latter three left with the express purpose of creating a safehouse for Mathews somewhere in the Southwest.[81]

Mathews never made it. FBI agents cordoned off the area around the three safehouses on Whidbey Island on December 7, 1984. Randy Duey, armed with a submachine gun, was arrested fleeing through the back door of one of the residences. At another, Robert and Sharon Merki were arrested without incident. In the last house remained Mathews and the Merki's sixteen-year-old son. Mathews allowed the teenager to flee to the waiting arms of police before opening fire. For two days Mathews held government agents at bay. Finally, on December 8, 1984, Mathews died as a result of flares that were fired into the house. Exploding ammunition stored in the house turned the flames into a firestorm.

The end of the Order came rather quickly after the fight at Whidbey Island. With Duey, Yarbrough, and Robert and Sharon Merki already in custody, authorities began concentrating on finding the remaining members. A nationwide search resulted in the arrests of virtually all of the Order members.[82] The killing of the Missouri state policeman by Order members Tate and Silva as they tried to reach the CSA encampment at Three Brothers, Arkansas led federal authorities to lay seige to the CSA compound.

At least twenty-eight persons affiliated with the Order were convicted for crimes committed in association with the group's activities. In April 1985, Charles Ostrout was indicted in federal court in San Francisco on racketeering charges relating to his assistance in the Ukiah robbery. He pled guilty and was sentenced to five years in prison.[83] The primary trial against Order members took place in Seattle during the summer and fall of 1985. Twenty-three members of the group were named in a twenty-one count indictment charging members with a variety of weapons violations, counterfeiting, possession of explosives, and other crimes.[84] The most important charges against this group, however, related to violations of the Racketeer Influenced and Corrupt Organizations (RICO) statutes (table 4.1)[85]

Unlike some leftist groups such as M19CO, which have been characterized by continued commitment in the face of official pursuit, the Order fell apart with the threat of prosecution. The ideological bond created by the Identity movement dissolved at Mathews's death. Numerous Order members testified against confederates at their trial; many later entered the Federal Witness Protection Program. The Silent Brotherhood was not so silent. Eleven of the twenty-three pled guilty before coming to trial.[86] An additional ten members were convicted in December 1985 and were sentenced to lengthy prison terms. Tate, charged with the murder of the Missouri state policeman, and Scutari, a fugitive, missed the Seattle trial. Tate was later convicted of murder and was never tried in federal court. Scutari pled guilty after his capture in March 1986. Jones and Norris were convicted of aiding the escape of Scutari, who was already under indictment.

When state authorities in Colorado decided not to pursue prosecution of Alan Berg's killers,[87] federal prosecutors decided to act. Since there is no federal murder statute, Lane, Pierce, Scutari,

Table 4.1 Federal Prosecutions of Order Members

NAME	AGE AT INDICTMENT	PLEA OR TRIAL	SENTENCE
1. Robert Jay Mathews[a]	31	Deceased	N/A
2. Bruce Carroll Pierce[a]	30	Trial	250 years[b]
3. Gary Lee Yarbrough[a]	29	Trial	60 years
4. Randolph George Duey[a]	34	Trial	100 years
5. Andrew Virgil Barnhill[a]	29	Trial	40 years
6. Denver Daw Parmenter[c]		Plea	20 years[d]
7. Richard Harold Kemp[a]	22	Trial	60 years
8. Richard Joseph Scutari[a]	39	Plea	60 years
9. David Eden Lane[a]	46	Trial	190 years[e]
10. Randall Paul Evans[a]	29	Trial	40 years
11. Robert E. Merki[a]	50	Plea	20 years
12. Sharon K. Merki[a]	47	Plea	20 years
13. James Sherman Dye[f]			Unknown
14. Frank Lee Silva[a]	27	Trial	40 years
15. Jean Margaret Craig[a]	51	Trial	40 years
16. Randall Eugene Rader[g]	34	Plea	6 years/ suspended
17. Kenneth Joseph Loff[a]	34	Plea	5 years
18. Ronald Allen King[a]	46	Plea	5 years
19. David Tate	22	Not tried[h]	
20. Thomas Bentley[a]	57	Plea	7½ years
21. Ardie McBrearty[a]	57	Trial	40 years

Table 4.1 *Continued*

NAME	AGE AT INDICTMENT	PLEA OR TRIAL	SENTENCE
22. Jackie Lee Norton[i]		Plea	Suspended
23. George Franklin Zaengle[j]		Plea	Suspended
24. William Anthony Nash[k]		Plea	Credit for time served
25. Ian Royal Stewart[a]	21	Plea	5 years, all but 6 months suspended
26. Charles Ostrout[l]	51	Plea	5 years
27. Mark Franklin Jones[m]		Plea	Suspended
28. Michael Stanley Norris[n]	26	Trial	5 years
29. Frank Scutari[o]		Plea	3 years

a. United States v. Pierce et al. (CR 85-001M), U.S. District Court, Western District of Washington, Seattle Division.

b. 100 years in the Seattle trial (CR 85-001, Western District of Washington) and 150 years in his conviction for violating the civil rights of Alan Berg by killing him (87-CR-114, District of Colorado), to be served consecutively.

c. United States v. Denver Daw Parmenter (CR 85-74), U.S. District Court, District of Oregon, Portland Division.

d. Parmenter was the primary witness against the rest of the Order members. He pled guilty before the trial in Seattle began.

e. 40 years in the Seattle trial (CR 85-001, Western District of Washington) and 150 years in his conviction for violating the civil rights of Alan Berg by killing him (87-CR-114, District of Colorado), to be served consecutively.

f. United States v. James Sherman Dye (CR 85-091-1), U.S. District Court, Eastern District of Washington, Spokane Division. Archived at Regional Federal Records Center.

g. United States v. Randall Eugene Rader (CR 85-095-1), U.S. District Court, Eastern District of Washington, Spokane Division.

h. He is serving a life sentence in the Missouri state penitentiary for murdering a state policeman.

i. United States v. Jackie Lee Norton (CR 85-131-1), U.S. District Court, Eastern District of Washington, Spokane Division.

j. United States v. George Franklin Zaengle (CR 85-132-1), U.S. District Court, Eastern District of Washington, Spokane Division.
k. United States v. William Anthony Nash (CR 85-133-1), U.S. District Court, Eastern District of Washington, Spokane Division.
l. United States v. Charles Ostrout (CR 85-0102 WHO), U.S. District Court, Northern District of California.
m. United States v. Mark Frank Jones (CR 85-HM-80-S), U.S. District Court, Northern District of Alabama, Birmingham Division.
n. United States v. Michael Stanley Norris (CR 85-00010 M), U.S. District Court, District of Utah, Central Division.
o. United States v. Frank Scutari (CR 85-0291), U.S. District Court, Northern District of California. Transferred to U.S. District Court, Southern District of Florida as CR 3-85-0111-FW.

and Craig were charged with violating Berg's civil rights. The subsequent trial centered on proving that Berg was killed because he was Jewish. Scutari and Craig were acquitted of the charges, but Lane and Pierce were convicted and sentenced to 150 years each for the killing.[88]

Activities of hard-core Order members did not cease with imprisonment. Several imprisoned leaders continue their efforts through membership in the Aryan Brotherhood, a neo-Nazi prison gang. Outside support for the group continues as well.

In January 1989, Lane, Pierce, and Scutari (the three killers of Berg) were involved in a plot to escape from the Federal Correctional Institution at Leavenworth, Kansas. Weapons were to be smuggled into the prison through a contact in the prison laundry. The escape was aborted when officials learned of the plan. The three men were subsequently transferred to the federal institution at Marion, Illinois.[89] Despite these setbacks, more right-wing terrorism shook America before the decade ended.

Chapter 5

Right-Wing Terrorists Try a Comeback

When "War in '84" resulted in "arrests in '85," several groups that had watched from the sidelines while Order, SPC, and CSA members were being prosecuted sprang into action. The prosecution of right-wing terrorists during the mid-1980s was viewed by these remaining groups as evidence of ZOG's commitment to destroy "God's chosen people." Instead of having a deterrent effect, some extreme-right groups redoubled their efforts to fight an unrighteous government. Among these groups were: 1) the Bruder Schweigen Strike Force II, also known as the Order II; 2) a small band of persons affiliated with the Arizona Patriots; and 3) the White Patriot Party.

Bruder Schweigen Strike Force II (Order II)

Arising from the ashes of the Order, a second version of the Silent Brotherhood appeared on the scene in Hayden Lakes. Members were current or former members of the Aryan Nations. Robert Pires, David Dorr, and Elden "Bud" Cutler provided the link between the original Order and its newer counterpart, Order II (Cutler had served as Butler's chief of security after Yarbrough went underground). Dorr was a member of the security force at the Aryan Nations, and he and his wife, Deborah, led the Order II. They were assisted by another couple, twenty-three-year-old Edward and twenty-seven-year-old Olive Hawley. The Hawleys moved in with the Dorrs in early September 1986 at their home near Athol, Idaho. The youthful Pires, twenty-one, and Kenneth

77

Shray completed the group. Pires later was implicated in the killing of Shray—a murder reminiscent of the execution of Walter West.[1]

The Dorrs' sympathies toward Order members first appeared in early 1985, when they assisted Yarbrough and his attorney in the preparation of his defense against federal criminal charges.[2] David Dorr also made such services available to Scutari and to Eldon "Bud" Cutler, who was arrested in August 1985 in the Martinez murder-for-hire scheme. Throughout 1985 and 1986, Deborah Dorr worked for Butler at the Aryan Nations compound. In December 1985, while Cutler was standing trial, David Dorr began purchasing the necessary supplies to continue the counterfeiting tradition begun by Mathews. By February 1986, he was passing counterfeit twenty-dollar bills.

Order II bombings began shortly after Cutler was convicted in federal court. On March 6, 1986 David Dorr had a bomb delivered to Gary Solomon, a local Jewish businessman and owner of Solomon Trucking.[3] Unsuccessful in that effort, they maintained a low profile for the next few months. In July 1986 David and Deborah Dorr worked at the Aryan Nations compound during the annual Aryan Nations Congress. Like Mathews, David Dorr was not content with simply preaching about the coming race war and seemed frustrated by Butler's unwillingness to use terrorism. As if revived by the religious fervor of the meeting, the couple renewed their short-lived reign of terror. On August 7 they pipe-bombed Fred Bower's Classic Auto Restoration, a local business in Kootenai County, Idaho, where the Aryan Nations compound is located. Two weeks later, David Dorr and Pires shot and killed Kenneth Shray because they suspected that he was an informant.

In early September, David and Deborah Dorr and Pires took time out from their terrorist activities to defend neo-nazism on the "Oprah Winfrey Show" in Chicago. In their absence the Hawleys moved into the Dorr's home near Athol, Idaho, continued the movement's counterfeiting operations, and traveled to Spokane where they passed approximately sixty of the bills. Upon the Dorr's return to Coeur d'Alene, bombings escalated. On September 16, they firebombed the home of Father William Wassmuth, an outspoken local critic of the Aryan Nations and pastor of the St. Pious X Roman Catholic Church. Ten days later two members of the group broke into the Aryan Nations compound and stole a computer and photographic and video equipment. Two weeks later, on September 29, 1986, the group committed its most spectacular crime.

Recalling the April 1984 diversionary bombing and subsequent robbery of a Continental armored truck by Mathews' group, the Order II implemented similar tactics. They set off four time bombs in Coeur d'Alene: one on the roof of the New Era Telephone Company, another in the parking lot of a local Jax Restaurant, a third at the Beneficial Finance Company, and the last at the local federal building.[4] The intent was to divert attention while they attempted to rob three facilities near Coeur d'Alene: a branch of the First National Bank of North Idaho at Rathdrum, the Idaho First National Bank, and an Idaho Army National Guard armory at Post Falls, Idaho. The effort was unsuccessful, and all five of the group's members were subsequently arrested.

Unlike the Order, which had drawn members nationally and used the diverse backgrounds of those members to launder counterfeit and stolen money, the Order II committed all of its crimes in one local area. Limited in imagination, the group imitated on a local scale what Mathews had attempted nationally. In February 1987, Pires pled guilty in Sandpoint, Idaho to first-degree murder in the death of Shray.[5] Although sentenced to life imprisonment, Pires agreed to testify to the activities of the other members and was placed in the Federal Witness Protection Program. All five members of the group were identified in a sixteen-count federal indictment issued in February 1988 that summarized their activities as violations of federal racketeering (RICO) statutes.[6] In October 1988 four of the five defendants pled guilty to some of the counts named in the indictment in exchange for dismissal of other counts. David Dorr was sentenced to twenty years imprisonment, while Deborah Dorr and Edward Hawley were sentenced to eight years each. Olive Hawley's six-year sentence was suspended, and she was placed on five years probation. It was not until January 9, 1990 that Pires pled guilty to the charges against him in this case. Like David Dorr, he was sentenced to twenty years in federal prison.[7] Without the ingenuity and charisma of Mathews, the Order II failed miserably. Born out of frustration over the Order's inability to achieve its stated aims and blinded by rage over the death of Mathews, the Bruder Schweigen Strike Force II struck back wildly and with little forethought. It did not prevail.

Arizona Patriots

While the Order II was busy trying to revive the dreams of the orginal Order, a violent chapter of the Arizona Patriots was busy trying to achieve the same results for SPC. The Arizona Patriots was founded in 1982 by Ty Hardin, former motion picture star during the heyday of westerns. Hardin left Hollywood, arguing that the motion picture industry had fallen under the control of wealthy Zionists.[8] In the mid-1970s, after experiencing difficulties with the IRS for failure to pay his income tax, Hardin moved to Prescott, Arizona and began a local anti-tax movement. In 1982 the group took the name Arizona Patriots and began publishing a monthly newsletter. Members of the group probably numbered about 200 at its height during the mid-1980s.

Like SPC, members of the Arizona Patriots considered government beyond the county level to be illegitimate. Consequently, federal authority, particularly the federal income tax, was detested. Many Arizona Patriot members had ties to other right-wing groups, particularly the Christian Patriot's Defense League and other survivalist groups associated with the Identity movement. Staunchly anti-Communist, many members believed that a Communist invasion from Mexico was inevitable. The movie *Red Dawn* was believed to be an accurate portrayal of these events and was shown repeatedly at group meetings.[9] In June 1984 the group attracted the attention of federal and state authorities when the Arizona Patriots issued an "indictment" against all elected officials in Arizona, demanding their resignation within thirty days. Almost immediately thereafter, the FBI began an intensive investigation into the activities of Arizona Patriot members.

Although most members of the Arizona Patriots remained nonviolent, by early 1985 it was evident that some members of local chapters had hopes of continuing where the Order and CSA had left off. Although Ty Hardin was implicated in several secretly taped conversations with extremist members of the organization, his role in these activities is not clear.

Among the most extreme of the Patriot members were sixty-one-year-old Jack Maxwell Oliphant and forty-one-year-old Foster Thomas Hoover. Reminiscent of James Ellison's beginnings with CSA, Oliphant and his wife, Margo, instructed a real estate agent to "find the roughest, most remote land possible" to build a "Christian retreat" for Identity adherents.[10] They located on 320 acres about twenty miles from Kingman, Arizona. Oliphant, who was also a member of the Christian Patriot's Defense League (CPDL), used Colonel Jack Mohr's CPDL newsletter to solicit funds and assistance for developing the remote site.[11]

Hoover lived with his wife on a dilapidated forty-acre ranch about forty miles north of Flagstaff. Although unemployed, Hoover had a steady income of slightly over $1,000 per month from a U.S.

Navy pension. As early as May 1985, Hoover, Oliphant, and others were meeting to discuss ways to further the revolution as well as support the building project on Oliphant's ranch. Plans were made to bomb a Jewish synagogue, the IRS Regional Complex at Ogden, Utah, and hydroelectric power plants on the Colorado River.[12] In June 1985, Hoover and Bill Sivils, an undercover agent who had already infiltrated the organization, traveled to Ogden, Utah to identify the best way to destroy the computing facilities at the IRS complex. Upon their return the small group began developing weapons to carry out their plans. They were joined in the scheme by a twenty-three year old, dishonorably discharged veteran named Monte Ross, who, working as a ranch hand on Oliphant's ranch, fell into the role of bomb maker. Oliphant eventually made a bomb-making video to distribute to other Identity groups.

In addition to Ross, Oliphant recruited thirty-one-year-old Patrick Schlect, who owned an auction house, and his wife, Rita, a nurse. They joined the small group in June 1986. Like Hoover and Oliphant, Schlect owned a ranch and raised horses. David Gumaer, Steve Christensen, Daniel Taylor, and two felons previously convicted for drug violations, J. R. Hagan and Tom Palmer, completed the conspiracy group.

If it were not for the seriousness of the acts planned by this group of Arizona Patriots, their actions would seem humorous. Perhaps because of the recent arrests of Order and CSA members, Oliphant and his band of followers were reluctant to carry out any of the crimes they boastfully planned. Nonetheless, in order to fund their terrorism and develop the paramilitary training camp on Oliphant's land, the small group devised a plan to rob an armored truck carrying money from the casinos near Las Vegas. Their plans were doomed from the beginning: discord, incompetence, indecision, infiltration by undercover agents, and inexperience characterized the group.

As early as mid-1985, undercover agents infiltrated the small band. In addition to the ten persons already identified, at least one, and sometimes as many as three, undercover agents were present at the group's planning sessions throughout 1986. Oliphant was so eager for competent members that he readily accepted an FBI agent who responded to Olipant's ad in the CPDL newsletter. When one agent aroused suspicion by suggesting a place for the armored truck robbery that was ideal for the FBI to arrest the group, a second undercover agent was so trusted that Oliphant readily believed him when he produced a fake rap sheet, showing the suspected agent's criminal record. On another occasion, when the group planned to test their bombs on a Jewish synagogue in Phoenix prior to robbing the armored truck, undercover FBI agents simply talked them out of it by arguing that it would arouse too much suspicion.

Not only was the group infiltrated from the outside, the organization was characterized by internal strife and disillusionment from within. Hoover, in particular, was concerned about the techniques being used to create the revolution. While Hardin and other leaders in the movement were advocating public action to draw members into the Patriot movement, Hoover was busy advocating the use of an underground cellular structure to ensure anonymity and the expansion of hands-on military training. The conversation between Hoover and Bill Sivils is indicative of the conflict:

> Sivils: Last night Ty (Hardin) was talking about, you know, he had ten guys in Prescott and he was training them. That's a bunch of. . . .
>
> Hoover: I don't call that really training them. Training requires field activity. . . .
>
> Sivils: All we do is B.S. each other.
>
> Hoover: I'm serious about what I'm doing. I want to go at it in a reasonable, logical, common sense fashion. But pure and simply, I want to stop them bastards (the IRS). I want to throw a wrench into their machinery. And if I can garbage out those . . . computer centers, I want to do it.[13]

While Hoover was busy complaining about the tactics of the movement, Oliphant became increasingly frustrated with the length of time it took to arrange the armored truck robbery. He had plenty to be frustrated about.

Oliphant began planning the robbery of the armored truck in January 1986. Week by week he and his compatriots worked out the details. They eventually settled on a Monday—any Monday would do—when the winnings from the previous weekend would be shipped. They first planned to fire a homemade mortar at the truck to open it up. However, after much discussion they decided that the resulting fire would also burn up most, if not all, of the money. By May 1986 the group decided to create an accident scene using two wrecked cars to block the road, then shoot some type of gas that would put the guards to sleep in the truck, winch the truck up onto a transport truck and take it to an isolated area in the desert. Once there, the money would be transferred to another vehicle, the armored truck would be buried using a bulldozer, and the guards would be released to later awaken out in the desert. Although much thought went into the plan, no logistics for such an operation were mapped out.

On June 2, 1986, the plotters contacted Jan Paulsen, who worked as a card dealer at one of the casinos across the state line in Laughlin, Nevada, to ask if he would provide the schedule of armored trucks leaving the casino where he worked. Paulsen agreed. A month later, however, Monte Ross blew off two fingers and a thumb while building pipe bombs for the group. The robbery had to be delayed but was rescheduled for late October.

Other setbacks followed. The Schlects were either tardy or did not show up at all for about half the meetings the group held to plan the robbery. Their horses got loose, or their truck broke down, or, as they explained to Oliphant on one occasion, they couldn't make it to the meeting because they had a realtor bringing a prospective buyer out to look at some property they were trying to sell.[14] Surprisingly, in a September meeting attended by the usually absent Pat Schlect, he enthusiastically reported that he could obtain a type of gas from a veterinary supply company in Tulsa, Oklahoma that would put the guards to sleep. But at a later meeting of the gang at Oliphant's ranch on October 10, Schlect said he did not have the gas yet because he couldn't remember the name of the gas he needed to order. Jack Oliphant was livid.

On October 21, 1986 Oliphant traveled to Laughlin, Nevada to finalize the timing of the operation with Jan Paulsen, their contact at the casino. Upon arriving, he found that Paulsen no longer worked there. Since they had no schedules to work with, Oliphant decided to conduct surveillance on armored trucks leaving the Laughlin casinos. Some terrorists never learn. Oliphant sent Pat Schlect to follow the trucks to record their routes and their time schedules. On three separate occasions in November, Schlect lost sight of the trucks on their route and had to discontinue the surveillance. The robbery was postponed again and rescheduled for mid-January 1987.[15]

With the patience of federal authorities wearing thin, the FBI arrested nine members of the Arizona Patriots on December 15, 1986. Oliphant, Patrick Schlect, Arthur, and Ross were identified in a seven-count indictment charging them with conspiracy to commit armed robbery and a variety of weapons violations. All four pled guilty in June and July 1987. Oliphant, Arthur, and the three-fingered Ross were sentenced to four-year federal prison terms. The inept Schlect was given five years probation.[16]

Rita Schlect probably would have avoided prosecution if she

had not assaulted an FBI special agent with a handgun in an effort to prevent her husband from being arrested. She was arrested with her husband on December 15, 1986 and was charged later in a separate two-count indictment, although the charges against her were later dismissed.[17] Based on information obtained during the investigation of this wing of the Arizona Patriots, Hagan and Palmer were charged with illegal possession of firearms. Hagan was sentenced to two years in federal prison on September 17, 1987, but his sentence was suspended and he was placed on five years probation. Tom Palmer pled guilty to the charges. However, his sentencing was delayed and his case was transferred to Federal District Court in Kansas, where there were outstanding warrants for his arrest.[18]

Hoover, the outspoken advocate of terrorist tactics, was named in a separate indictment for three counts of violating weapons laws pertaining to the manufacture of a homemade mortar he planned to develop and use. At his trial, in March 1987, the jury found him guilty of two of the three counts. He was sentenced to five years probation.[19] Upon learning that Gumaer and Christensen had illegally bought eight Uzi machine guns for members of the group, a separate indictment was issued in Colorado. Christensen was arrested, convicted, fined $6,000, and placed on five years probation. Gumaer remains a fugitive. Extremist factions of the Arizona Patriots have remained silent since Oliphant's conviction.

White Patriot Party

On other fronts, Frazier Glenn Miller, the charismatic leader of the White Patriot Party, continued a long association with the American white supremacy movement. Miller joined the Army as a teenager, served twenty years, and was subsequently discharged for distributing Nazi literature to an undercover military intelligence officer.[20] Retiring to Angier, North Carolina, Miller's involvement in neo-Nazi activities escalated when he became a member of the National Socialist Party of America. From his experiences with this group, Miller realized that negative public sentiment about nazism severely limited his ability to attract large numbers to the movement. He subsequently decided that by diminishing the Nazi connection but cloaking white supremacy in issues touching the nerve of white discontent, massive numbers could be drawn to his organization. In 1980 Miller formed the Carolina Knights of the

Ku Klux Klan. The recession of the late 1970s fueled new, broad opposition to affirmative action, busing, and welfare, and Miller's group reaped the benefits of white frustration in the early 1980s. During this time Miller became acquainted with members of small but growing bands of survivalists who adhered to Christian Identity theology. Attracted to the paramilitary training advocated by these groups, and with nostalgic memories of his own experiences from the Army, Miller rapidly moved to alter the image of the Carolina KKK by changing the group's apparel to the more appealing military-style fatigues of the survivalist movement.

Miller appears to have been heavily influenced by either Robert Mathews' charisma or his new-found money. On April 24, 1984, one day after the Order committed its first major robbery, Mathews sent word to Robert Miles that he wanted to meet with Frazier Glenn Miller.[21] Mathews subsequently sent two Order members to visit Miller in North Carolina, provided him with a $1,000 contribution, followed later with a much larger contribution.

Drawn into Mathews' web, Miller and a small cadre of Klansmen began stockpiling weapons in the summer of 1984. Stephen Miller (no relation to Glenn Miller), the thirty-four-year-old "chaplain" and second-in-command to Glenn Miller, and three other White Patriot Party members met with Robert Norman Jones to arrange for the theft of U.S. military weapons and equipment. Although Jones was the catalyst for much of Stephen Miller's criminal activities, little is known about him. He was named only as an unindicted co-conspirator in court documents. A resident of Fayetteville, North Carolina, Jones appeared to have numerous contacts with active army personnel at Fort Bragg. During the fall of 1984 Jones was hired to conduct military training for the Carolina Klan.

After Mathews was killed in December 1984, the arrests of Order members dominated the news during the first three months of 1985. Glenn Miller, armed with contributions estimated at nearly $300,000 in stolen money from the Order, turned increasingly violent. That spring, he changed the name of the Carolina Knights of the Ku Klux Klan to the White Patriot Party.

Through Jones and an active-duty U.S. Army serviceman, Miller used the services of military personnel sympathetic to WPP's cause to assist with paramilitary training.[22] It was, perhaps, Miller's greatest mistake. Morris Dees, the outspoken critic of the extreme Right and the director of The Southern Poverty Law Center in Montgomery, Alabama, filed a lawsuit demanding a Defense Department investigation of the U.S. military's links with WPP paramilitary operations.[23] Alarmed by this use of active duty military personnel, a federal court judge in North Carolina issued a court order prohibiting Miller from conducting any paramilitary training.

Although having received substantial quantities of stolen military equipment through Robert Jones, the relationship between the WPP and the mysterious Jones began to sour in July 1985. Jones was arrested while trying to buy C-4 plastic explosives from an undercover Fayetteville, North Carolina police officer. The paramilitary training did not stop, however, and in the spring of 1986 Glenn Miller and Stephen Miller were charged with violating the federal court order. When his trial began, Glenn Miller decided Morris Dees had to be killed. WPP member Simeon Davis was told that Dees was "a 'thorn' in the side of the White Patriot Party and needed to be 'plucked out.'"[24] Although no immediate attempt was made to kill Dees, WPP members did conduct surveillance on his residence, his vehicle, and the home of the attorney with whom he was staying during the trial. Glenn Miller and Stephen Miller were convicted that summer but remained free pending a series of appeals.[25]

If Glenn Miller actually received approximately $300,000 of the Order's stolen money, he did not share it with his friends. While Miller stood trial in Raleigh, other members of his group sought ways to raise money for the movement. Stephen Miller and thirty-eight-year-old Wendell Lane took to driving up and down Interstate 95 looking for people to rob. They finally decided to rob the manager of the local Pizza Hut in Fayetteville, North Carolina when he transported the day's earnings to The People's Bank and Trust Company. On September 27, 1986, Lane and another WPP member were arrested in the parking lot of the Highsmith Rainey Hospital in Fayetteville while waiting to begin the robbery.[26]

With their arrests, pieces of the puzzle began to come together for federal prosecutors. On January 17, 1987, Stephen Miller and four others were named in a three-count indictment issued in federal court in Fayetteville. By this time Glenn Miller had all but exhausted appeals of his earlier conviction. In late March, Glenn Miller went underground with two WPP members. On March 31, 1987 they showed up in Monroe, Louisiana, where they rented an apartment. On April 6, the day Stephen Miller's trial was to begin in North Carolina, the three men wrote their own "Declaration of War." Similar to the declarations drafted by the Order and CSA, Miller's document included an assassination point system for the killing of Jews, blacks, and federal judges. Morris Dees' name topped the list.[27] Armed with fully automatic weapons and home-made fragmentation grenades, the band travelled from Louisiana to Ozark, Missouri, just across the Arkansas state line. There they rented a mobile home at the Country Side Manor Trailer Court and plotted how to get the revolution off the ground. Anthony Wydra, who had been acquitted of conspiracy charges in Fayetteville, North Carolina on April 13, joined them later that month. Seeking to publicize their goals, they mailed their declaration of war to a local newspaper in Springfield, Missouri.[28] That clever act made it easy for authorities to track the men down, and they were arrested on April 30, 1987.

Shortly after the capture of Glenn Miller in Missouri, Stephen Miller and three of his co-conspirators pled guilty in federal court in Fayetteville. Stephen Miller was sentenced to ten years in prison, while the remaining indictees received substantially shorter sentences.[29] The fifth defendant in the case, Wydra was acquitted of taking part in the conspiracy.[30] In Missouri, Frazier Glenn Miller and his two sidekicks were charged in a nine-count indictment with conspiracy and other weapons violations. Refusing to accept a plea agreement, Miller's two colleagues were convicted and sentenced to twenty years in federal prison.[31] Glenn Miller, who was also named in the Missouri indictment, was also charged in a separate indictment in North Carolina with having mailed "threatening communications" to WPP members regarding his desire to assassinate attorney Morris Dees.[32] After extensive negotiations, Miller agreed to plead guilty to charges in both indictments in exchange for a lesser sentence. He pled guilty January 4, 1988 to one count of possessing illegal hand grenades and to having mailed the declaration of war and death threats against Morris Dees. He was sentenced to five years in prison with an additional five years probation. As part of his plea agreement, he agreed to testify in the ongoing federal trial in Fort Smith, Arkansas against national leaders of the white supremacy movement. The White Patriot Party disbanded soon thereafter, and its remaining members merged with the National Democratic Front, a white supremacy group active in Maryland.

Same Song, Second Verse

With the demise of the Order and the Order II, the disbanding of the White Patriot Party, and the closing of the armed camps of SPC and the CSA, federal authorities appeared to have successfully dismantled the leadership of the violent groups associated with the white supremacy movement. Federal prosecutors realized, however, that three major figures in the violent outbreak of the mid-1980s remained untouched. Robert Miles, the pastor of the Identity-affiliated Mountain Church; Richard Butler, the head of the Aryan Nations; and Louis Beam, the Klansman turned ambassador-at-large for the Aryan Nations; all remained free. Even though the convicted leaders of the various extreme-right groups repeatedly named these men as catalysts behind the revolution of the '80s, they had somehow managed to steer clear of criminal complicity. That changed in August 1986.

One year after his conviction as leader of the CSA, James Ellison decided he had seen enough of federal prison. In an effort to have his sentence reduced, Ellison detailed an extensive plan by Miles, Beam, and Butler to foster civil unrest and distrust of the federal government through a series of terrorist acts. Ellison's unfolding story revealed two conspiracies previously untried by federal prosecutors. The first involved a conspiracy to assassinate U.S. District Judge H. Franklin Waters and FBI Special Agent Jack Knox, both of whom were involved in the investigation that led to the death of SPC member Gordon Kahl. The second conspiracy implicated Beam, Butler, and Miles as leaders of a national movement to get the revolution under way. The Order, under Robert Mathews, was to conduct a national campaign of terror, while the CSA would serve as the primary depot and supply channel for weapons and equipment.[33]

In April 1987, Miles, Beam, Butler and eleven others were named in a five-count indictment in federal court in Fort Smith, Arkansas. Many of the others indicted were already serving lengthy prison terms: Order members Scutari, Pierce, Barnhill, McBrearty, and Lane and CSA murderer Snell were brought in from state and federal prisons across the country to stand trial. Previously unindicted CSA members William Wade and his son, Ivan; Lambert Miller; and Jim Ellison's own son-in-law, David Michael McGuire; rounded out the extremists who were charged.[34] Beam fled to Mexico but was captured in Guadalajara in November 1987. After numerous delays the trial finally got under way in February 1988.

The prosecution paraded former members of extremist groups from all over the country before the jury. Ellison told of secret meetings involving himself, Beam, Butler, and Mathews at the 1983 Aryan Nations Congress in Hayden Lakes, where they plotted strategy for the "War in '84" that was to involve all of the violent, right-wing extremist groups. Denver Parmenter, the Order member who became the star prosecution witness at the Order trial in Seattle, repeated his testimony about the Ukiah armored car robbery. Order member Soderquist and CSA leader Ellison testified that Miles "wouldn't mind to receive tithes for his church from the robberies."[35] Having pled guilty a couple of weeks earlier, Glenn Miller testified that he received $200,000 of the Order's stolen money.[36] Zillah Craig, the mother of Robert Mathews' out-of-wedlock son, and Tom Martinez described the cutting, distribution, and laundering of counterfeit money.

Despite the extensive testimony presented, the jury remained unconvinced. All fourteen of the men were acquitted of all charges on April 7, 1988. Beyond the possibility that the jury simply did not believe the men were guilty of the crimes, two additional explanations have been offered for the acquittal. According to federal prosecutors, the jury may have perceived that many of these men were being retried for crimes for which they had already been convicted.[37] The second explanation suggests that the testimony rendered by former members of these groups may have been regarded as suspect by the jury, given in an effort to reduce their own sentences. Both of these possibilities were raised by defense attorneys during the trial. Whatever the reason, leaders of the extreme Right were jubilant. Beam, Butler, and Miles continue to make speeches to white supremacy and anti-tax groups throughout the country. In the final analysis, perhaps Butler's assessment that "Mathews made his move too soon"[38] was apropos.

The Future of Right-Wing Terrorism

Despite the obvious success of the government in combatting the violent excesses of the extreme Right, a number of disturbing scenarios leave reason for alarm. First, the continued prison ministry of Identity-affiliated churches remains a potent source for recruiting extremists of the right. Second, a large volume of the money stolen during Order robberies remains unaccounted for and is suspected to be in the hands of surviving right-wing groups. Third, there is evidence that some right-wing terrorists may turn to drug distribution and sales to generate funds. Finally, despite recent setbacks among white supremacists using "skinheads" as a front for racial violence, efforts to attract "marginal" youths into the white supremacy movement continue unabated. All of these activities are related to the terrorists' two fundamental probems: the recruitment of new members and the funding of terrorist activities.

Recruiting for the Right

Although members of the extreme Right continue to draw crowds at local rallies,[39] the terrorist extremes of the movement have found an additional source of potentially violent members inside prisons and within the skinhead movement. Prison recruitment is not a new phenomenon for terrorist organizations. In Italy and Ireland, the Armed Proletarian Nuclei (NAP) and the Provisional Irish Republican Army have used prisons as a source of new members for many years. In the United States in the 1960s and 1970s, the Black Liberation Army and the New World Liberation Front found California's prisons a fertile source of politically and ideologically eager inmates. Through the Aryan Brotherhood and similar local chapters in state and federal prisons, the white supremacy movement has also developed an effective strategy to draw violence-prone men and women into terrorist activity.

As early as 1971, KKK leader Robert Miles was mailing Identity-related materials to white inmates throughout the United States. The mailings ended after his conviction for bombing school buses in Pontiac, Michigan. Upon his release from prison in 1979, Miles immediately initiated a new campaign to provide Identity doctrine to white prisoners. That year Richard Butler began a similar "ministry" from the Aryan Nations headquarters in Hayden Lakes. In the mid-1980s Butler turned most of his mailing lists over to Robert Miles, who has become the major source of right-wing extremist literature available to prisoners. Miles' newsletter, "Beyond the Bars . . . The Stars!" reportedly reaches between 1,500 and 2,000 inmates.[40]

Order members currently behind bars continue the recruitment tradition as well. Frank Silva, who was sentenced to forty years in prison for his participation in Order robberies, has become a leading spokesperson for prison recruitment from his cell. Even while awaiting trial in 1985, Silva was busy spearheading efforts to recruit other inmates in the Pierce County, Washington jail.[41] Similarly, Gary Yarbrough said after his trial and conviction that he "plans to spend his years in federal prison telling his beliefs about the white race to anyone who will listen. 'Let me talk to them a half-hour. They'll change their minds.'"[42] Although efforts by correctional administrators to restrict inmate literature deemed likely to cause violence have been successful, recent federal lawsuits brought by inmates against correctional institutions attempting to restrict neo-Nazi and Identity literature have resulted in inmates being granted the right to receive "religious" and ideological literature that does not expressly advocate violence.[43]

An equally rich source of violent-prone youths has been discovered by the neo-Nazi movement—not behind bars, but in white, lower-class housing areas and in America's college classrooms. Since 1986, John Metzger, the son of White Aryan Resistance leader Tom Metzger, has been a prominent leader in the Aryan Youth Movement (AYM). The AYM reportedly has over twenty chapters on college campuses across the United States.[44] In November 1988, skinheads associated with Metzger's group fatally beat an Ethiopian immigrant, Mulugeta Seraw, to death with a baseball bat. To mark the 100th birthday of Adolf Hitler, Richard Butler held the "first national neo-Nazi skinhead conference" at Hayden Lakes on April 20, 1989. Butler, still trying to disassociate himself from the failures of the extreme-right coalition of the mid-1980s, sees the skinheads as a completely new source for "Aryan warriors." In reference to the skinheads, Butler stated "they're the last hope, the only hope, of the white race."[45]

However, the skinhead movement has run head-on into a double-barrelled blast of aggressive federal criminal prosecution and private civil rights attorneys. Following outbreaks of skinhead violence against minorities in Dallas, Texas and Tulsa, Oklahoma, federal indictments resulted in the convictions of seventeen skinheads associated with the Confederate Hammerskins in Dallas. Another seventeen skinheads in Tulsa have pled guilty to similar criminal charges. Following the latest guilty pleas in Tulsa, Attorney General Dick Thornburgh commented:

> Skinhead groups strike against the fundamental freedoms that countless Americans have lived and died to preserve— life, liberty, and the pursuit of happiness. The Department of Justice stands firm in its commitment to enforcing the civil rights laws of this nation while protecting innocent Americans from the poisons of bigotry.[46]

Even more devastating to the movement has been a California jury's decision to award the family of Mulugeta Seraw $12.5 million in a civil suit brought by Morris Dees against Tom Metzger's White Aryan Resistance.[47] Already, Metzger's bank accounts have been seized and his home prepared for the auction block. As a result, his newspaper, cable TV program, and telephone hotlines are on the verge of financial collapse.[48]

What Money Might Buy

While many persons may be ideologically committed to right-wing terrorism, the ability to conduct a lengthy campaign of terror requires money—lots of it. The immediate future of the extreme right lies in the fruits reaped by Bob Mathews. Only about 10 percent of the $4 million stolen by the Order has been recovered. Although a large portion of the money was indirectly recovered when the property of Order members was forfeited during federal prosecution,[49] probably 25–50 percent of the money ended up in the hands of other extremist groups. The significant point is that one successful robbery can finance terrorist organizations for extended periods. A continuing campaign of traditional robbery is unnecessary if the group has the skills to conduct one or two highly successful heists.

Lacking such skills, however, the extreme right may turn to an increasingly popular method of financing terrorist operations—drugs. Examples of terrorists in the United States using this strategy abound. Left-wing and international terrorists have found drug trafficking a remarkably successful economic venture. In the United States, the Provisional IRA, Palestinian terrorist Fawaz Younis, Omega 7, and the El Rukns used illegal-drug operations as a source to finance future terrorism. Although most adherents of Christian Identity doctrine abhor the use of drugs, the violent offshoots of the movement have attracted those willing to use illegal-drug money as the lesser of two evils to achieve a more "noble" result. Convicted money launderer Tom Martinez recounted conversations with Bob Mathews in which Mathews expressed interest in cultivating links to known drug dealers in South America.[50] Members of some of the groups already have drug connections.[51] Given the type of person attracted into the terrorism-prone groups of the extreme Right, the expansion of the movement into drug dealing is more than just a possibility, it is an almost certain probability.

Chapter 6

Leftist and Single-Issue Terrorism

The inclusion of single-issue terrorism with left-wing terrorism in this chapter is more a matter of convenience than ideological or empirical similarity. While the extreme left has grasped at issues as a means of generating support for its positions, single-issue terrorism in America has not been committed exclusively by leftists. Although the extreme left did find the war in Vietnam and, for a while, the anti-nuclear movement to be sources of public support, there is little publicly available evidence linking the extreme Left to the single-issue environmental and animal rights activists who recently have found terrorism a viable weapon. It may very well be that animal rights and eco-terrorists are politically leftist, but at this point we simply do not know.

To most Americans leftist extremism reached its peak in this country from 1963–1973—the civil rights movement, urban unrest and street rioting, the "Days of Rage" and opposition to the Vietnam war all conjure up visions of leftist influence. Groups like the Weathermen (later changed to the less sexist Weather Underground), the Black Panther party, the Black Liberation Army, and Students for a Democratic Society are to Americans vivid examples of leftist fervor turned violent. In contrast, many Americans equate the 1980s Reagan era with extremism from the right. Yet while it is true that right-wing terrorism dominated the news in the 1980s, left-wing terrorism was also alive and well. Particularly ominous was the resurgence of names and groups long believed to have disappeared or to have joined the Establishment. Noted leftists Raymond Levasseur, Joanne Chesimard, Marilyn Buck, Linda Evans, Susan Rosenberg, and William Morales all made dramatic reappearances in headlines of the eighties. In addition to the return of these familiar faces, the 1980s saw the emergence of environmental and animal rights terrorists. In particular, the Animal Liberation Front and the Evan Mecham Eco-Terrorist International Conspiracy became significant players in the terrorist game after 1985.

Misconceptions Regarding Leftist Terrorism in America

Although most Americans were left with the impression that American terrorism in the eighties was largely rightist, the actual number of acts of terrorism committed by left-wing groups accounted for about three-fourths of all officially designated acts of domestic terrorism in America. About half of these leftist acts were committed by Puerto Rican groups, while the rest were committed by traditional leftist terrorist groups like M19CO.

Additionally, and despite much debunking of the idea, leftist terrorist groups appear to be interrelated. Several noted scholars have expressed criticism of the hysteria created by a belief in the existence of an international terrorist conspiracy. Regardless of the threshold used before conceding the existence of a network of terrorists, it is abundantly clear that substantial cooperation has existed among leftist white, black, and Puerto Rican terrorist groups in the United States. Although the FBI categorizes Puerto Rican terrorism apart from left-wing terrorism, there are several reasons why they should be considered together. Although this is discussed in Chapter 3, the most important reasons are recapitulated here for clarification.

First, leftist groups in America like M19CO and the UFF share similar ideological beliefs with Puerto Rican extremist groups such as the Macheteros, the Armed Forces of National Liberation, and the Organization of Volunteers for the Puerto Rican Revolution. Second, both leftist, student radical groups and Puerto Rican terrorists have received sanctuary or support from the same source: Fidel Castro's Marxist government in Havana.[1] The revolutionary training and literature received by radical members of Students for a Democratic Society who went to Cuba in the late 1960s as part of the Vinceremos Brigades is common knowledge. More recently, Castro has provided sanctuary to leading figures in both Puerto Rican terrorism and leftist, student radical holdovers from the 1960s. JoAnne Chesimard, considered by many to be the heart and soul of the BLA, somehow evaded capture following her escape from a New Jersey prison in 1979, only to reappear in Cuba, where she still lives. Similarly, William Morales, fugitive leader of the FALN, also has been given sanctuary in Cuba.[2]

Finally and most importantly, Puerto Rican terrorist groups and leftist extremists in America have cooperated on joint ventures. The most damning evidence of a link between the groups is provided in the 1979 escape of captured FALN leader William Morales. While receiving treatment at the Bellevue Hospital prison ward in New York, he escaped with the assistance of Dr. Alan Berkman, a member of M19CO. Whisked away to a safehouse in New Jersey, Morales was cared for by M19CO members, especially Marilyn Buck.[3] He later fled to Mexico, where he was arrested and imprisoned for the murder of a Mexican police officer. Released in June 1988, he was granted asylum by Cuba despite efforts to extradite him to the United States. These bizarre events and the relations that existed between members of the various groups have come to light only since the trial of M19CO members concluded in 1990.

May 19th Communist Organization

Although the full story involving the activities of M19CO members may never be known, pieces of the story have been obtained by reviewing the radical student groups that flourished in the United States in the 1960s—from SDS to the Black Panther party and the Student Non-Violent Coordinating Committee. These organizations provided the ideological motivation and peer support for most of the terrorists who later pooled their skills as M19CO terrorists. In addition, the biographies of the young men and women, black and white, who eventually turned to terrorism through M19CO provide classic examples in criminological literature of how one learns not only techniques for committing crime but also the motivations for doing so.[4] For many of these terrorists, the story began with Students for a Democratic Society (fig. 6.1).

Although it only lasted a decade, SDS had a profound effect upon an entire generation of college and university students. Created in 1959 from the remnants of the Socialist League for Industrial Democracy, SDS began the student leftism of the 1960s. Jane Fonda's former husband, Tom Hayden, served as one of its founding and most ardent supporters. His 1962 Port Huron Statement became the basis for student political activism: opposition to racism, militarism, nationalism, and capitalist exploitation of third-world countries characterized the political ideology of SDS members.[5] The initial thrust of the organization was to provide as-

Profile in Terror
Linda Sue Evans

Date of birth:	May 11, 1947
Place of birth/ childhood home:	Fort Dodge, Iowa
Socioeconomic status:	Upper-middle class
Parents' occupations:	Father: partner in a construction firm Mother: school teacher
Education:	Michigan State University, 1965–1967
Initial links to radical left:	Left MSU in 1967 to devote full-time to anti-war movement. Became editor of a radical newspaper and an SDS organizer for high schools and colleges in Michigan and Ohio.
Turning points:	Went to Hanoi, North Vietnam in June, 1969 as part of anti-war delegation invited by North Vietnamese government. Arrested in October 1969 for her involvement in the "Days of Rage" demonstrations and riots in Chicago, Illinois. Forfeited bond, but re-arrested and convicted in 1971.
In the interim:	During the early 1970s, Evans was heavily involved in support for various leftist groups: the Black Panther party, the Wildcat Revolutionary Union, and other organizations. Lived in rural Arkansas organizing efforts against use of farm pesticides (not coincidentally, Marilyn Buck was arrested and convicted during this period for buying weapons in Arkansas and providing them to Black Liberation Army members in California).
	Evans moved to Texas in 1975, where she worked for prisoners' rights, and was a member of various radical organizations in Austin. In 1977, she learned to operate offset printing presses as part of the Red River Women's Press—a skill she would later use to great advantage as a member of M19CO.

	She worked extensively with black organizations in the Austin area, including the Black Citizens Task Force, and she was a founding member of the John Brown Anti-Klan Committee.
Terrorist ties:	Although never charged in the Chesimard escape in 1979, Evans' fingerprints were found at the safehouse where Chesimard and William Morales were both taken after their escapes.
	Similarly, Evans was not charged in the 1981 Brinks robbery, although her fingerprints were also found on a map in the glove box of one of the getaway cars.
	Evans was subsequently indicted for utilizing a fake ID and driver's license to buy machine guns and other weapons in Gretna, Louisiana, on February 10, 1983. The weapons were later found in the possession of M19CO members Alan Berkman, Elizabeth Duke, Laura Whitehorn, Marilyn Buck, and Timothy Blunk.
The pipe dream bursts:	Evans was arrested with Marilyn Buck on May 10, 1985, one day before her 38th birthday. She is now serving sentences totaling forty years for federal convictions in New York, Louisiana, and Washington, D.C.
Sources:	"Defendant Linda Evans' Memorandum in Aid of Sentencing" and "Plea Agreement," United States v. Whitehorn, et al. (CR 88-0185), U.S. District Court, District of Columbia; "Indictment" and "Judgment and Probation/Commitment Order," United States v. Linda Sue Evans (CR 85-337 F), U.S. District Court, Eastern District of Louisiana.

Figure 6.1 Profile in Terror/Linda Sue Evans

sistance to the growing civil rights movement. When Huey Newton and Bobby Seale formed the Black Panther party in Oakland, California in 1966, SDS lined up to provide support for the party. Espousing Marxism-Leninism, Newton, Seale, Eldridge Cleaver and other black leaders in the party joined forces with the Student

Non-Violent Coordinating Committee in early 1968, bringing the added influence of Stokely Carmichael and Hubert Geroid "H. Rap" Brown to the fold. Within only a few years the ideological ties had been formed that carried the more radical, black and white leftists into the violent terrorism of M19CO.

1968 was a turning point for students wavering on the ideological fence. In April of that year, Mark Rudd, the founder of the Weathermen, emerged as a radical SDS leader during demonstrations at Columbia University. That summer, protests at the Democratic National Convention in Chicago led to the arrests of the Chicago Seven.[6] During the spring and summer of 1969, factional disputes within the leadership of SDS surfaced over the extent to which violence would be used as a means to attain the group's goals. The final break came in early October 1969, during the trial of the eight activists who had organized the demonstrations that led to rioting during the national convention. During the four "Days of Rage" that followed, several SDS members who subsequently joined the Weathermen were arrested and charged with inciting to riot. Among them were Linda Evans and Laura Whitehorn, who reemerged in the 1980s as prominent members of M19CO.[7] The Revolutionary Youth Movement, composed of the more radical leftist core of SDS and led by Mark Rudd and Bernadine Dohrn, subsequently broke off from the splintering remnants of the organization to form the Weathermen.[8]

Instructed by the failures of Che Guevara, the advocacy of Castro, and the writings of Carlos Marighela, the Weathermen turned to the Tupamaro model of urban guerrilla warfare using clandestine cellular structures (called "focals"). Realizing that "mass revolutionary violence was not a viable strategy in the United States" at that time, Weathermen purged most of their members and went underground, changing their name to the Weather Underground in the process.[9] During the next five years Weather Underground claimed responsibility for at least nineteen bombings, most of which took place on the East and West coasts. In 1974 the group published *Prairie Fire: The Politics of Revolutionary Anti-Imperialism*, in which Weather Underground leaders explained their rationale for terroristic violence. Weather Underground used the volume to advocate a brand of Marxist socialism attainable only through a violent dialectic. Having identified world capitalism as its enemy, the group saw the United States as the core of this evil economic system:

> Our intention is to disrupt the empire . . . to incapacitate it, to put pressure on the cracks, to make it hard to carry out its

bloody functioning against the people of the world, to join the world struggle, to attack from the inside.

Our intention is to forge an underground . . . a clandestine political organization engaged in every form of struggle, protected from the eyes and weapons of the state, a base against repression, to accumulate lessons, experience, and constant practice, a base from which to attack.[10]

In addition to listing a number of bombings the group had committed, the document also acknowledged the group's support for organizations fighting U.S. imperialism, particularly members of Puerto Rican independence groups like the FALN. Although claiming responsibility for bombings must have seemed like a positive way to publicize Weather Underground's goals, the result was entirely negative. With the publication of *Prairie Fire*, the WU attracted the attention of every law enforcement agency in the United States. The leaders of the Weather Underground scattered and went into hiding, and the organization dissolved. In 1977 the stress and difficulty of living a clandestine lifestyle led Mark Rudd to surrender to authorities.[11]

While many of the leading figures in the Weather Underground abandoned the violent prescriptions of *Prairie Fire*, others bitterly resolved to continue the fight. Some members on the West Coast emerged as the Prairie Fire Collective, an organization advocating nonviolent political strategy. However, most of the members of the East Coast faction turned once again to terrorism. M19CO was formed in the late 1970s, taking its name from the joint birthdays of Ho Chi Minh and Malcolm X. Its membership (at least those known to law enforcement) read like a Who's Who in leftist terrorism (table 6.1). The primary role of M19CO, according to a FALN informant, was to be "an above-ground organization used to support the . . . underground terrorist groups," which included the FALN, the remaining Weather Underground members, and the Black Liberation Army.[12] Most of M19CO's members (e.g., Judy Clark, Kathy Boudin, Marilyn Buck) had been in the Weather Underground or prominent black radical groups like the Black Panther party, the Black Liberation Army, or the Republic of New Africa (e.g., Sam Brown, Samuel Smith, Nathaniel Burns, JoAnne Chesimard). Law enforcement agencies had not seen or known the whereabouts of many of these people for over a decade. As evidence of the egalitarianism they espoused, M19CO's members were gender and racially mixed. About half were female, mostly white, while about three-fifths were black.

Within a year of its formation, M19CO embarked on a three-

Table 6.1   1981 Brinks Robbery Participants

NAME	BACKGROUND
Silvia Baraldini	Legal aide to leftist attorney Susan Tipograph.
Dr. Alan Berkman	Physician who aided escape of FALN leader William Morales.
Timothy Blunk	27-year-old M19CO associate of Susan Rosenberg.
Kathy Boudin	Weather Underground bomber, last seen in 1970 prior to robbery.
Sam Brown	Black Panthers, Black Liberation Army member.
Marilyn Buck	SDS, Weather Underground, leader of M19CO.
Nathaniel Burns	Black Panthers; fled to Algeria in 1969. Returned as part of Republic of New Africa.
Judith Clark	SDS, a founder of Weather Underground.
JoAnne Chesimard (a k a Assata Shakur)	Black Liberation Army leader who escaped from prison in 1979.
Cheri Laverne Dalton	Black associate of the Republic of New Africa.
Linda Sue Evans	SDS, Weather Underground; noted for ability to produce false IDs.
Cecil Ferguson	Republic of New Africa.
Dave Gilbert	White SDS organizer at Columbia University in mid-'60s. Father of Kathy Boudin's child.
Eddie Joseph	Black Panthers.
Susan Lisa Rosenberg	SDS, Weather Underground; drove get-away car at Chesimard prison break.
Samuel Smith	With Williams, leader of the Republic of New Africa. Killed in shootout with police, 10/23/81.
Donald Weems	Black Liberation Army; had escaped from prison prior to Brinks crime.
Jeral Wayne Williams (a.k.a. Mutula Shakur)	Leader of Republic of New Africa.
Laura Whitehorn	SDS, Weather Underground.

stage campaign. First, M19CO wanted to free selected "political prisoners" held in American prisons. The far Left had suffered significantly from the loss of key leaders to imprisonment or flight to foreign countries to avoid prosecution. The second stage of the campaign called for the appropriation of capitalist wealth to fund the third stage: a series of bombings and terrorist attacks planned to arouse the collective consciousness of the proletariat. Impatient and unwilling to let the dialectic naturally achieve its inevitable result, the small band of revolutionaries hoped to speed things up in an effort to achieve the society they envisioned.

The group wasted no time before launching a series of bold strikes to free imprisoned revolutionary leaders. In 1979 three black members of M19CO walked into the visitors section of the New Jersey State Prison at Clinton, took two guards hostage, and freed JoAnne Chesimard, the infamous leader of the Black Liberation Army. Chesimard was serving a life-plus twenty-six- to thirty-three-year sentence for murdering a New Jersey state trooper. She and her comrades went to a prearranged location, where the hostages were released. There Chesimard was met by Marilyn Buck, a fugitive member of the now-defunct Black Liberation Army, and Susan Lisa Rosenberg. Buck and Rosenberg escorted Chesimard to a safehouse rented by Buck in New Jersey. She remained there for several months while Buck and others made arrangements for her successful flight to Havana.[13] They were assisted in the escape and subsequent planning by Silvia Baraldini, a legal aide to Manhattan attorney Susan Tipograph. Buck's own "escape" from prison in 1977 had involved her receiving a furlough from prison to see Tipograph about legal matters. She simply never returned from her meeting with the leftist lawyer.

Buck's efforts did not stop with the Chesimard escape. With the help of Alan Berkman, a physician at Bellevue Hospital and a member of M19CO, she arranged the 1979 escape of famed FALN leader William Morales. Morales had been apprehended following the explosion of a FALN bomb factory in Queens, New York. His hands were severely disfigured as a result of the blast. While being treated at Bellevue for his injuries, he escaped with the help of Buck and Berkman. He was driven to the same safehouse in New Jersey that had been occupied by Chesimard, and Buck personally cared for his wounds for four to five weeks.[14] He eventually made it safely to Mexico, only to be arrested for shooting a Mexican police officer. Paroled in 1988, he also is now in Cuba. Having completed the first stage of its campaign, M19CO members embarked on a series of armed robberies. Their most infamous attack took place in Nyack, New York, on October 20, 1981. Members of the group robbed a Brink's armored truck while it was parked at the Nanuet Mall, twenty miles north of Manhattan. Killing a guard and wounding the armored truck driver, they escaped with $1.6 million. Less than a minute later, they abandoned the van they were driving and, with assistance from four persons in a small Honda, they switched to a U-Haul truck. Suspicious neighbors notified police, and the two vehicles were stopped minutes later as they entered the New York State Thruway. The M19CO members opened fire, killing two police officers. The assailants then jumped into the Honda and an Oldsmobile that had been following the U-Haul. The police gave chase and finally arrested the occupants of the Honda after the driver lost control of the vehicle and crashed. All of the money was recovered. The identity of the four persons arrested sent chills through the nation's law enforcement community: Judy Clark, a well-known member of the old Weather Underground; Sam Brown, a member of the defunct Black Panther party; Dave Gilbert, an anti-war activist leader at Columbia University in the mid-1960s; and last, but certainly not least, Kathy Boudin, last seen over a decade before running naked from an exploding, makeshift Weather Underground bomb factory in Greenwich Village.[15]

Using the license plate number of the escaping Oldsmobile, police within three days located one of the groups' safehouses in East Orange, New Jersey. It was the current residence of Marilyn Jean Buck, a leading member of the Weather Underground and believed by some to be the only white member of the BLA. Since her disappearance following her furlough, Buck had been on the FBI's Most Wanted list for over four years. Although Buck could not be found, clues found at Buck's apartment led officials to other safehouses in Brooklyn, provided the fingerprints of known BLA members like Donald Weems, and positively linked M19CO to other terrorist organizations, such as the Republic of New Africa and FALN.

In a shootout with police three days after the robbery, one of the robbers, Samuel Smith, was killed, and Nathaniel Burns was wounded. Both had been members of the Black Panthers. Ultimately, police learned that the leader of the group was Jeral Wayne Williams, a long-time black fugitive now using the name Mutula Shakur. Police also learned that Buck had accidently shot herself in the leg during the robbery and had been taken to a hideout in Mount Vernon, New York. There she was treated by Berkman, the physician who assisted in the escape of FALN leader William Morales two years earlier. The investigation also revealed the extent to which group members had been involved in the

Chesimard and Morales escapes. Evidence obtained during the investigation enabled authorities to obtain convictions and lengthy sentences for some of those involved in the Brinks robbery.[16] Despite these convictions, other figures in the robbery—Williams, Buck, Berkman, Rosenberg, and Cheri—remained at large and joined the remaining members of M19CO who were not directly involved in the Brinks robbery in the third stage of the campaign.

Approximately fourteen months after the Brinks robbery, this group bombed the federal building in Staten Island, New York. They used the name "Revolutionary Fighting Group" to claim credit for the damage. Changing their name to the Armed Resistance Unit, the group committed three more bombings during 1983. They bombed the entrance to the National War College at Fort McNair in Washington, DC, on April 26, the Washington Navy Yard Computing Center on August 18, and the United States Capitol building on November 7, 1983. Altering their name once more, the group kept up a steady pace, committing one bombing every three months—the "Red Guerrilla Resistance" claimed responsibility for all of the bombings in 1984. They hit the Israeli Aircraft Industries Building in New York City on April 5, the Washington Navy Yard Officer's Club on April 20, and the South African Consulate in New York City on September 26, 1984.[17]

M19CO received a major setback, however, when on November 3, 1984 two of its youngest members, Susan Lisa Rosenberg, 29, and Timothy Blunk, 27, were arrested at a mini-warehouse they had rented in Cherry Hill, New Jersey. Police recovered over 100 blasting caps, nearly 200 sticks of dynamite, over 100 cartridges of gel explosives, and 24 bags of blasting agent.[18] Fleeing the Connecticut area where the group had been hiding, the remaining members relocated near Baltimore. The group committed its last bombing on February 23, 1985 at the Patrolmen's Benevolent Association in New York City. The bombings came to a screeching halt when M19CO members Linda Evans and Marilyn Buck were arrested in New York on May 10. Two weeks later police caught up with Berkman and Elizabeth Duke in Doylestown, Pennsylvania. Laura Whitehorn, a thirty-nine-year-old former SDS organizer, was arrested by FBI agents at the Baltimore apartment she shared with Evans.

Prosecutions of M19CO members were conducted almost continuously during the 1980s in federal courts on the East Coast. From the cases of Kathy Boudin and her comrades following the Nyack robbery in 1981 until the capture of Jeral Williams (Mutula Shakur) in February 1986, prosecution of the various indictments were not completed until a negotiated plea was reached in November 1990. As is typical with terrorism cases because of their high priority, prosecutors rushed to bring charges against the defendants. Unfortunately, their efforts to obtain quick convictions frequently precluded thorough, comprehensive trials of M19CO members. Initial indictments were often issued on relatively simple offenses and were usually fairly easy to prosecute. Many involved presumed-liability statutes not requiring proof of intent. Mere possession of an illegal weapon, for example, is considered prima facie evidence of the intent to possess. Consequently, United States attorneys were faced with a dilemma: should prosecutions proceed with the initial charges, which have relatively minor sanctions, or should the FBI be given time to investigate and assist in developing more serious conspiracy charges, with greater penalties for conviction? Given the ability of M19CO members to stay underground, prosecutors decided to seek convictions for relatively straightforward offenses to avoid the possibility that members might be released on bail during more lengthy, complicated trials.

In the months immediately before police rounded up Buck and her comrades in 1985, Rosenberg and Blunk stood trial in New Jersey for possession of explosives. Despite a defense handled by Buck's close friend and attorney, Susan Tipograph, the trial was completed in less than four months after their arrest, and on March 18 the jury returned a guilty verdict for each defendant on eight counts of a nine-count redacted indictment. Receiving consecutive terms on most of the counts, Blunk and Rosenberg were each sentenced to fifty-eight years in prison on May 20, 1985, just ten days after the capture of Buck and Evans.[19]

The following year Laura Whitehorn was convicted in New York for making a false statement on a passport application. Using the name Sharon Scott, Whitehorn, with the help of Buck and Evans, intended to produce passports for the group in order to escape the country. She began a two-year sentence in federal prison in February 1987 and was placed on parole one year later.[20]

Shortly after Evans' arrest in New York in May 1985, she was named in three separate indictments in different federal jurisdictions.[21] On November 21, 1985, she was convicted in federal court in New York of harboring a fugitive (Buck) and was sentenced to five years in prison. Shortly thereafter, Evans was named in an eleven-count indictment in Louisiana charging her with illegally using false identification to buy weapons. Although Evans' role in the 1981 Brinks robbery was never clearly established (despite her fingerprints being found in one of the getaway cars and at one of the safehouses), it became obvious as the trials progressed that Evans was a key player in M19CO's ability to perform the crimes it committed. Implicated in the Austin robbery of the explosives found in the possession of Rosenberg and Blunk, she was also responsible for having bought many of the weapons used by group members. Using her skills as an offset printer, she assumed the name of Louise Robinette, a deceased woman from Oklahoma with a birthdate close to her own, and produced false identification cards and a driver's license. With the driver's license, Evans was able to buy a number of weapons, including three Uzi submachine guns. Many of the weapons were later found in the possession of M19CO members and in the safehouses searched by police. A jury found her guilty of all counts of the Louisiana indictment in April 1987. She was sentenced to consecutive five-year sentences on nine of the eleven counts.[22]

In 1987 Berkman was convicted of possession of illegal weapons, explosives, and the use of false identification. He was sentenced to ten years in prison.[23] Buck and Shakur, the most important and the most dangerous M19CO members, were tried and convicted in 1988 for assisting in the JoAnne Chesimard escape and participating in the 1981 Brinks robbery, in which three persons were killed. They received lengthy sentences for murder, armed robbery, and RICO violations.

To avoid influencing the trial of the last two participants in the 1981 Brinks robbery, federal prosecutors waited until the day after the Buck and Shakur convictions in Manhattan to announce the indictment of Buck and six others for the bombing spree that took place from 1983 to early 1985. All but two of the indictees were already in federal prison. Elizabeth Duke, who had been arrested with Berkman in Doylestown, Pennsylvania in May 1985, was allowed, ridiculously, to post bond over prosecutor's objections. She fled and remains a fugitive. Whitehorn had completed one year of a two-year sentence and was out on parole when indicted on the additional charges. The remaining defendants were all in prison: Buck, Evans, Rosenberg, Blunk, and Berkman. Berkman by this time had contracted Hodgkins disease and was in extremely poor health.

The five-count indictment recapitulated the conspiracy M19CO began in 1982 and concluded with the bombing of the Patrolmen's Benevolent Association in New York in 1985. Unfortunately, some of the indictees had already been tried for many of the acts specified in the indictment. Defense attorneys argued that no new charges had been identified for at least three of the defen-

Table 6.2   Results of Final Conspiracy Trial of M19CO Members[a]

DEFENDANT	OUTCOME	SENTENCE
Laura Whitehorn	Pled guilty to 2 counts, plus an "information" in District of Maryland	20 years
Marilyn Jean Buck	Pled guilty to 2 counts	10 years (consecutive to earlier 50-year sentence)
Linda Evans	Pled guilty to 2 counts	5 years (consecutive to earlier 35-year sentence)
Susan Rosenberg	Case dismissed; indictment ruled double jeopardy	Returned to federal prison
Timothy Blunk	Case dismissed; indictment ruled double jeopardy	Returned to federal prison
Alan Berkman	Case dismissed	Returned to federal prison
Elizabeth Duke	Remains a fugitive[b]	

a. United States v. Whitehorn et al. (CR-88-0145), U.S. District Court, District of Columbia.
b. Regarding Duke's ingenuity at living underground, an assistant U.S. attorney involved in the case said, "She's probably a stockbroker in Philadelphia by now."

dants. Initially overruled, a U.S. Supreme Court ruling on double jeopardy eventually precluded prosecution of Rosenberg and Blunk (table 6.2).[24]

After numerous delays Buck, Evans, and Whitehorn each pled guilty to two counts of the indictment: a conspiracy charge and the bombing of the U.S. Capitol. In exchange, the prosecution dropped all remaining charges against Rosenberg and Blunk. In addition, all charges against Berkman were dismissed after he completed a scheduled series of chemotherapy treatments at the Washington, DC, General Hospital. Laura Whitehorn, the only one of the six who went to trial who was not already in prison, was sentenced to twenty years.[25] For the three revolutionaries who began as SDS organizers, were transformed into Weathermen, and finally turned to all-out terrorism through M19CO, their dream had become a nightmare. Their remaining hope was that their convictions would radicalize those marginal supporters who had not yet taken up the fight. Defiant to the end, the three women raised their hands in clenched fists and saluted the approximately fifty supporters who jeered the judge's sentencing decision.[26] Some of those in the gallery were members of the remnants of Mutulu Shakur's small band of revolutionaries known as the Republic of New Africa.

Republic of New Africa (New African Freedom Fighters)

The Republic of New Africa (RNA) was founded by the small band of former Black Panthers and Black Liberation Army members who were involved in the 1981 Brinks robbery. Their goal was to create a separate black nation carved from the southern states of Alabama, Georgia, Louisiana, Mississippi, and South Carolina.[27] When finally captured in Los Angeles in February 1986, Shakur, the leader of the group, had been on the FBI's Ten Most Wanted list since the Brinks robbery in 1981. Shakur was described by his Los Angeles attorney as "a black patriot dedicated to the liberation of the New African nation."[28] From his small "clinic" in Harlem that served as the headquarters for the Black Acupuncture Association of North America as well as a front for the Republic of New Africa, Shakur attracted a small cohort of black radicals. Many had former ties to the BLA and the Black Panthers, had extensive criminal records, and supported themselves through theft and robbery. Others, however, were highly educated and held full-time jobs in the private or government sectors. Almost all of the members of the RNA were practicing Moslems. The most radical elements of the group were convicted and given lengthy prison sentences for their involvement in the 1981 Brinks robbery. Those members who remained above ground soon decided to take a more active role in the organization. Assuming the role of the "military wing of the Republic of New Africa," they came to be known as the New African Freedom Fighters.

Led by a forty-one year old Harvard doctoral student named Randolph Simms (a.k.a. Coltraine Chimurenga), the group plotted an attack on the Brooklyn courthouse, where Donald Weems was being tried for his role in a June 1981 robbery that had netted over $290,000 for the BLA and M19CO. They also made plans to undertake additional armored truck robberies and to free Nathaniel

Burns, the former Black Panther convicted in the Brinks robbery, from prison. Two days before the Weems trial ended in Brooklyn, FBI agents raided four houses in different sections of New York City. The ten persons eventually arrested reflected a picture of successful, black, middle-class businessmen and women, rather than a gang of violent terrorists. In addition to doctoral student Simms, two of the persons arrested were attorneys and two others were employees of New York City's Department of Housing Preservation and Development (table 6.3).

A search of the residences uncovered several handguns, an Uzi submachine gun, bulletproof vests, two bombs, sawed-off shotguns, prison guard uniforms, and assorted false identification papers. Howard Bonds quickly turned state's evidence to avoid prosecution. The others were named in a fifty-one count indictment charging them with conspiracy to commit robbery, illegal possession of weapons, and a variety of other offenses.[29]

The proceedings that followed were anything but ordinary. While the National Council of Churches scrambled to make bail for Chimurenga and his followers, the group availed itself of help from leftist attorneys and spokespersons. Susan Tipograph, representing Kelley, argued that the defendants were political activists in the black community who were the victims of FBI surveillance and harassment.[30] During the trial, prosecutors presented videotapes of a rehearsal for an armored truck robbery directed by Chimurenga. The videotape included a conversation in which Chimurenga gave explicit directions to kill the victims.[31] U.S. attorneys also presented as evidence FBI surveillance, wiretapped telephone conversations detailing the plot, illegal weapons, and drawings of the courtroom and prison that the group intended to attack. Unfortunately, prosecutors were unable to convince the jury that some overt act in preparation for the crime accompanied the plans they allegedly had made. FBI spokesperson Lee Laster acknowledged that the Weems trial was within two days of completion and that law enforcement officials simply could not afford to wait any longer. They believed the attack would take place the next day: "We acted now to avoid possible bloodshed . . . we did not want one shot fired."[32]

After a two-month trial and five days of deliberations, the jury acquitted all of the defendants of the conspiracy charges but convicted them on lesser charges of illegal weapons possession. Several jurors hugged the defendants as supporters cheered.[33] Prosecutors were still optimistic, however, since each of the counts for which a guilty verdict was rendered carried a maximum five-to-ten year penalty. They were shocked, therefore, when on January 16, 1986 U.S. District Judge Robert Carter suspended the sentences of

Table 6.3 Members of the New African Freedom Fighters Indicted for Conspiracy in 1985 Attempted Rescue of Donald Weems

NAME	AGE AT INDICTMENT	BACKGROUND
Coltraine Chimurenga (a.k.a. Randolph Simms)	41	Harvard University doctoral student
Yvette Kelley	32	Graduate of Rutgers Law School; public defender in East Orange, NJ
Roger Wareham	35	Graduate of Columbia Law School; worked in law office of Leonard Boudin, father of Kathy Boudin, the Weather Underground member
Viola Plummer	47	Resident of Queens and employed by New York City's Department of Housing Preservation and Development
William (Omowale) Clay	38	Employed by New York City's Department of Housing Preservation and Development
Robert Taylor	29	Resident of Queens; son of Viola Plummer
Ruth Carter	40	Resident of Brooklyn; worked at a Fifth Avenue book store
Collette Pean	25	Lived with Ruth Carter; originally identified herself to police as Paulette Jackson
Howard Bonds	33	Unemployed Brooklyn resident who turned state's evidence
Jose Rios	33	Bronx resident; acquitted of robbery charges

all of the defendants except one and placed them on probation for periods of two to three years. As part of their probation, each defendant was required to perform between 200 and 400 hours of community service. The only defendant sentenced to prison was Collette Pean, and she received three months in prison, 200 hours of community service, and a $1,561.10 fine.[34]

The United Freedom Front

Like M19CO, the UFF was started by former SDS members. The UFF was not a large group and never had more than eight members. Yet despite its small size, it was the most prolific left-wing terrorist group in the United States from the mid-1970s until its demise in 1985. Marxist in orientation and opposed to U.S. militarism and U.S. foreign policy in Central America, members of the UFF were characterized by their attorney, William Kuntsler, as striving for "a whole different system of distributing economic wealth in this country and an end to American imperialism."[35]

The UFF grew out of early SDS efforts to radicalize prisoners and organize prison strikes. Several of the members had extensive prison records. The group was led by Raymond Luc Levasseur, a Vietnam veteran who later served two years in Tennessee's maximum security prison for drug dealing. Upon his release, he enrolled in the University of Maine, where he majored in political science. While there he helped organize the Maine chapter of the Vietnam Veterans Against the War. By the mid-1970s, Levasseur was heavily involved, with his common-law wife, Patricia Gros, and Thomas and Carole Manning, in a number of prison reform groups such as the Red Star North Brigade and the Statewide Coalition Alliance for Reform.[36] In late 1975 the small group formed the Sam Melville-Jonathan Jackson Unit. The name itself reflected the group's ideological stance regarding "political" prisoners: Jackson was killed in 1970 during the now infamous escape attempt and kidnapping at a San Rafael, California courthouse; Melville was killed during the Attica prison uprising while serving time for bombing corporate offices in New York City during the 1960s.

In 1975 the small group adopted the name United Freedom Front. Four other members were added to the UFF over the next few years.[37] The UFF was undoubtedly the most successful of the leftist terrorists of the 1970s and 1980s. They were subsequently also the most widely sought group of terrorists. FBI spokesperson James Greenleaf described the search for the UFF as the "most

Table 6.4   Expropriations and Bombings Committed by the
United Freedom Front

	DATE	LOCATION	VICTIM	CRIME
1.	10/04/75	Portland, ME	Northeast Bank of Westbrook	Robbery
2.	12/12/75	Augusta, ME	Bank of Maine	Robbery
3.	04/22/76	Boston, MA	Suffolk County Courthouse	Bombing
4.	06/21/76	Lowell, MA	Middlesex County Courthouse	Bombing
5.	07/04/76	Revere, MA	First National Bank of Boston	Bombing
6.	12/12/76	Needham, MA	Union Carbide Corporation	Bombing
7.	03/12/77	Marlboro, MA	Ideal Roller and Graphics	Bombing
8.	10/27/78	Wakefield, MA	Mobil Oil Corporation	Bombing
9.	10/27/78	Waltham, MA	Mobil Oil Corporation	Bombing
10.	02/27/79	Eastchester, NY	Mobil Oil Corporation	Bombing
11.	06/25/81	New Britain, CT	New Britain Bank & Trust	Robbery
12.	04/02/82	Burlington, VT	Chittenden Trust Company	Robbery
13.	06/25/82	Onondaga, NY	Syracuse Savings Bank	Robbery
14.	12/16/82	Elmont, NY	South African Airways	Bombing
15.	12/16/82	Harrison, NY	IBM Building	Bombing
16.	02/23/83	Utica, NY	Marine Midland Bank	Robbery
17.	05/12/83	Uniondale, NY	Roosevelt Army Reserve Center	Bombing
18.	05/12/83	Queens, NY	Naval Reserve Center	Bombing
19.	07/06/83	Rotterdam, NY	Marine Midland Bank	Robbery
20.	08/21/83	Bronx, NY	J. Muller Army Reserve Center	Bombing
21.	10/18/83	Dewitt, NY	Onondaga Savings Bank	Robbery
22.	12/13/83	East Meadow, NY	Navy Recruiting Office	Bombing
23.	12/14/83	Queens, NY	Honeywell Corporation	Bombing
24.	01/29/84	Queens, NY	Motorola Corporation	Bombing
25.	03/19/84	Harrison, NY	IBM Building	Bombing
26.	04/26/84	Norfolk, VA	First VA Bank of Tidewater	Robbery
27.	06/05/84	Norfolk, VA	Sovran Bank	Robbery
28.	08/22/84	Melville, NY	General Electric Corporation	Bombing
29.	09/26/84	Tarrytown, NY	Union Carbide Corporation	Bombing

intensive and longest investigation in New England."[38] For nearly
a decade the small group successfully evaded police and FBI agents
while committing an almost endless string of robberies and bombings (table 6.4).

From the fall of 1975 until the last bombing in September
1984, the UFF is known to have committed at least nine bank rob-

beries and twenty bombings and is suspected of committing others, as well.[39] Highly committed to its ideology, the UFF perfected the successful use of urban guerrilla tactics. By using mail drops and public telephones to communicate with one another and by maintaining an extensive series of safehouses and the appearance of "normal" American families, UFF members evaded detection for years. When surveillance on possible targets was completed, the group selected the next bombing victims at regular meetings called "sets," where extensive notes were kept in which members were referred to by aliases. As fugitives, members of the group generally lived in suburban areas of major cities. Normally the residences of each of the three married couples in the group would be located within 20–30 miles of each other. Raymond Levasseur and his wife, Patricia Gros, and Karl Laaman and his wife, Barbara Curzi, each raised three children during the ten years they were underground.

The suburban life ended on November 4, 1984, when police arrested Levasseur and his wife as they rode in a van with their children in rural Deerfield, Ohio. Less than an hour later police located Laaman and Curzi and their three children at a home approximately thirty miles away in west Cleveland. An added bonus for law enforcement officers was the discovery of Richard Williams at the Laaman home. Thomas and Carol Ann Manning, who lived in nearby Ashtabula County, fled before agents found their home. It was nearly a year later before the Mannings were arrested.

In a strategy that characterizes the prosecution of terrorism cases, UFF members were tried repeatedly for crimes committed in different federal and state jurisdictions. As with the prosecutions of M19CO and right-wing Christian Identity members, prosecutors of UFF members had many crimes they could choose to prosecute. Before the group's major trial for conspiracy in 1989, all of the members had been convicted of related offenses in separate trials. At her arrest in 1984, Patricia Gros was charged in a six-count indictment with harboring her "Top Ten" fugitive husband, Levasseur.[40] Convicted of four of the six counts, she was sentenced to five years in the federal penitentiary on April 2, 1985.[41] Thomas Manning, finally arrested with his wife in 1985, was tried and convicted in state Superior Court in New Jersey in the 1981 shooting death of state trooper Philip Lamonaco. He was sentenced to life imprisonment.[42]

The first major federal trial of the group resulted from a March 1985 indictment in New York charging the UFF members with conspiracy in the bombings of eleven corporate and government buildings. On March 4, 1986 seven of the members were convicted and sentenced to prison terms from fifteen to fifty-three years.[43] Soon after the trial, all eight members of the group were indicted in a federal court in Massachusetts in 1987 in a three-count indictment charging them with seditious conspiracy and RICO violations.[44] Black activist Richard Williams' trial eventually was separated from the remaining members, since he was not charged with the RICO violations. He pled guilty in December 1987 to one count in exchange for a dismissal of the other two counts, a prosecutor's recommendation that he receive no more than seven years imprisonment, and an agreement that he would not serve as a government witness.[45] Carol Manning also pled guilty and was sentenced to five years imprisonment and fined $300,000.[46]

The remaining UFF members went to trial in January 1989. In scenes similar to those that characterized the trials of M19CO members in Washington, D.C., and the NAFF in New York, leftist political rhetoric filled the air. Jay Manning referred to the trial proceedings as "a zoo," demanding, "we are political prisoners, we demand political lawyers . . . we've built up a certain momentum. We've presented our politics well . . . and the government is trying to break up that momentum."[47] Chaos marked the proceedings. Bomb threats postponed the trial on occasion. William Kuntsler, the attorney chosen by the group to represent them, was ejected from the courtroom. Vocal supporters regularly interrupted the trial. During the ten-month long trial, charges against Thomas Manning and Jaan Laaman were dropped, and Barbara Curzi's trial was separated from the others. Finally, on November 27, 1989, the jury returned not-guilty verdicts on most of the counts. Two days later the judge declared a mistrial when jurors said they were deadlocked on the remaining charges. All of the defendants, except Patricia Gros (who had already served 3 1/2 years for harboring a fugitive and was now out on bail), were returned to prison as quickly as possible so they wouldn't miss any more of their taxpayer provided college classes.[48]

Puerto Rican Terrorism

If the sheer volume of completed acts of terrorism is used as an indicator of the success of terrorist organizations, the Puerto Rican groups would be judged the most successful American terrorists. During the latter half of the 1980s, Puerto Rican terrorists com-

mitted over 60 percent of all completed acts of terrorism in the
United States and Puerto Rico.[49] Although a number of different
Puerto Rican violent extremist groups exist, they share similar
goals and ideological motives: All reflect the nationalist-separatist
goals of the major Puerto Rican terrorist groups and are opposed to
perceived U.S. imperialism and the American military presence in
Puerto Rico. Marxist, pro-Communist ideology characterizes the
most violent of these organizations, and some of the groups maintain close ties to Cuba. The Macheteros, for example, are strongly
supported by members of the Marxist-Leninist Puerto Rican Socialist party, which is led by Jose Mari Bras, a confidant of Fidel
Castro.[50]

Although several groups have claimed responsibility for the
acts of terrorism committed by Puerto Rican terrorists during the
past fifteen years, the overwhelming majority were committed by
six different organizations:

1. the Armed Forces of National Liberation;

2. the Organization of Volunteers for the Puerto Rican Revolution;

3. Ejercito Popular Boricua–Macheteros;

4. the Armed Forces of Popular Resistance;

5. the Guerrilla Forces of Liberation;

6. the Pedro Albizu Campos Revolutionary Forces.

All six of these groups are politically leftist, strongly influenced by
Castro's brand of Marxism-Leninism, and advocate the separation
of Puerto Rico from the United States with the creation of a social-
ist-communist government to replace the present political structure. In addition, close ties exist among the groups, with some
members belonging to more than one. Consequently, a large number of the terrorist acts committed by Puerto Rican terrorists involved joint operations among the groups.

Of these groups all but one are based in Puerto Rico. The
FALN, unlike the others, operated on the continental United
States and conducted most of its bombings during the late 1970s in
New York and Chicago. The FALN first surfaced in 1974 and
gained national prominence the following year with the bombing of
the Fraunces Tavern in New York City in which four persons were
killed and fifty-four were wounded. During the next six years
FALN members committed over 100 bombings in the United

States. In 1977 the leader of the FALN, William Morales, was severely injured in an explosion at a FALN bomb factory in Queens. He lost most of his teeth, his jaw, and fingers in the explosion.[51] He escaped to Mexico two years later with the help of the M19CO. In 1980 the FALN suffered major setbacks when more than a dozen members were convicted for terrorist acts.[52]

Morales, however, continued to direct the activities of remaining FALN members from his hideout in Mexico. Authorities finally closed in on him in 1983 when they learned that FALN members in Chicago were maintaining communication with Morales from a pay phone in Puebla, Mexico.[53] He was arrested on May 26, 1983 at an international telephone while awaiting a call from Alejandrina Torres in Chicago. Torres and three other FALN members were subsequently indicted and convicted for sedition relating to approximately twenty-five bombings in the Chicago area during the previous eight years. With Morales' arrest in Mexico and subsequent conviction on a murder charge there, FALN-claimed bombings ceased.

The rest of the active Puerto Rican terrorist groups base their operations from Puerto Rico. Three of the five groups (the Macheteros, FARP, and OVRP) emerged in 1978 and rose to prominence the following year with the December 1979 ambush of a Navy bus at Sabana Seca, Puerto Rico in which two Navy personnel were killed and nine others wounded. The Guerrilla Forces of Liberation (GFL) and the Pedro Albizu Campos Revolutionary Forces (PACRF) did not appear on the scene until the late 1980s. These groups differ in the targets they select. The Guerrilla Forces of Liberation, for example, were responsible for all seven of the officially designated acts of domestic terrorism in the United States in 1987. All of their bombings were against non-military targets. They struck four banks, a department store, and two government buildings that housed the U.S. Customs and the U.S. Postal Service.

The Pedro Albizu Campos Revolutionary Forces were responsible for four of the seven terrorist acts in the United States in 1988. As with the GFL, none of their bombings included military targets. The PACRF bombed Citibank and the Mexican Travel Agency in Rio Piedras, Puerto Rico, in January 1988. They later issued a communique demanding that FALN leader William Morales not be extradited to the United States, and they were jubilant when Mexican authorities refused the U.S. extradition request. Morales was allowed to join other leftist terrorists exiled in Cuba. Picking up on issues they believed would attract local support, in

December 1988 PACRF bombed two U.S. corporations, Motorola and International General Electric, as punishment for "contributing to the environmental pollution of Puerto Rico."[54]

But of all the Puerto Rican groups, the Macheteros and OVRP have been the most prolific, daring, and violent. Combining forces in numerous attacks and bombings, these two groups have consistently struck U.S. military targets in Puerto Rico. Following the Sabana Baca ambush in 1979, the Macheteros staged one of the most daring terrorist attacks in U.S. history. On January 12, 1981, they blew up nine military planes belonging to a wing of the Puerto Rican National Guard at Muniz Airport on Isla Verde, Puerto Rico. Later that year they ambushed four U.S. Navy enlisted men on shore leave from the USS *Pensacola*, killing one and wounding the other three.[55] The Macheteros and OVRP spent most of 1983 searching for funds to continue their terrorism. From 1984 to 1986, the two groups continued their rampaging violence in Puerto Rico. OVRP took the initiative in 1984 with five terrorist attacks, most against U.S. Army recruiting offices on the island. In 1985, they joined forces with the Macheteros to fire a light anti-tank weapon at the federal courthouse in Old San Juan. Later that year OVRP terrorists shot a U.S. Army major stationed in Puerto Rico as he walked near his residence.[56] In 1986 OVRP and the Macheteros were responsible for ten terrorist incidents on the island: one was committed by the Macheteros, two by OVRP, and the remaining seven were joint operations by the Macheteros, OVRP, and FARP. In April that year, OVRP bombers detonated a pipe bomb on the campus of the University of Puerto Rico. Two weeks later OVRP claimed responsibility for the assassination of Alejandro Malave, a former Police of Puerto Rico officer, in a drive-by shooting.

On October 28, 1986 the three groups merged to plant ten pipe bombs at military targets throughout Puerto Rico. Two of the bombs exploded—one at a Navy recruiting station, the other at Fort Buchanan. Additional bombs were discovered prior to detonation at Army Reserve recruiting stations in Santurce, Aguadilla, and Cayey as well as at an Army Reserve center in Aguadilla, a National Guard armory in Mayaguez, and an Army-Navy recruiting office in Bayamon. Apparently intended to discourage young Puerto Ricans from joining the American military, these bombings—as well as one by the Macheteros less than a week later—included directions telling of the location of the bomb. The Macheteros also included instructions on how to dismantle the bomb located at the National Guard Armory at Puerta De Tierra.[57] All of these incidents required supplies and equipment, and it was the job of the Macheteros to obtain money to procure them.

While M19CO and the Order preferred Brinks and Continental armored cars as funding sources, the Macheteros fancied Wells Fargo. The Macheteros began modestly on September 1, 1982 when several members opened fire on a Wells Fargo truck carrying more than $800,000 from San Juan to Naranjito. The robbery attempt was unsuccessful, and none of the assailants was captured. Ballistic experts, however, matched one of the rounds fired at the scene to the weapon that was used to kill a Navy enlisted man four months earlier, an incident for which the Macheteros claimed responsibility.

The group struck again on November 16, 1982 when they robbed a supermarket in Carolina, Puerto Rico. After taking $12,000 from the store, they herded the customers and employees into a stockroom and settled down to wait for a Wells Fargo armored truck that was due to arrive shortly. When it arrived, the members of the group robbed the driver and guard of approximately $300,000, killing an innocent civilian at a gas station across the street in the process.[58] The following spring they tried the same technique. This time, however, they were less successful and fled before the armored vehicle arrived. They reappeared at Rio Piedras, Puerto Rico on July 15, 1983 where members of the Macheteros killed the driver of a Wells Fargo truck and absconded with nearly $600,000 in cash and checks. The funds they accumulated supported the outbreak of Puerto Rican terrorism that took place between 1984–1986. But the Macheteros were not through with Wells Fargo.

Given the Macheteros' inclination to restrict their activities to the island, neither Wells Fargo nor federal authorities had any idea that the group would strike next nearly 3,000 miles away. On September 12, 1983 a twenty-five-year-old part-time employee of Wells Fargo in West Hartford, Connecticut placed a gun to the head of the depot manager and walked out with $7.1 million in cash. At first authorities believed the heist was just the work of a lone gunman working for minimum wages who was unable to control the temptations of handling millions each day. What puzzled police and federal authorities, however, was how the suspect, Victor Gerena Ortiz, had so easily disappeared without a trace.

Hartford, Connecticut, the "insurance capital of the world," has a large Puerto Rican population, mostly lower income and impoverished. Some elements of the Puerto Rican community maintain strong ties with the independence movement in Puerto Rico. Unknown to Wells Fargo at the time of his employment, Gerena had, during his college years at the now-defunct Annhurst College, openly critized American involvement in Puerto Rico and described

American capitalism as a system that "sucked the blood from the poor."[59] The stolen money was out of the country before federal authorities made the link between Gerena and the Machetoros. In a series of shipments in 1984, the funds were gradually transferred to Mexico with the help of attorney Paul Weinberg, the only non-Machetero known to be involved in the crime.

On the anniversary of the robbery one year later, the Macheteros claimed responsibility for the expropriation. Gerena, now safely hiding in Cuba, sent postcards to the media in which he promised them a videotape for television use that would explain his relationship with the Macheteros and his ideological beliefs about U.S. exploitation of Puerto Rico. It was another year before FBI agents made any arrests in the case, but in late August 1985 over 200 federal agents combed the island, warrants in hand, and rounded up several leading figures associated with the Macheteros.

Federal prosecutors shocked the Puerto Rican populace when it released an indictment naming the nineteen persons arrested during its raid on August 30, 1985 (table 6.5).[60] Most of the indicted were members of what one assistant U.S. attorney described as the Puerto Rican intelligentsia.[61] Many of those arrested were college-educated professionals—businessmen, attorneys, and teachers—along with several prominent farmers and other highly respected community members. The most important figure among the group was Filiberto Ojeda Rios, a fifty-three-year-old musician and the legendary founder of the Macheteros. He was also the main link between the Macheteros and other Puerto Rican terrorist groups. Educated at the University of Puerto Rico and trained in urban guerrilla tactics in Cuba, Ojeda maintained close ties to Castro's Communist government. Gerena was not among those arrested; he had been spirited away to Mexico late in September 1983. He remains on the FBI's Ten Most Wanted list.

Although most Puerto Ricans support the American presence in Puerto Rico and disdain the use of excessive violence by the island terrorists, prosecuting Puerto Ricans involved in the independence movement has been an extremely difficult task. Filiberto Ojeda Rios, who shot and partially blinded an FBI agent during his arrest in 1985, was charged in a separate eight-count indictment relating to those crimes in 1989. Much to the chagrin of federal prosecutors and the FBI, a jury acquitted Ojeda of all counts on August 26, 1989.[62] In 1990, while awaiting trial for his involvement in the 1983 Wells Fargo depot robbery, Ojeda went underground; he remains a fugitive.

Given the relative immunity of the Puerto Rican terrorists from prosecution on the island, the Wells Fargo robbery presented

Table 6.5 Macheteros Members Indicted for 1983 Robbery of Hartford, CT, Wells Fargo Depot

NAME	AGE AT INDICTMENT	BACKGROUND	CASE OUTCOME
Victor Gerena	27	Part-time employee of Wells Fargo	Fugitive
Filiberto Ojeda-Rios	53	Musician; founder of the Macheteros	Fugitive
Orlando Claudio	38	Farmer and carpenter; founder of Macheteros	Trial pending
Juan Enrique Segarra Palmer	40	Harvard graduate; founder of Macheteros	Convicted; fined $500,000, 65 years
Paul Weinberg	38	Attorney; only non-member indicted	Pled guilty; 1 year
Fernandez Diamante	46	Graduate of U. of P.R. in political science	Trial pending
Jorge Farinacci Garcia	41	Labor attorney in P.R.	Trial pending
Avelino Claudio	NK	Brother of Orlando	Fugitive
Norberto Claudio	NK	Brother of Orlando	Fugitive
Luis Alfredo Colon-Osorio	37	Graduate of U. of P.R. in political science	Fugitive
Carlos Ayes-Suarez	26	Graduate of U. of P.R. in anthropology	Acquitted
Norman Ramirez Talavera	29	Artist for Caribe Graphics, believed to be a front for EPB	Convicted; fined $50,000, 5 years
Roberto Maldonado-Rivera	50	Well-known attorney in Puerto Rico	Convicted; fined $100,000, 5 years

Table 6.5 *Continued*

NAME	AGE AT INDICTMENT	BACKGROUND	CASE OUTCOME
Antonio Camacho Negron	40	Automotive mechanic	Convicted; 15 years
Elias Castro Ramos	NK	Teacher in P.R.; has master's degree in natural sciences	Trial pending
Luz Berrios	36	Female occupational therapist	Pled guilty; 5 years
Isaac Camacho Negron	NK	Owner of locksmith business in P.R.	Trial pending
Ivonne Melendez Carrion	NK	Graduate of U. of P.R. in sociology	Trial pending
Angel Diaz Ruiz	NK	Husband of Ivonne Carrion; painter, handyman	Trial pending

federal authorities with a unique opportunity to prosecute the Macheteros in a different venue—and they took advantage of it. The nineteen defendants were charged with seventeen counts relating to the theft. The indictment itself was also unique. Because the stolen money actually belonged to four banks in the Hartford area, rather than to Wells Fargo, prosecutors were able to charge the defendants with four separate counts of robbery. These counts were linked to four additional counts of assaulting the depot manager while taking the money. The remaining charges related to the interstate transportation of the stolen goods from Hartford to Mexico and eventually to Cuba.

The principal defendants in the case include Victor Gerena Ortiz, who is still a fugitive, and the three founders of the Macheteros: Filiberto Ojeda Rios, Juan Segarra Palmer, and Orlando Gonzalez Claudio.[63] Five of the nineteen defendants, including Palmer, went to trial in August 1988.[64] After a lengthy trial complete with political rhetoric and a gallery filled with supporters, a federal jury in Hartford convicted him and three others.[65] Raising a clenched fist and shouting "Puerto Rico libre!" to the gallery of chanting supporters, Palmer was led from the courtroom after being sentenced to sixty-five years in prison and fined $500,000.[66] Extensive continuances have delayed the trials of the other defendants. Of the $7.1 million taken in the robbery, only about $80,000 has been recovered.

El Rukns

Among the extremist groups dedicated to the use of violence to oppose perceived U.S. imperialism, El Rukns are an anomaly. Unlike other leftist organizations that started as a result of political grievance or youthful idealism, the El Rukns are, first and foremost, a traditional criminal gang. Unknown to most lay students of criminology, the El Rukns began as the Blackstone Rangers, an infamous black street gang that was heavily involved in drug trafficking in Chicago in the late 1960s. From its inception, the Blackstone Rangers and its contemporary counterpart, the El Rukns, have had only one leader, Jeff Fort.

Fort's first leadership role in gang activities was as an underling to Eugene Hairston when they formed the Rangers in 1963. When Hairston went to prison in 1965, Fort assumed complete control and never relinquished it. Having claimed as his territory the area around Blackstone Street on the southside of Chicago where he grew up, Fort immediately changed the name of the group to the Blackstone Rangers. In 1968, at the age of twenty-one, he consolidated his power on Chicago's Southside by incorporating twenty-one different black gangs into the newly formed Black P. Stone Nation. The leaders of each of those groups were "generals" and formed the "Main 21," the governing body of the organization.[67]

While the El Rukns may seem different from other terrorist groups of the Left, in actuality their move from traditional criminality to the fight against American imperialism followed classic Marxist theorizing about the class struggle. The Blackstone Rangers, as they became the Black P. Stone Nation, epitomized the politicalization of the criminal underclass in America, the development of class consciousness among Marx's *lumpenproletariat*, and the shift from self-serving thievery to altruistic revolutionary activism. In 1968, Fort was considered a legitimate leader in the black community. Although his organization was routinely involved in criminal activities during the late 1960s, he nonetheless became a "center chief" in the Woodlawn-area job training project funded by the federal Office of Economic Opportunity.[68] Later in 1968, however, Fort refused to honor a subpoena to testify before a U.S. Senate subcommittee investigating possible misuse of government funds and was convicted of two counts of contempt of Congress. In 1972 Fort and other members of the Black P. Stone Nation were convicted of making false statements to the federal Office of Educational Opportunity in order to obtain money through a federal grant for the impoverished. Sentenced to the federal penitentiary at Leavenworth, Fort's conversion to Islam while there signaled an end to his "legitimate" efforts to work for the benefit of black people through federally funded programs. His conviction and subsequent imprisonment radicalized the organization. In 1976 he changed the group's name to the El Rukns, a name borrowed from the cornerstone of the Kaaba, an Islamic shrine in Mecca, Saudi Arabia.

The El Rukns epitomized the worst elements of what criminologists Richard Cloward and Lloyd Ohlin characterize as "conflict" and "criminal" subcultures.[69] While retaining an air of legitimacy within the community through business and political contacts, the group's drug clientele found them to be violent and relentless. To maintain its place in the community and attract new recruits, the El Rukns bought an old theatre on South Drexel Street and renamed it "El Rukn Sunni Muslims Masjid Al Malik," or simply "the Fort"—for its appearance, and in honor of the group's leader. The organization bought several other pieces of property in the South Chicago area, including at least four apartment buildings.

By the mid-1980s Fort had reduced his Main 21 to five top "generals" who ran the day-to-day operations of the enterprise. The generals—Melvin Mayes, Alan Knox, Sammy Knox, Tramell Davis, and Henry Leon Harris—led an organization that maintained an active membership of about 250, who responded to Fort's orders through a hierarchy of "ambassadors," "officers" (or "mufti"), and "generals." However, in 1983 Fort and two of his generals were convicted on federal drug charges in Mississippi after trying to arrange shipments of marijuana from the southern United States to Chicago for resale. Fort was sentenced to thirteen years in prison in December 1983. He was assigned first to the federal correctional institution at Terre Haute, Indiana, where prison authorities were alarmed after it became apparent that Fort continued to run the El Rukn operations via telephone from the prison. He was subsequently transferred to the federal prison at Bastrop, Texas, where it was thought he would be unable to continue his leadership role in the organization.

Despite federal correctional officials' efforts to monitor and limit Fort's control of his organization, the El Rukn leaders devised an elaborate code and series of "call forwarding" procedures whereby Fort maintained daily contact with his generals in Chicago. On March 11, 1986 four of Fort's top lieutenants, Reico Cranshaw, Leon McAnderson, Charles Knox, and Yvonne King, flew from Chicago to Casablanca then on to Tripoli, Libya on tickets paid for by the Libyan government. There they attended the Second General Mathaba Conference sponsored by Moammar Kaddafi. The purpose of the conference was to provide a forum for the discussion of revolutionary and terrorist strategies to combat American imperialism.[70] Cranshaw and McAnderson promoted the El Rukns as able to carry out acts of political violence in the United States as a show of their support for Libya. Before leaving, the Libyan leader promised $2.5 million in exchange for their services. Kaddafi personally called the Chicago headquarters to solidify the deal. The call was patched through to a pay phone at the federal penitentiary in Bastrop so Kaddafi could speak directly to the incarcerated Jeff Fort.

Fort and the El Rukns soon discovered that Kaddafi's money wasn't as easy to get as the funds in federal programs had been. Kaddafi expected action, so the El Rukns came up with a five-fold plan to convince him of their allegiance. The first phase involved placing threatening phone calls to the U.S. Capitol Building from cities throughout the country in order to give the impression of general public discontent about Washington's relations with Libya.[71] The second phase involved producing a videotape for public release showing the El Rukns professing support for Libya. Mayes filmed the video while the "generals" posed behind Fort's "throne" at the El Rukn headquarters. In Fort's absence, the best the group could do was to have a picture of Fort behind the group, between posters of Kaddafi. The video and newspaper accounts of the threatening phone calls were delivered by Reico Cranshaw to Libyan diplomats in Panama on May 4, 1986. Kaddafi, however, remained unconvinced. He wanted violent action, such as the bombing one month earlier of TWA flight 840 on its trip from Athens to Rome.[72]

In response, the El Rukns suggested three additional phases to the original plan to convince Kaddafi: (1) telephoning an airline claiming a bomb was set to explode; (2) assassinating a political figure who had spoken out against Kaddafi; and (3) actually destroying government buildings by bomb or missile attack. Throughout April 1986, Libyan contacts demanded that an assassination be committed on their behalf. Charles Knox selected Harout Sanasarian, a local Milwaukee politician and critic of Kaddafi. Although the assassination never took place, surveillance on Sanasarian's movements was conducted extensively by members of the El Rukns.

Fort hoped to procure weapons and training for El Rukn members by sending them, ten at a time, to Libya for training. In particular Fort, through his generals in Chicago, asked Kaddafi for a light anti-tank weapon, or LAW rocket. In an FBI-intercepted call from Mayes to Fort on May 25, 1986, Fort was told that the deal with the Libyans for the LAW had been postponed. Fort wanted one anyway and instructed Mayes to find it. FBI undercover agents readily complied. On July 31, 1986 Special Agent Willie Hulon sold an inert LAW rocket to Knox and Mayes in a Holiday Inn parking lot in Lansing, Illinois. The weapon was taken to an El Rukn-owned apartment building on South Kenwood in Chicago and stored with other weapons in a makeshift arsenal in the basement. FBI agents raided El Rukn buildings on August 5 and confiscated weapons, explosives, and ammunition. Knox and Davis were arrested at the site. Within a month after the raid, Mayes, Fort's chief aide, made his way to Morocco, then Libya, where he remains a fugitive.

In September 1986 a fifty-count indictment named Fort, Mayes, Knox, Davis, Cranshaw, McAnderson, and Roosevelt Hawkins as principals in a conspiracy in the terrorism-for-hire scheme.[73] Only Mayes, the fugitive, was not convicted. The case is remarkable because, according to Assistant U.S. Attorney John Podliska, it represented the "first convictions of U.S. citizens for conspiring to commit terrorist acts in this country for a foreign government in exchange for money."[74] Approximately fifty El Rukns have been convicted of state or federal crimes and two members are on death row in Illinois prisons. The sentence given Jeff Fort is indicative of the danger to society that federal authorities believed he was. Convicted of forty-nine of the fifty counts, Fort was sentenced to one year on each of forty-four counts of using interstate commerce (a telephone) to carry out illegal activities, plus five years on the conspiracy charge and ten years on each of three illegal weapons charges. Given consecutive sentences on each count, Fort received a total sentence of eighty years in addition to a $255,000 fine.[75]

Special Interest or Single-Issue Terrorism

Although terrorists—leftist terrorists in particular—have committed acts supportive of special interests like the anti-nuclear movement, an understanding of the single-issue or special interest terrorist should not be clouded by the political rhetoric of the Left or Right. The activities of special interest terrorists in America are analyzed best by accepting them at face value—as attempts to change *one* aspect of the social or political arena through terrorism.

In the 1980s in America, increasing concern over environmental issues led some extremists to turn to terrorism. Guided by a philosophy that is still evolving, environmental extremists contend that human efforts to sustain and improve the quality of human life have led to the suffering and extinction of other species. More importantly, these groups exhibit a world view similar in its fatalism to that of their left- and right-wing cousins, contending that, if left unchecked, humans will eventually bring the world to a cataclysmic end. Within the United States, environmental terrorists have had two major concerns: (1) the expanding use of nuclear power, and (2) the use of other species to further human ends. The Evan Mecham Eco-Terrorist International Conspiracy has violently opposed the use of nuclear power in the United States, while the Animal Liberation Front has been concerned primarily with what they believe to be the inappropriate use of animals for scientific research.

Although anti-nuclear, environmental, and animal rights extremists have been active in the United States for over two decades, their actions did not attract the attention of official terrorism labelers until the late 1980s. With the exception of Norman Mayer's threat to blow up the Washington Monument with a van laden with explosives on December 8, 1982, none of the officially labeled acts of terrorism prior to 1987 could be attributed to environmental terrorists. However, between 1987–1990 nearly a third (six out of twenty-one) of those acts have been committed by either EMETIC or ALF. In addition, the FBI prevented four planned acts of terrorism when four EMETIC members were arrested in 1989.

The Evan Mecham Eco-Terrorist International Conspiracy

EMETIC, an Arizona-based organization, selected its name as a sarcastic slap at Evan Mecham, a former governor of the state. The group was formed from the radical elements of the environmental movement known as Earth First. David Foreman, who informally directed the activities of Earth First after its inception in 1980, was also the leader of EMETIC. EMETIC is best understood as an outgrowth of Foreman's philosophy and leadership regarding environmental protection. In 1981, less than a year after forming Earth First in his home in Tucson, Arizona, Foreman attracted national attention by placing a long strip of black plastic down the wall of the Glen Canyon Dam that gave the appearance of a huge crack in the structure.[76] Four years later he published *Ecodefense: A Field Guide to Monkeywrenching*,[77] which described techniques for interrupting logging operations as well as construction and development in pristine areas. Foreman borrowed the term *monkeywrenching* from his mentor, Edward Abbey, who a decade before had published *The Monkeywrench Gang*.[78] Even Foreman's idea about the Glen Canyon Dam was borrowed from Abbey: the gang in Abbey's novel plotted to blow up that dam. Foreman's book, which also described the "spiking" technique used widely on trees in the Northwest to prevent logging operations, brought him celebrity status. He appeared on numerous national talk shows, including "60 Minutes" in March 1990.[79] As the Earth First movement grew rapidly during the late 1980s, Foreman turned to practicing some of the more violent monkeywrenching tactics. In October 1987 David Foreman, Mark Davis, Margaret Millet, Marc Baker, and Ilse Asplund formed EMETIC to conduct sabotage against nuclear power plants in the Southwest.[80] All four of Foreman's associates in EMETIC were in their mid-thirties when the group was active. Their backgrounds were diverse: Margaret Millet worked part-time for the local Planned Parenthood; Ilse Asplund was the divorced mother of two and worked in Yauapai County, Arizona; Marc Baker had a Ph.D. in botany from Arizona State University and was married with two children.[81]

Although the group probably was responsible for the May 1986 destruction of power lines at the Palo Verde Nuclear Generating Station, EMETIC issued no communiques claiming responsibility. They made their first "official" appearance on November 7, 1987, when the management at Fairfield Snow Bowl ski resort received a letter advising them that the chairlifts at the resort had been damaged. Over $20,000 damage had been done to the bolts that anchored the power lines on the lift, and EMETIC further threatened that if the trees were not allowed to grow back and if ski operations were not discontinued, they would strike again.[82]

Nearly a year later, the group resurfaced, this time destroying power lines feeding uranium mines near the Grand Canyon. Thirty-four power poles at two locations on the north and south rims of the canyon were damaged, causing power outages at two uranium mines owned by Energy Fuels Nuclear. Two days later, on September 28, 1988, a radio station in Flagstaff received a typed letter from EMETIC claiming responsibility for the vandalism. Less than a month later, they struck again, returning to the scene of the crime at the Fairfield Snow Bowl, where they used an acetylene torch to cut through a pole supporting the chairlift.

On May 30, 1989 the first EMETIC members to be arrested were apprehended near Wenden, Arizona. Three members of the group were caught cutting through a support tower that delivered electricity to a local substation. Davis and Baker were apprehended at the scene. Millet fled but was apprehended the following day. David Foreman was named with the others in the federal indictment released the following month. Charged with conspiracy (among other things), the group apparently intended to use the May 30 vandalism at Wenden, Arizona as a practice session before simultaneously attacking the power transmission lines at three separate nuclear facilities in California, Arizona, and Colorado.[83]

Unfortunately for Foreman and other EMETIC members, the group had been infiltrated by Michael Fain, an undercover FBI agent who made more than 800 hours of tape recordings. Gerry Spence, the noted environmentalist lawyer from Jackson Hole, Wyoming who won the Karen Silkwood case against Kerr-McGee, volunteered to defend members of the group.[84] Although the case was repeatedly delayed, all five eventually pled guilty. With the exception of Mark Davis, group members recieved relatively minor punishments.[85] Unlike any of the other terrorists in our study, formal sentencing for Foreman has been delayed until 1996; if he complies with the conditions of his probation, he will be allowed to enter a guilty plea to a misdemeanor charge.[86]

In August 1991, one month before pleading guilty in the conspiracy case, Foreman announced his resignation from Earth First. Claiming that Earth First had become part of the left-wing politics of the group's California wing,[87] Foreman maintained he could not ally himself with the leftist social causes that were becoming part of the Earth First movement. Mike Roselle, a leader in the California wing of Earth First, referred to Foreman as an "unrepentant right-wing thug."[88] One way or another, single-issue terrorists eventually get caught up in the political rhetoric of extremism.

The Animal Liberation Front.

Unlike EMETIC, which is localized in the southwestern United States (although it claims international support), Animal Liberation Front supporters have committed acts of vandalism both in the United States and overseas. Despite the fact that ALF members have committed nearly 100 crimes, including the theft of lab equipment and animals, the destruction of research records and data, and the vandalism or arson of university buildings that house animal labs, it was not until 1987 that the FBI officially began to label their acts as terroristic. Since that time, ALF has committed three officially designated acts of terror.

All three acts took place on the campuses of major research universities. The first occurred on April 16, 1987, when ALF members set fire to the new Veterinary Medicine Research Building at the University of California-Davis, causing more than $3.5 million in damages. ALF's anonymous calls to local television stations and its spray-painting of vehicles on campus with the words "Animal Liberation Front" and "Stop the Torture" linked the group to the fire. Although the group remained fairly quiet in 1988, in April 1989 they stole more than 1,000 lab animals from the University of Arizona, then set fire to two buildings on campus: the Pharmacy Microbiology Building and the Office for the Division of Animal Resources. Three months later members of the group broke into the Health Sciences Center at Texas Tech University and released lab animals, destroyed lab equipment, stole the records and data for lab experiments, and painted animal rights slogans on the walls. As a show of support for the efforts of People for the Ethical Treatment of Animals (PETA), another animal rights activist group, ALF members claimed credit for the Texas Tech vandalism via a news release to PETA the day after the incident.

Federal authorities are seriously examining ALF's relationship with PETA.[89] As such, ALF's threats to continue vandalizing research facilities housing lab animals cannot be taken lightly. In mid-June 1991, ALF claimed credit for the arson of a barn housing 1,300 lab animals and the destruction of research equipment at Oregon State University.[90] The Animal Liberation Front probably poses a much more viable threat in the 1990s than does EMETIC. For one thing, ALF has a much larger support base through less radical fringe groups like PETA. In addition, their goals allow them to focus on targets that remain fairly soft. While the antinuclear efforts of EMETIC have been forced to confront an industry that is highly security conscious, the Animal Liberation Front is able to concentrate its attacks against university campus buildings that typically have minimal security and are easily accessed. The Animal Liberation Front may prove to be a formidable foe to universities and private labs in the next decade.

Summary and Conclusions

The activities of left-wing and environmental terrorists during the 1980s were substantially different from the actions of right-wing terrorists in several ways. First, left-wing terrorists in this country during the past decade were much more ideologically committed than right-wing terrorists. Substantially fewer left-wing terrorists turned state's evidence and testified against their comrades than did right-wing terrorists. Secondly, the underground support networks of leftist terrorists appear to be much more sophisticated than those of right-wing terrorists. While few, if any, right-wing terrorists from the 1980s have evaded apprehension, several left-wing terrorists have avoided capture. Much of this difference results from Cuba's willingness to harbor American fugitives. Members of the Macheteros, the Black Liberation Army, and the FALN have found sanctuary there. Others, like M19CO's Elizabeth Duke, remain unaccounted for. Finally, environmental terrorists promise to be a major threat before the turn of the century. Although the FBI successfully infiltrated right-wing groups and snared left-wing terrorists through good detective work during the 1980s, less has been learned about the inner workings of environmental terrorist groups. Until law enforcement agencies develop the necessary information to combat this type of terrorism, environmental terrorists may contribute a unique brand of violent extremism well into the 21st century.

Chapter 7

International Terrorist Activity in America

Although domestic terrorists committed most terrorist acts in the United States during the 1980s, it was the threat of international terrorism that held America's attention. Although Israel was the primary target of international terrorists during the 1960s and 1970s, American property and citizens increasingly became a favorite target of the international terrorists during the 1980s.[1] With Israel's tightened security and fabulous successes in retaliatory strikes such as the one at Entebbe in 1976, international terrorists sought alternative targets. Although Israel remained the desired target for some of the more spectacular terrorist incidents of the 1980s (e.g., the Rome and Vienna Airport massacres and the Achille Lauro hijacking of 1985), Americans witnessed the displacement of much international terrorism from Israel to its chief proponent, the United States. By 1985 nearly a quarter (22 percent) of all international terrorist attacks were directed against U.S. citizens or property.[2] After the bombings of the U.S. Embassy in Lebanon and the Marine Corps barracks at Beirut Airport in 1983, Americans realized, probably for the first time, the magnitude of the problem Western Europeans had been experiencing during the past twenty years.

Following the Marine Corps barracks bombing President Reagan swore that if a "smoking gun" could be found America would retaliate.[3] On April 5, 1986, the United States intercepted communication between Tripoli and the Libyan Embassy in East Germany authorizing a strike against American servicemen in West Germany. Within hours the LaBelle Disco, a favorite haunt of American GIs in West Berlin, was bombed. Two were killed, one an American soldier. Seventy-nine more Americans were injured. President Reagan had found sufficient probable cause.[4] Within weeks, the United States mounted a retaliatory strike against Libyan targets in Tripoli and Bengazi, destroying Moammar Kaddafi's headquarters and causing substantial damage to civilian sections of the city as well.[5] The escalation brought international terrorism closer to home.

Despite the escalation of attacks against Americans overseas, Americans at home remained fairly safe from international terrorists. It is difficult to explain why we have been relatively immune from international terrorist strikes within the United States. Security experts such as Brian Jenkins have suggested that the lack of isolated, disenfranchised ethnic groups within the United States has prevented the development of a base of operations for international terrorists.[6] The sheer proximity of nations in Western Europe, which is home to a large number of displaced Palestinians, has made it a fertile ground for international terrorism.[7] The physical isolation of the United States may have been as great an inhibitor to international terror as any social or political strategy. With oceans on either side and friendly allies to the north and south, the United States, despite its open arms and general lack of security, was seemingly insulated from the international network of terrorists during the 1980s.

With the exception of an assassination and a couple of bombings by Croatian and Armenian terrorists, the United States was faced with only one major group committing acts of international terrorism within our borders during the early 1980s.[8] Yet even this organization, Omega 7, was not foreign supported, nor was it composed of members with links to international terrorism in western Europe. By the late 1980s, however, the United States witnessed a number of non-citizen, foreign terrorists parade before the federal courts.[9] From Japanese Red Army member Yu Kikumura to IRA gunrunners, from Libyan intelligence agents to Syrian bombers, Americans were exposed for the first time to the types of terrorists that had forced Europeans to make changes in their courtroom practices and methods of judicial administration. Recent changes in federal law grant the U.S. jurisdiction over some acts of terrorism overseas, and in 1989 America had its first prosecution of an international terrorist brought to this country for trial.[10]

Most of the persons arrested for international terrorism-related activities in the United States never committed an act of terrorism. The most active of the groups, the Provisional Irish Republican Army, primarily has used the United States as a resource for

the procurement of weapons. Omega 7, however, successfully completed a number of bombings and won the distinction of being the
most violent international terrorist group in America in the 1980s.
Federal indictments against members of six "international" groups
attracted the attention of Americans during the 1980s.[11] Omega 7
members, Provo gunrunners, a group of Libyan agents, one Palestinian member of the Shiite group Amal, Yu Kikumura of the
Japanese Red Army, and three members of the Syrian Social Nationalist party were indicted by the U.S. government.

Characteristics of International Terrorists in America

Russell and Miller's widely cited description of the international
terrorist as being between twenty and twenty-three-years of age
has become the accepted characterization of the typical terrorist.[12]
An examination in Chapter 3 of persons arrested for domestic terrorism revealed, however, the typical domestic terrorist to be approximately thirty-five at the time of indictment, considerably
older than previous estimates. Lest one think this may have been
an anomaly, persons indicted for acts of international terrorism or
terrorism-related activities in the United States also tend to be
much older than usually depicted. In fact, their average age of
thirty-six is slightly older than that of their domestic counterparts
(table 7.1).

The skeptic might suggest that age at indictment does not
reveal when the individuals turned to terror, only when they were
caught. However, with the exception of Omega 7 (which had a
lengthy period of operation), the overwhelming majority of acts
that resulted in indictment of international terrorists took place
only a year or two prior to indictment. Clearly the average age of
these persons is at least a decade older than Russell and Miller
suggested. Even Omega 7 members, who operated for eight years
before anyone was captured, were in their thirties when they began operations. Eduardo Arocena was nearly thirty-two when he
formed the group in late 1974, and most of the other members were
older than that. An examination of indicted members of more traditional and widely known international terrorist groups like the
Japanese Red Army and the Provos reveals similar trends. Yu Kikumura of Japanese Red Army fame, for example, was thirty-six
when arrested in New Jersey in 1988. The average age of indicted
Provo members in the United States was thirty-five.

All of the persons indicted in federal courts for international

Table 7.1   Demographic Characteristics of International Terrorists[a]

Average Age at Indictment	36 Youngest, 23; oldest, 48
Sex	All males
Education	Moderate Only 8% had a college degree; Over half (56%) had never attended college.
Occupation	Varied Most Libyans were posing as students; Only Omega 7 members held routine, full-time employment.
Ethnicity	50% Irish 34% Arab/Middle Eastern 13% Hispanic 3% Oriental

[a]Includes members from the following groups or nationalities: Provisional Irish Republican Army, Japanese Red Army, Omega 7, Amal, Libyans, and the Syrian Social Nationalist party.

terrorism or terrorism related activities were male. Half of these men were married, compared to nearly three-fourths (73 percent) of persons indicted for domestic terrorism. Members of the Provisional IRA accounted for half of the indictees, while a third were of Arab or Middle Eastern origin. International terrorists in America have been less educated than either American left-wing or right-wing domestic terrorists, although differences between the international terrorists and the rightists are minimal. A major difference between domestic and international terrorists in America is their occupations. Due to the non-citizen status of many of the international terrorists they are unable to hold traditional jobs in the work force. Many transient Provo members held part-time jobs, while some Provo members obviously received funds from some other source. Similarly, most of the Libyans were students or they worked for the Manara Travel Agency, a Libyan-owned enterprise that hired its own agents. The only U.S.-based international terrorist group, Omega 7, was also the only group whose members held traditional, full-time employment.

Omega 7

Organized September 11, 1974 by Eduardo Arocena, Omega 7 was one of the most active international terrorist groups on American soil in the late 1970s and early 1980s. Between 1974 and 1982, Omega 7 members committed over fifty bombings and assassinations against Cuban diplomats, governments, and businesses sympathetic to Communist Cuba and corporations trading with Cuba. It is ironic that under different circumstances Omega 7 members and U.S. government officials might have found themselves working for the same cause.

The rise of Omega 7 reflected the frustration of thousands of Cuban Americans. Having lost everything to Castro's brand of socialism, unhappy expatriate Cubans have been unable to mount either an internal overthrow of his dictatorship or to convince the United States that external support would result in a successful overthrow of Castro's government. Consequently, these expatriates have waited in the wings, hoping for an opportunity to return home in the event of Castro's fall. Unfortunately some, like Arocena, became too impatient. He formed two cells of Omega 7 with members drawn from the large Cuban populations in Miami and New Jersey. Virtually all of its members suffered at the hands of Castro's redistribution of wealth, collectivization of private farms, and nationalization of the industrial base of the island. The New Jersey cell consisted of Arocena and six others: Pedro Remon, Andres Garcia, Eduardo Losada-Fernandez, Jose Julio Gracia, Alberto Perez, and Eduardo Ochoa. The name Omega 7 probably was derived from the number of original members in the group. The background of these men provides insight into their motivation and goals.

Like most of the members of Omega 7, Eduardo Arocena was born in Cuba. He lived in Caibarien, Cuba as a child and attended school there until he quit when Castro obtained control of the island in 1959. Very athletic, he worked as a stevedore and later became a Cuban wrestling champion who aspired to compete in the Olympics. Benefitting from his status as an athlete, he was selected by the government cooperative where he worked to study aviation in the Soviet Union. By this time, however, Arocena was already participating with other Cuban expatriates in clandestine guerrilla activities against Castro, monitoring Soviet troop movements, burning cane fields, and destroying planned industrial sites. Fearing that his anti-Castro sentiments would be exposed if he refused to go to the Soviet Union for schooling, Arocena fled to the United States in 1965 at the age of twenty-two. He settled in Elizabeth, New Jersey, married, and went to work as a merchandise selector for Wayfirm, a large food warehouse.[13]

Pedro Remon lived and was educated not far from where Arocena was born. He received an associate's degree in accounting in Cuba before fleeing to the United States in 1963. He lived in Miami and later relocated to the West Orange, New Jersey area in 1965. A more severe story unfolded for Jose Lopez. Born in 1938 in Placetas, Cuba, he and his mother managed to turn their farm into one of the most prosperous plantations in the region. Unwilling to go along with the Communist party movement in Cuba when the Batista regime fell, Lopez spent the next five years in prison. Upon his release in 1965, he and his mother fled to the United States. When his wife was able to join him, he settled in North Bergen, New Jersey, where he became a supervisor of shipping and receiving at Foldtex, a textile distributor.[14] Like Arocena and Lopez, Omega 7 members were intensely anti-Communist and had almost as great a hatred for the Soviet Union as they did for Fidel Castro.

The roles of group members were clear and well defined. Arocena assumed the tactical role of commander, while also lending his expertise in the procurement and development of explosives. He claimed to have been trained in 1967 by American military or CIA personnel somewhere in the Florida Everglades. Court documents do indicate that Arocena left his job at Wayfirm in 1967 and moved to the Miami area for a short time. He claimed to have been taught infiltration techniques, guerrilla tactics, and the art of bomb making.[15] Whatever the source of his training, Arocena was skillful in using high explosives and demonstrated knowledge in the creation of fairly sophisticated remote-controlled explosive devices.

Pedro Remon was the most active participant in most of the violent bombings and assassinations committed by the group during their eight-year romp through New York, New Jersey, Florida, and Canada. It was Remon who also placed the anonymous calls to radio station WCBS in New York following each bombing or assassination. Other members played lesser roles. Losado-Fernandez provided the upstairs portion of his Fruit-Meat King grocery store as a place where weapons were tested and bombs were built. Andres Garcia frequently acted as the driver while Remon actually made the hit or placed the bomb.[16]

Omega 7 was highly active from its formation in September 1974 until Arocena's arrest on July 22, 1983. They opened their campaign by bombing the Venezuelan Consulate in New York City on February 1, 1975 because of Venezuela's sympathetic support for Castro. The group then waited a year before bombing the Cuban delegation to the United Nations in June 1976. Two months later they bombed the Soviet ship *Ivan Shepetkov* at Port Elizabeth, New Jersey. Throughout 1977 and 1978 WCBS radio in Manhattan received Pedro Remon's calls claiming responsibility for bombings of travel agencies in New Jersey and a sporting goods store near Madison Square Garden. Remon lamented that the media were not paying enough attention to the group's cause. In late 1978 the bombings became more indiscriminate and held the potential for greater destruction. On December 28 the group bombed Avery Fisher Hall at Lincoln Center for the Performing Arts in downtown Manhattan.

1979 and 1980 proved to be Omega 7's most active years. In March 1979 Arocena purchased a ticket and placed a time bomb with his luggage on board a TWA flight to Los Angeles. Remon's call, which warned of the bomb's presence, was intended to reveal to authorities that the group had the capacity to carry out their threats. In December they bombed the Cuban Mission to the United Nations and followed this up one month later by bombing the Aeroflot Soviet Airlines ticket office on Fifth Avenue in New York City.

In March 1980 Omega 7 stepped up their actions against Cuban diplomats when they planted a remote-controlled bomb in the car of the Cuban ambassador to the United Nations, Raul Roa. The plastic explosives were attached to the vehicle by magnets. Although the explosive device was quite sophisticated, the magnets were not strong enough and the bomb fell off the vehicle. It lay in the street for some time before an unsuspecting citizen threw it in a nearby garbage can, and it was ingloriously hauled away in a city garbage truck.[17] The remote control was later found in Eduardo Arocena's hideout in Miami.

Undeterred, Omega 7 stepped up their efforts to assassinate Cuban diplomats. The group bought a MAC-10 machine gun, and test-fired it over Losada-Fernandez's store, and Remon used it to gun down Felix Garcia-Rodriguez, an attaché to the Cuban Mission to the United Nations.[18] The same day, September 11, 1980, Remon placed his traditional call to WCBS saying that Omega 7 had "eliminated" a member of the Cuban delegation to the United Nations. This was followed by a plan to kill Cuban Interests Section Ambassador Ramon Sanchez Parodi in Washington, DC. On September 14, Arocena drove Remon and Losada-Fernandez to Belleville, New Jersey, where they were to steal a car to drive to

Washington, but Remon and Losada-Fernandez were arrested for auto theft before leaving the scene.[19] The group began to fall apart shortly thereafter as the FBI closed in.

After fleeing to Florida, Arocena established a Miami cell of Omega 7. Remon continued the New York operations, evading FBI scrutiny until he was caught returning illegally from Canada after bombing the Cuban Consulate in Montreal in December 1980. Believing that Remon had divulged his activities to FBI agents in New York, Arocena agreed to talk to a federal grand jury on September 2, 1982. He promptly went into hiding after his testimony and remained a fugitive until his arrest on July 22, 1983.

To supporters of the anti-Castro movement, many of Omega 7's activities may have seemed legitimate. However, as the investigation unfolded it became clear that Omega 7 funded its activities through murder and extortion often in association with illegal drug traffic. In March 1984 an indictment filed in federal court alleged that Omega 7 members were hired by major narcotics suppliers in the New York area to murder Luis Fuentes and Raymond Vanyo for having failed to pay for a narcotics delivery.[20] As hired guns, Omega 7 used arson and physical force to extort money from nonpaying drug customers. Payments for such services were then funneled into Omega 7 coffers to cover travel expenses, hotel bills, and the purchase of weapons for terrorist acts in the Northeast, Canada and Florida.

On November 9, 1984 Arocena was sentenced to a mandatory life sentence for the first-degree murder of a diplomat. Convicted on twenty-five counts of a twenty-six count indictment, Arocena also received consecutive twenty- and 10-year sentences for RICO violations, his placement of a bomb near an aircraft, and numerous other offenses.[21] Although some sympathizers, like Jose Lopez, the Cuban expatriate, were jailed for refusing to testify before the federal grand jury, remaining members of the New York cell were arrested and brought to trial. When Arocena later refused to testify, Remon, Garcia, and Losada-Fernandez were allowed to plead guilty in exchange for a lesser sentence. On April 10, 1986, each of the three was sentenced to ten years for conspiracy to murder a foreign diplomat.[22]

Provisional Irish Republican Army

Sixteen of the thirty-two persons indicted as a result of investigations into international terrorism were members of PIRA, or Provos—the provisional wing of the outlawed Irish Republican

Army. They have found the Irish-American population in New England to be a major source for support and funding. The dispute between the Catholic population of Ireland and the English-supported Protestant population has gone on for centuries. When England broke away from the Catholic church to form the Anglican church in the late 1500s, the predominately Catholic-Irish population experienced periods of severe persecution. The "official" IRA was formed to fight the British presence in Ireland. In 1921 the moderate wing of the official IRA, led by Sean MacBride, renounced violence and accepted the Anglo-Irish Treaty of 1921. The treaty established the Irish Free State, formed from twenty-six Catholic counties in southern Ireland. Northern Ireland, which was predominately Protestant, remained part of the United Kingdom.

Catholics in northern Ireland, however, experienced tremendous economic and political hardship. In the late 1960s radical nationalists in northern Ireland formed the "provisional" Irish Republican Army to fight the British presence in northern Ireland as well as discrimination against Catholics by the Protestant majority there. Provos' split from the remaining members of the "official" IRA in 1969 reflected significant philosophical and tactical differences between the two groups. While the majority of IRA members desired a political solution to the problem in northern Ireland, members of Provos advocated a return to militant action and terrorism. They launched their terrorist campaign of indiscriminate bombings in Ireland and England in 1970, but Provos has avoided engaging in actual terrorist acts in the United States. Instead, it has used the United States as a source of funding, weapons procurement, and political support. Two major gun-smuggling schemes involving IRA members in the United States attracted the attention of FBI and customs officials during the 1980s.

The *Valhalla* Incident

In April 1984 seven men associated with the Provos and led by Joseph Murray, Jr., then 38, and Patrick Nee, 40, began buying large quantities of weapons, rockets, weapons manuals, bulletproof vests, and other pieces of military equipment. They bought the equipment from dealers all over the United States: the rocket warheads from Barnicle Wharf Trading Company in Newark, Ohio; the weapons manuals from Sierra Supply Company in Durango, Colorado; ammunition cans from Jolly Roger Surplus in Roxbury,

Pennsylania; and the vests from Professional Image Uniform in Woburn, Massachusetts. Deliveries were made via UPS to Pat Mullen, in care of the Columbia Yacht Club, South Boston. Then individual members of this group began to buy one or two rifles or pistols each during May and June 1984, primarily from Ivanhoe Sports Center in Watertown, Massachusetts and Roach's Sporting Goods in Cambridge, Massachusetts.[23]

In July 1984 a corporation known as Leeward, Inc. bought the *Valhalla*, an oceangoing fishing boat, at a U.S. Marshal's Service auction of confiscated property. Little did the Marshal's Service know that the *Valhalla* would be returned to its service in criminal activities here in the United States. Leeward hired Robert Andersen, one of the seven conspirators, to captain the boat. On September 14 Andersen and two other members of the conspiracy, John Crawley and John McIntyre, left Gloucester, Massachusetts supposedly to fish off the Grand Banks. Two weeks later the *Valhalla* was spotted by Irish naval authorities in international waters off the coast of Ireland. They observed as weapons and other military items were transferred to another boat, the *Marita Ann*.[24] Two days later the *Marita Ann* was seized by Irish law enforcement authorities in Irish territorial waters. Over 150 firearms, including many new assault rifles, over 71,000 rounds of ammunition, and various other military hardware, were confiscated. American authorities were notified to watch for the return of the *Valhalla*. The boat was seized in October 1984 after docking at Pier 7 in Boston Harbor.

As the investigation unfolded, it was discovered that, like many other terrorist groups, this group financed its operations through drug trafficking. Joseph Murray and Robert Andersen were convicted in 1987 of smuggling more than 1,000 pounds of marijuana into the country in addition to violations of the Export Administration Act and RICO statutes.[25] They were originally sentenced to ten- and four-year sentences, but their sentences were later reduced. Nee was given a four-year sentence for his participation in the conspiracy, and Crawley is now in prison in Ireland.

The Redeye Buyers

In March 1985 another group of Provo sympathizers sought to sell weapons to the Provos in Belfast, Ireland. Noel Murphy, 26, and Cairan Hughes, 23, would negotiate the deal with the Provos, provide money to buy the weapons here in the United States, and even make a small commission off each weapon sale for themselves.[26] Apparently, the scheme was one the men had used before. Several years before, the two men had been involved in a scheme to buy firearms stolen from homes in New York, but some of their brokers had been caught by federal treasury agents. This time they hired John McDonald, 36, to find a seller-supplier in the United States.

Murphy and Hughes wanted to upgrade their operation by buying large quantities of military hardware—M-16 assault rifles and MP-5 machine guns—rather than the potpourri of sporting rifles and handguns they had previously bought. MacDonald made contact with a person who said he had 100 M-16s, two MP-5 submachine guns, each with 100 rounds of ammunition, that he was willing to sell for $60,000. They finally agreed on a selling price of $73,000 on condition that a Redeye missile would be included in the deal. Unfortunately for MacDonald, the seller was an undercover FBI agent.

Murphy and Hughes hired Roy Willey to inspect the weapons before shipment to ensure that they were in firing condition. Four other men, James Boyle, John Fitzgerald, Steven MacDonald, and Michael McLaughlin were hired to accompany the shipment to Belfast, offload the weapons, and deliver them to PIRA representatives. On May 20, 1986, over one year after the original contacts were made, Murphy and Hughes were taken to Hanscom Field to inspect the 100 M-16s, a Redeye missile, and 5,000 rounds of ammunition loaded aboard a jet aircraft. At the same time, the remaining Redeye buyers were meeting in Bedford, Massachusetts with the sellers to discuss the logistics of loading and offloading the weapons. All eight men were arrested at that time and later charged in a four-count indictment.

In October, 1986 the five hired hands and MacDonald pled guilty to one count each in exchange for dropping one additional charge. The five men hired to load and accompany the weapons to Ireland were each sentenced to six-month sentences. MacDonald received eighteen months for his part in the conspiracy. Murphy and Hughes were not offered leniency, and both opted for a jury trial. On October 23, 1986, they were convicted of illegal arms dealing. Murphy was sentenced to nine years, and Hughes was sentenced to eight years in the federal penitentiary.[27]

The Libyan Threat

When Americans think or speak of terrorism, the names most likely to be mentioned are Libya and its charismatic leader, Moammar Kaddafi. America enjoyed diplomatic relations with Libya until the Iranian takeover of the U.S. Embassy in Tehran in 1979. In December 1979, the American Embassy in Libya was burned and was never reopened. On May 6, 1981, the United States closed the Libyan Embassy in Washington, thereby breaking any remaining formal diplomatic ties between the countries. In 1982, as Kaddafi shouted threats at President Reagan during rallies staged for maximum media exposure, Reagan prohibited the importation of crude oil from Libya. Kaddafi responded by saying that terrorist hit-teams would be dispatched to the United States to assassinate President Reagan. Although unsuccessful in conducting large-scale terrorism in the United States, Kaddafi continued to support leftist terrorism in western Europe, primarily through Abu Nidal's Fatah Revolutionary Council.

In January 1986 President Reagan signed two executive orders dealing with the Libyan threat. The first prohibits all commercial dealings between U.S. citizens and Libya. This prohibition includes any transactions involving travel to or from Libya.[28] The second order blocks all transfers of property in which the government of Libya has an interest.[29] These two orders directly affected Kaddafi's efforts to transport terrorism to the United States through Libyan students studying in America. Later that year, Kaddafi bombed the LaBelle Disco in West Berlin in retaliation. President Reagan responded in kind on April 14, 1986 by bombing the Libyan cities of Tripoli and Bengazi.

Following the closing of the Libyan Embassy in Washington in 1981, the Libyan government immediately formed the People's Committee for Students of Libyan Jamahariya (otherwise known as the People's Committee for Libyan Students, or simply PCLS). The organization's stated purpose was to assist Libyan students in the United States with their academic, personal, and legal needs. The Manara Travel Agency opened for business in Washington shortly thereafter. Both organizations were manned by intelligence agents of the Libyan government. Five Libyan agents, Milad Shibani, Mahdi Mohammed Abousetta, Ramadan Belgasem, Salem Zubeidy, and Saleh Al-Rajhi, posed as students and served as officers of the PCLS. Two additional agents, Mousa Hawamda and Manhal Ben Mohammed worked for or were part-owners of the Manara Travel Agency.

Their conspiracy involved three primary objectives: the collection and transmission of intelligence data to Libya, the assassination of high-ranking government officials, and the support of radical domestic groups in the United States. To further the first of these goals, Saleh Al-Rajhi, using the PCLS facilities, was able to obtain the names of over one thousand federal employees of the CIA, FBI, Defense Intelligence Agency, Defense Department, and the armed services.[30] The names were to be transmitted to Libya. One of them was Oliver North. North, who was fired from his National Security Council job in November 1986 for his part in the Iran-Contra affair, was targeted by PCLS for having been involved in planning the April 1986 bombing of Kaddafi's headquarters in Tripoli.[31] Mousa Hawamda, a naturalized American and co-owner of the Manara Travel Agency, apparently directed the conspiracy objective to murder North and other American officials.

In an effort to create civil unrest in the United States, the PCLS, using the Manara Travel Agency as a front, funded the First International Conference of the Red Indians of the Americas in Tripoli, Libya in April 1986. In 1987, the Manara Travel Agency provided the arrangements for selected American dissidents to attend a "peace gathering" in Libya. During 1986 and 1987 Libyan funds paid for the travel of numerous well-known American radicals, including Bill Means, Kwame Ture (Stokely Carmichael), Vernon Bellecourt, and Bob Brown.[32] Illegally using PCLS funds, Saleh Al-Rahji, Hawamda, and Mohammed organized and paid the expenses for a demonstration in front of the White House on April 14 and 15, 1987 to protest the 1986 U.S. bombing of Libya.

In July 1988 a forty-one count indictment was returned in federal court in Alexandria, Virginia against the eight men. They were charged on a variety of conspiracy charges, aiding and abetting, and wire and credit card fraud. Mousa Hawamda subsequently fled the country. On October 14, 1988, six of the defendants pled guilty to one count of conspiracy and were each fined $100,000 and deported from the United States. The remaining defendant, Saleh Al-Rajhi, was also fined $100,000, received a five-year prison sentence to be suspended if the fine was paid, and was allowed to remain in the United States.[33] The investigation against the PCLS continued, with additional indictments being returned against PCLS members in February 1989.[34] Despite these successes against Libyan agents, terrorists from other countries also paid visits to the United States during the late 1980s.

Syrian Social Nationalist Party

The United States has been targeted by a number of international terrorist organizations from the Middle East. Few, however, have been successful in infiltrating American soil and committing acts of terrorism within the United States. The United States support of Israel and its support for the Christian faction in Lebanon led most Moslem terrorist groups in the Middle East to take a staunchly anti-American stance. The Middle East has literally hundreds of small guerrilla organizations in Lebanon fighting to gain political control as well as numerous Palestinian groups allied in their fight against Israel.

In 1972 Kamal Jumblat, the leader of one of the largest factions in Lebanon, the Druze, formed a leftist coalition of six major organizations within Lebanon. One of these six groups was the Syrian Social Nationalist party. The party is composed of Muslims who support greater Syrian involvement and control of Lebanon. Its militias fought in the recent civil war in Lebanon against the Lebanese Christian government. More ominously, its members have responded favorably to news of the violent actions of exiled Palestinian groups against Israel and the United States.[35] From 1987 to 1990 the United States witnessed a number of attempts by pro-Palestinian groups to gain access to the United States—to bring international terrorism to our own front door.

On October 23, 1987 the chief of police in Richmond, Vermont detained a naturalized Canadian citizen for having crossed the border into the United States illegally. As was customary, he returned him to the U.S. Border Patrol. When searched, the suspect was found to have illegally transported firearms and explosives across the border. The subsequent investigation revealed that Walid Nicholas Kabbani had been assisted in his illegal entry by two other men, Walid Magib Mourad and Georges Fouad Younan, all members of the Syrian Social Nationalist party. They all had been born in Lebanon but had moved to Canada, where they obtained citizenship. Little is known about what the three men intended to do with the weapons and explosives, but obviously some type of bombing was being planned. The target of the bombing was never revealed, nor was their extent of contact with radical elements of the Syrian Social Nationalist party. However, some Shiite factions of the Syrian Social Nationalist party, such as the Movement of the Disinherited, are allied with Iran.[36] Such linkages suggest that Kabbani, Mourad, and Younan were receiving orders from an outside source.

Kabbani, Mourad, and Younan were named in a five-count indictment in federal court in Vermont on November 5, 1987 charging all three with illegal interstate and foreign transfer of firearms and explosives. Kabbani also was charged with illegal entry, while Mourad and Younan were charged with aiding Kabbani in the border crossing.[37] Younan pled guilty and was sentenced to eight years imprisonment. One week later Mourad and Kabbani went to trial and were found guilty on all four of the counts against each of them. They received identical consecutive sentences totaling 16 ½ years.[38]

Japanese Red Army

Perhaps more than any other terrorist group, the Japanese Red Army brings to mind the argument of an international terrorist network.[39] On April 12, 1988, Yu Kikumura, a known JRA member, was arrested on the New Jersey Turnpike with three pipe bombs in his possession. The nation was shocked. Somehow Americans at home, up to this point, had escaped the wrath of one of the most infamous international terrorist groups. That spell had now been broken.

The Japanese Red Army was formed in 1971 by Fusako Shigenobu and her husband; the organization arose from the leftist student movement in Japan during the late 1960s. In 1971 she and a small contingent left Japan and moved to Beirut, Lebanon where they were to be a liaison between the Japanese Red Army Faction in Japan and the PFLP in the Middle East. While in Beirut and with the support of George Habash, Wadi Haddad, and the PFLP, the JRA was born with a core of no more than twenty-five members. With a strong Marxist orientation, the group became strongly anti-American through the indoctrination of PFLP leaders. During the next year JRA members trained in guerrilla warfare alongside PFLP members in Syria and Lebanon. In 1972 the JRA repaid the Palestinians for their hospitality by sending three of their members on one of the bloodiest massacres of the decade.

The three Japanese deplaning at Lod Airport in Israel opened fire when they entered the terminal. They killed twenty-six, including sixteen Americans. Two of the terrorists were killed. Kozo Okamoto, the sole surviving terrorist, was captured, tried, and imprisoned.[40] He was later released in an exchange with other Palestinian terrorists for three Israeli army officers captured in Lebanon.[41] The JRA remained fairly active during the 1970s, committing a number of hostage takings, airline hijackings, and bombings. With the 1978 death of Wadi Haddad, the PFLP's chief of operations, the Japanese Red Army became significantly less active.

Still under Shigenobu's leadership, they emerged again in

May 1986 when Yu Kikumura was arrested at the Schiphol Airport in Amsterdam for having a bomb in his luggage.[42] Later that month JRA member Tsutomu Shirosaki, 38, fired a mortar at the U.S. Embassy in Jakarta, Indonesia. In June 1987 JRA members detonated a car bomb across the street from the U.S. Embassy in Rome, then fired two rockets at the Embassy compound. In April 1988, they planted a bomb in front of the U.S. servicemen's club in Naples, Italy. Five people were killed.[43] The bombing was planned to coincide with the anniversary of the U.S. raid on Libya in 1986, leading U.S. officials to suspect that the JRA had found a new source for funding their terrorist activities in Moammar Kaddafi.

Despite the attacks on American targets overseas, the JRA had never sent its terrorists to the United States. But in late February 1988, Yu Kikumura came to visit. Kikumura, 36 in 1988, has been a long-time member of the Japanese Red Army. He was a student activist in the 1960s and a member of Kuro Hero (Black Helmet), a radical Marxist political organization that joined forces with the JRA in the summer of 1971.[44] His arrest in May 1986 at Schiphol Airport in the Netherlands signaled the resurgance of the JRA. He was ordered deported to Japan for carrying a bomb in his luggage during the incident and was later released from Japanese custody on a minor legal technicality. Authorities learned that he kept an apartment in Athens and had a Swiss bank account in Zurich. He fled Japan shortly after his release and returned to Lebanon in late 1986. While there, according to U.S. intelligence, he underwent training in Palestinian guerrilla training camps in the Bekaa Valley in late 1986 and early 1987.

Using a faked passport, Kikumura left Paris en route to the United States on February 29, 1988. He traveled widely during his month-long stay in the States, visiting thirteen states and logging more than 7,000 miles. Kikumura's visit was timed to coincide with the April 14, 1986, anniversary of the U.S. bombing of Libya. Federal authorities suspected that his target was a Navy recruiting center in midtown New York City. The bombing was apparently to take place simultaneously with a bombing in Naples, Italy. New Jersey State Police arrested Kikumura, however, with three pipe bombs in his possession just two days prior to the anniversary of the Tripoli bombing.[45] Although Kikumura's bombing was prevented, the bomb in Naples went off as scheduled—five persons were killed. Another JRA member, Junzo Okudaira, is wanted in connection with that bombing.[46]

On July 22, 1988, a federal grand jury in Newark, New Jersey returned a twelve-count indictment against Kikumura charging him with the unlawful transportation of explosive materials; possession and transportation of unregistered firearms, none of which had serial numbers; use and misuse of a passport; and fraud in obtaining a visa.[47] William Kunstler, the noted defender of other indicted terrorists, represented Kikumura during his November 1988 trial. The jury was not impressed by Kunstler's courtroom dramatics,[48] and Kikumura was found guilty of all twelve counts on November 29, 1988.[49] U.S. District Judge Alfred Lechner sentenced him on February 7, 1989 to thirty years imprisonment.

Amal

Lebanon has provided the world with more than its share of international terrorists. In addition to the JRA and the Syrian Social Nationalist party, at least one other terrorist group from this small, war-torn country played a major role in America's response to terrorism in the late 1980s. Terrorists from the radical fringes of the Shiite group Amal forever changed how America responds to international terror.

Two major divisions exist within the Moslem religion. The overwhelming majority are Sunni Muslims; a small minority, approximately 10 percent, are Shiites. Generally, Shiism has been the religion of the poor and downtrodden within Moslem countries. Ever since Mohammed's grandson led an army against overwhelming odds and certain death at Karbola a millenium ago, the Shiites have reenacted his death at Karbola every year at ceremonies throughout the Middle East. To the Shiite, the Karbola metaphor occurs every day; it is a certainty and not to be avoided. Through this religion of martyrdom, the Shiites have raised suicide bombing to an art. Within the Shiite sect are three main factions: Amal, the mainstream faction; Hizballah, otherwise known as the Party of God; and Islamic Amal. Although Hizballah has largely been responsible for most of the hostages taken in Lebanon during the past decade, Amal members have actively committed acts of terrorism as well. They were responsible for two airliner hijackings in June 1985 and have since been indentified in a number of other Middle East acts of terror.

The first of these hijackings is of particular significance, because it represented the first time an international terrorist who committed an act of terrorism overseas was brought back to the United States to stand trial. Although the United States has always had jurisdiction over acts of terrorism occuring within its borders, federal law did not grant jurisdiction over criminal acts outside the United States or its territories. It was left to "host" foreign governments to protect American citizens living or visiting overseas. Out of concern for terrorist attacks abroad, Congress passed the Comprehensive Crime Control Act of 1984, which provides federal jurisdiction over hostage takings of American citizens. Then in 1986 President Reagan authorized the CIA to identify terrorists who had committed crimes against American citizens overseas and to bring them to the United States to stand trial.[50] Later that year Congress passed the Omnibus Diplomatic Security and Antiterrorism Act of 1986. The act created a new section of the federal code and granted extraterritorial federal jurisdiction over assault, homicide, and conspiracies related to these crimes.[51] In addition, the FBI was granted authority to investigate and arrest persons involved in acts of international terrorism when American citizens were victimized by crimes covered under the new act.

On June 11, 1986, twenty-five-year-old Fawaz Younis, and at least four other heavily armed men, boarded Royal Jordanian Airlines flight 402 at Beirut, Lebanon and seized control of the plane. Three Americans were on board. The hijackers directed the plane to be flown to Larnaca, Cyprus, then to Tunis, Tunisia and finally to Palermo, Sicily. The following day the plane returned to Beirut Airport.[52] Although their demands were never clearly articulated, Younis read a statement to the press publicizing Amal's demands for the removal of Palestinian refugees from Lebanon. Although several Jordanian sky marshals aboard were severely beaten, all of the passengers and crew were eventually released. Following Younis' prepared statement to the press, the plane was blown up as the hijackers opened fire on it with assault rifles.

In a sealed indictment on October 1986 Younis was indicted in federal court in Washington, DC, for taking American hostages and on four other counts, relating to destruction of the aircraft and the beating of the sky marshals. It would be nearly two years, however, before the United States could catch up with him.

After the U.S. bombing of Kaddafi's headquarters in Tripoli in 1986, President Reagan boasted: "You can run, but you can't hide." American agents tried to fulfill Reagan's promise by stalking Fawaz Younis. Younis was an important figure in Amal, having also been involved in the hijacking of TWA flight 847 in which Navy diver Robert Stetham was murdered and his body thrown onto the tarmac.[53] Younis lived openly in Beirut, was known by many residents as a man who had sold used cars in Beirut for the past six years, was married, and had two small children.

By February 1987, the Drug Enforcement Administration and CIA had compiled volumes on Younis' movements and friends. By sheer luck, the CIA had an informant who was an old friend of Younis'. Younis, now unemployed, jumped at the chance to make some money dealing drugs with his old friend. On September 12, 1988, Younis and the informant stayed at the Sheraton Hotel in Limassol, Cyprus. Later that night they caught a speedboat to a luxury yacht conveniently anchored in international waters several miles offshore. Instead of closing a major drug deal, Younis was slammed to the deck, breaking both wrists in the process, and informed of his arrest. Four days later he was flown in a U.S. Navy jet to the United States for trial.

Even non-residents of the United States have the same constitutional rights to due process as American citizens enjoy. Consequently, when Younis appeared before U.S. District Judge Barrington Parker, questions regarding Younis' physical injuries and subsequent four days at sea in an isolation cell raised important constitutional issues about the acceptability of his taped confession. Subjected to continuous interrogation in a stifling cell, Younis not only suffered from his untreated broken wrists but from dehydration and seasickness, as well. Judge Parker eventually disallowed the confession, saying that Younis lacked the "will necessary to waive his rights."[54]

Even without Younis' confession, substantial evidence was available, including his videotaped press statement prior to blowing up the plane and a taped account of Younis bragging to Jamal Hamdan (the informant) about his role in the hijacking. He finally was brought to trial in March 1989. An American jury convicted Younis of three of the five counts against him: conspiracy, air piracy, and hostage taking. The jury refused to convict on the remaining two charges: placing explosives aboard an aircraft and assaulting the sky marshals of flight 402. Apparently, the jury believed that the plane was destroyed by exploding jet fuel ignited by rifle fire, rather than by an explosive device. Nor was the jury convinced that assaulting the sky marshals endangered the lives of the American passengers. On October 4, 1989, Younis was sentenced to five years for conspiracy to commit air piracy, thirty years for taking American hostages, and twenty years for aircraft piracy. The sentences were to run concurrently.[55]

Summary and Conclusions

During the last half of the 1980s America witnessed its first real exposure to terrorism as surrogate warfare. Libya, in particular, chose this strategy in lieu of fighting a conventional war it could not win. America's response was twofold. First, President Reagan elevated Libya's acts of terror to "military-like operations" when American military force was used to respond. But the use of military force is a two-edged sword; to many it suggests that terrorists, when caught, should be treated as political prisoners or as prisoners of war. While this may be practical—the use of America's military might has certainly dampened Libya's willingness to attack American citizens and property—the use of military force to combat terrorism raises disturbing questions about appropriate *political* responses to *criminal* activities.

Second, America responded to international terrorism in the 1980s by laying claim to legal jurisdiction over crimes committed on foreign soil. Despite the retributive desires these laws may satisfy, they may do more harm than good. These laws immediately created friction between the United States and Italy when the United States attempted to forcefully extradite the Achille Lauro hijackers from Italian soil. The incarceration of international terrorists in America's prisons may spawn new rounds of terror and demands for the release of those imprisoned. With the incarceration of Younis and Kikumura in federal prisons in the United States, a new chapter in American involvement in international terrorism has begun. The 1980s witnessed the success of state, federal and local law enforcement in combatting terrorism. Occasionally tempered with a lot of luck (as in the Kikumura and Kabbani cases), the United States thwarted most external terrorist threats from abroad. Our luck ran out in February 1993, when a truck bomb exploded in the underground garage of the World Trade Center, killing five and injuring hundreds more. While some may consider the New York bombing merely an isolated incident, the arrests less than a month later in St. Louis of four suspected members of Abu Nidal's Fatah Revolutionary Council gives one reason to reconsider. The support groups capable of fostering international terrorism on American soil appear to be materializing.[56]

Chapter 8
Criminalizing Terrorism: Problems Without Easy Solutions

Although the academic literature on terrorism has been largely atheoretical, explanations of the causes and consequences of this phenomenon can be derived from sociological theories. Within sociology the major frameworks used to examine societal change have been 'consensus' and 'conflict' models.[1] Developed by Emile Durkheim and Karl Marx, respectively, these perspectives have served as the major impetus for sociological theorizing for over a century. Although criminological theorists have shifted away from these polar models, contemporary perspectives on terrorism, as well as on virtually every other form of socially questionable behavior, reflect the influence of Durkheim or Marx. The two models represent opposite extremes regarding beliefs about human nature, the utility of social institutions, and the rate and type of social change beneficial to society. Although, as Austin Turk notes, "a growing number of sociologists eschew both extremes and are working from and toward a model of social reality as variable and dialectical,"[2] a basic understanding of the polar models is essential as a starting point for theoretical exploration. At the risk of oversimplification, the dominant themes of the two perspectives are presented below to demonstrate their polarity. An examination of contemporary legal and social responses to terrorism utilizing conflict/consensus as a variable rather than an assumption may create a model capable of predicting governmental response under varying conditions.

Marx and Durkheim on Social Change

Karl Marx was optimistic of human nature, believing that people could create a utopian existence on earth. Unfortunately, a shortage of goods and services forced humanity into competition and conflict. As societies progressed through a series of economic-driven political systems (primarily feudalism and capitalism), the working class increasingly became separated from 'ownership of the means of production.' The advent of capitalism found the small businesses of independent craftspersons replaced by factories owned by entrepreneurs who invested nothing more than capital in the production of goods and services. These middlemen later came to be known as the middle class, or bourgeoisie, not because of their income level but as a result of their intercessory role as the buyers of labor from the working class and the sellers of goods to the upper class. Lacking only political power to protect their economic interests, early capitalists in Europe incited social revolutions of the late eighteenth and early nineteenth centuries in Europe that produced the political power desired by the nouveaux riches. Solidifying their hold over society, capitalists further corrupted social institutions, such as the political and legal systems, to control the economic have-nots. Workers increasingly experienced what Marx referred to as "alienation"—a social position as well as an effect that describes the helplessness of the worker when separated from the means of production. Consequently, Marx advocated the rapid dissolution of these social institutions so that a restructured and more equitable economic system could arise. Revolutionary change, violent if necessary, was seen as necessary to accomplish this dialectic. Terrorism, while not advocated by Marx, was viewed by some of his followers as one way to develop class consciousness, thereby inciting the proletariat to revolution.

In contrast, Emile Durkheim believed that people possessed insatiable desires and viewed social institutions (which Marx disdained) as necessary to control the evil impulses of humans.[3] Furthermore, Durkheim focused on the way in which these social institutions adapted to technological and social change. The adverse effects of the industrial revolution in the late nineteenth century led him to conclude, in contrast to Marx, that social change should progress slowly and naturally, thereby giving society time to adapt to disfunctional relations between institutions that might produce pathological manifestations of social deviance. Not surprisingly, perspectives derived from the conflict model tend to be suspicious of governmental actions, while adherents of the consensus framework generally assume that the polity acts in the best interests of its constituents.

Generally, examinations of terrorism from these two perspectives have focused on two issues: 1) the causes of terrorism and 2) a government's response to terrorism. Regarding the first issue, authoritative examinations of the causes of terrorism from either a consensus or conflict perspective have been rare. While consensus theorists have hinted that terrorism reflects the revolutionary's inability to adapt to the strains of a society experiencing disjunction between cultural goals and means to achieve,[4] conflict theorists have suggested that terrorism indicates excessive frustration over the speed with which social change is progressing.[5] Although a discussion of the causes of terrorism from both of these approaches is warranted (in fact, badly needed), our purpose is an examination of the second issue—the polity's response to terrorism. Consequently, while passing reference may be made to causative factors (indeed, governmental response and the labeling of terrorism may be viewed as causative), this work is most concerned with the manner in which conflict and consensus theories might interpret and predict governmental reactions to terroristic violence.

Consensus Explanations
of Governmental Response

To Durkheim, a certain level of crime as well as other forms of deviant conduct (and, for our purposes, including terrorism) were viewed as "normal" in any society.[6] Only when levels of deviance reached disruptive proportions were they percieved as indicative of social pathology.[7] Crime and deviance came to be seen as functional—performing some useful purpose for the maintenance of social order. Using this line of reasoning, Kai Erikson wrote:

> Deviant forms of behavior, by marking the outer edges of group life, give the inner structure its special character and thus supply the framework within which the people of the group develop an orderly sense of their own cultural identity.[8]

If deviant behavior is to some extent tolerated because of its "utility," under what conditions does society say enough is enough, and in what manner does society say it? Erikson maintains that "we invoke emergency measures when the volume of deviance threatens to grow beyond some level we have learned to consider 'normal.'"[9] His analysis of crime waves in seventeenth century Puritan society suggests two things: first, that "emergency" social responses to deviance occur when society is threatened if the behavior is allowed to continue; and second, that the response is apt to be highly publicized and punitively more severe than that toward other deviants.

The application of this approach to governmental responses to terrorism is identical to that provided by Erikson's deviating Puritans: certain types of terror may be "condoned" (as long as it is not too violent, too destructive, or too organized). The FBI routinely addresses this issue in officially labeling some acts as terroristic while ignoring other acts that appear equally harmful. However, once the bounds of "acceptability" are crossed, the government will muster all possible resources to publicly condemn the offenders. The prosecutor will give the terrorism case the highest priority as investigative and law enforcement assets are called in to assist in bringing the offenders to justice. At trial, the terms *terrorism* and *terrorist* would peal throughout the courtroom, and demands for maximum sentencing become common. According to the consensus model, the theme of any governmental response to terrorism is to restore the "symmetry and orderliness of nature itself,"[10] to bring society back into a state of equilibrium and thwart social change that might accelerate into anarchy.

Conflict Explanations
of Governmental Response

Although revolutionary terrorists articulate Marxist rhetoric about the government's response to terrorism when put on trial, few systematic conflict analyses of this phenomenon exist. Most Marxist analyses have focused on the structural causes rather than governmental response to terrorism. Although only alluding to terrorism in passing, Richard Quinney's analysis of the distinction between crimes of the *lumpenproletariat* and crimes of resistance illustrates contemporary Marxist thinking about governmental response.[11]

Quinney divides crimes into two basic types depending upon the motive of the perpetrator: crimes that are intended for purely personal profit are referred to as *lumpen* crimes, while crimes that reflect increased social consciousness are referred to as "crimes of resistance." Although the crimes committed may be identical (i.e., robbery may be either a *lumpen* crime or a crime of resistance),

Quinney suggests that governmental responses vary depending on the motive and intended victim. Consequently, if the victim of the robbery is simply another member of the working class and the motive is personal profit, the governmental response would be substantially different than if the victim were a member of the corporate community and the stolen money was to be used to fund a worker's revolution. The latter offense would, of course, be defined as terrorism and subject to more intense law enforcement and prosecutorial efforts.

Aside from the general proposition about different government treatment of crimes with political motives that one might deduce from the previous discussion, purely Marxist analyses of the relation between terrorism and governmental response tend to be tautological. The terrorists give detailed accounts of governmental misconduct at trial while subsequent Marxist analyses tend to accept the terrorists' reasoning at face value, assuming, as Karl Klockars so aptly described, that anything government does has an ulterior, evil motive.[12]

Conflict and Consensus as Variables

In recent years a number of non-Marxist or "non-partisan"[13] conflict perspectives have arisen as an alternative to Marxist analyses. These perspectives arose because many theorists, despite being non-Marxist, saw evidence of continuing conflict in a society supposedly characterized by overwhelming stability and consensus. As Murray Edelman noted:

> We have compelling evidence from a variety of kinds of observation that political beliefs, demands, and attitudes, far from being fixed and stable, are frequently sporadic in appearance, fluctuating in intensity, ambivalent in composition, and therefore logically inconsistent in pattern and structure.[14]

Although non-partisan conflict theory (or cultural deviance theory, as older versions in criminology are known) has a long tradition in the criminological literature, that perspective has assumed a more prominent place in sociological theory within the past two decades.[15] While retaining the basic assumptions of political and economic conflict inherent in the Marxist model, empirically based versions of conflict theory are devoid of the ideological, non-empirically based presumptive conclusions of Marxism. Although these models still tend to be highly suspicious of governmental motives, non-partisan conflict theories have incorporated more readily than either Durkheimian or extreme Marxist analyses a view of conflict and consensus as variable.

Of the few non-partisan conflict discussions of the response to terrorism that are available, Austin Turk's model of political criminality provides the most comprehensive examination of the types of behavior one might expect the judicial system to exhibit in responding to terrorism.[16] In particular, he describes three distinguishing features of political crimes: 1) explicit politicality; 2) exceptional vagueness; and 3) greater permissiveness regarding law enforcement. Regarding the criminalization of terrorism, Turk is straightforward: "Politicality, vagueness, and permissiveness in the legal definitions of political criminality are especially apparent in the growing preoccupation with terrorism."[17]

On some issues, Turk's hypotheses are similar to the suggestions of Erikson's consensus approach. For example, both perspectives agree that when political authority is threatened, governmental agents are apt to focus upon the "consensual rather than the coercive foundations of law,"[18] maintaining that the prosecution of terrorists is for the common good. Consequently, the terrorist who commits murder is defined as an "assassin," the arsonist is guilty of "sabotage," and some minor offenses may be transformed into "conspiracy to overthrow the government," "sedition," or "treason." In other places, Turk seems to contradict this basic argument by suggesting that political offenders (such as terrorists) are frequently charged with non-political crimes to avoid giving the public the impression that a serious social problem exists. The consistency with which government officials have persuaded the federal courts that persons charged with assassination or attempted assassination of the president should be committed to mental institutions is cited as evidence of this approach to governmental intervention.[19] How can two seemingly contradictory governmental responses (explicit politicality and exceptional vagueness) be theoretically consistent with Turk's conflict model? The answer lies in the extent to which social conflict is perceived.

The question thus remains: Under what conditions will prosecutorial agents explicitly politicize a terrorist's offense? Are these conditions significantly different from those occasions when prosecutors subsume the criminal charges against terrorists under traditional criminal offenses and attempt to avoid raising the spectre of terrorism before the public eye? In general, *the greater the perceived consensus that a particular group threatens society and*

*deserves condemnation, the greater the probability that prosecutors
in a given locality will explicitly politicize the terrorists' crimes.* The
absence of anti-government or pro-terrorist demonstrators, pro-
government media reporting of the events, and general media condemnation of the terrorists' actions may be used by prosecutors as
indicators that explicit reference to the defendants as terrorists
may be beneficial to the government's chances to convict. Explicitly politicizing a crime under such conditions may be intended to
reinforce the legal boundaries of acceptable behavior in addition to
bringing added stigma to the accused.

In contrast, the social support for terrorists by non-criminal
citizens adds legitimacy to the political arguments advanced by
any terrorist group. Therefore, *the greater the perceived social conflict regarding the danger that a particular group poses to society,
the greater the probability that prosecutors in a given locality will
resort to exceptional vagueness tactics to achieve convictions.* Under
such conditions, the government is apt to avoid explicit references
to the offenders as terrorists. Instead, those charged will be tried
under traditional criminal statutes and no mention of the political
motives or ideology will be raised by prosecutors. If possible, prosecutors will attempt to use strict- or presumed-liability statutes to
avoid even raising the issues of motive and intent.

The relationship between governmental responses and perceived levels of "moral" or social support for their actions is depicted in figure 8.1. Characteristics of each of the polar responses
are identified beneath the response categories. The third alternative, greater permissiveness regarding law enforcement, is not depicted since it appears to be invoked by the level of perceived
threat to governmental authority, rather than perceptions of the
extent of social conflict or consensus. It may be, and is, used in
combination with either of the other two responses.

Exceptional Vagueness

The use of 'exceptional vagueness' is strongly related to the development of anti-terrorism statutes in America.[20] Confronted by international terrorists abroad, left- and right-wing revolutionaries
at home, and sensationalist media practices in local and national
reporting, terrorism reached the forefront of American consciousness. Consequently, the nearly universal disdain for terrorism
among the general public provides an excellent subject for political
officials seeking to elicit voter support. Perceiving tremendous

HIGH LEVELS OF CONSENSUS	HIGH LEVELS OF SOCIAL CONFLICT
<———————————————————————————————————>	
Explicit Politicality	Exceptional Vagueness
*Public condemnation of terrorism	*Avoidance of mention of terrorist label
*Use of statutes which allow/ require discussion of terrorist's ideology/motives	*Use of statutes that allow conviction without mention of motive/ proof of intent
*Conspiracy, sedition predominant charges	*Illegal possession of weapons/ explosives most frequently used charges

Figure 8.1 Governmental Responses and Perceived Levels of Social Conflict/Consensus

public consensus on this issue, many politicians and legislators apparently have come to believe that terrorism provides a constructive and fruitful issue on which few constituents would disagree.

As a result, the 1970s subsequently were characterized by efforts to create terrorism-specific statutes that met acceptable definitions of terrorism while appropriately identifying essential elements of the crime that would meet constitutional tests. That trend continued throughout the 1980s. By 1990, half of the states had enacted terrorism-specific statutes. Unlike state assemblies, federal legislators avoided this trap, focusing instead on closing loopholes in existing national law (table 8.1).

Recognizing the conceptual problems in reaching a legally acceptable definition of terrorism, none of the statutes eventually enacted into law actually deal explicitly with terrorism. Most are modeled after the American Law Institute's exemplar called "terroristic threatening."[21] Enacted into legislation with the promise of "doing something about terrorism," these statutes do little more than criminalize verbal threats. If severity of sanction can be used as a rough gauge of deterrent value, these statutes have had little preventive effect. Relegated to misdemeanor or minor felony status, these statutes have been used only once or twice during the past decade to prosecute crimes that might be labeled "terror-

Table 8.1 States with Terrorism-Specific Statutes

STATE	FELONY OR MISDEMEANOR	WHEN ENACTED OR EFFECTIVE	STATUTORY CITATIONS	
Alaska	Felony	1980	Terroristic Threatening Alaska Stat.	11.56.810 (1980)
Arkansas	Felony	1975	Terroristic Threatening Ark. Stat. Ann.	41-1608 (1977 Replacement)
California	Felony	1977	Terrorist Threats Cal. Pen. Code	11.5.422/422.5 (Deering 1977)
Colorado	Felony	1984	Terrorism Co. Rev. Stat. Ann.	18-9-120
Connecticut	Misdemeanor	1971	Terrorizing Conn. Gen. Stat. Ann.	53a-62 (1971)
Florida	Felony	1990	Terrorism Fla. Stat. Ann.	874.01 (1991)
Georgia	Felony	1974	Terroristic Threats or Acts Ga. Code	26-1307 and 1307.1 (1974)
Hawaii	Misdemeanor/ Felony[a]	1972 (Amended 1979)	Terroristic Threatening Hawaii Rev. Stat.	707-715 (1979)
Idaho	Felony	1987	Terrorism Idaho Code	18-8103 (1987)
Iowa	Felony	1978 (Amended 1981)	Terrorism Iowa Code Ann.	54-708.6 (West 1981)
Kansas	Felony	1970	Terroristic Threat Kan. Crim. Code Ann.	21-3419 (Vernon 1970)

Kentucky	Misdemeanor	1975	Terroristic Threatening Ky. Rev. Stat.	508.080 (1975)
Louisiana	Misdemeanor	1978	Terrorizing La. Rev. Stat. Ann.	14:40.1 (West 1978)
Maine	Misdemeanor/ Felony[b]	1977	Terrorizing Me. Rev. Stat. Ann. tit.	17 210 (1977)
Michigan	Felony	1974	Terror Mich. Com. Laws Ann.	750.204a
Minnesota	Felony	1971	Terroristic Threat Minn. Stat.	609.713 (1971)
Mississippi	Misdemeanor	1958	Terrorism Miss. Code Ann.	45-19-51-65 (1958)
Montana	Misdemeanor	1983	Terrorism Mont. Code Ann.	45-8-103 (1983)
New Jersey	Misdemeanor	1979	Terroristic Threats N.J. Stat. Ann.	2c:12-3 (1979)
Pennsylvania	Misdemeanor	1973	Terroristic Threats 18 Pa. Cons. Stat. Ann.	2706 (Purdon 1973)
Rhode Island	Felony	1981	Threat by Terror R.I. Gen. Laws	11-53-2 (1981)
Texas	Misdemeanor	1974	Terroristic Threat Tex. Penal Code Ann.	5-22.07 (Vernon 1974)
Utah	Misdemeanor/ Felony[c]	1973	Terroristic Threat Utah Code Ann.	76-5-107 (1973)
West Virginia	Felony	1990	Terrorism W. Va. Code	11-21-62
Wyoming	Felony	1982	Terroristic Threats Wyoming Stat. Ann.	6-2-505 (1982)

[a]Primarily if threat involves public official or if a dangerous instrument is used to communicate threat.
[b]If evacuation of public facility occurs.
[c]If evacuation of public facility is intended.

istic."[22] If anything, they open the door for governmental overreaction, enabling local officials to label selected offenders as terrorists.

The problem in criminalizing terrorism lies in translating academic definitions into legally permissible definitions of terrorism. To adequately study the phenomenon of terrorism, most academicians add a number of qualifying characteristics to their definitions. For example, Jordan Paust argues that any definition of terrorism must consider the outcome, violence used, motivation, and goals of the terrorist to define adequately the concept.[23] Likewise, Grant Wardlaw notes that "for a definition of terrorism to be universally accepted it must transcend behavioral description *to include individual motivation*, social milieu, and *political purpose*."[24] Unfortunately, these salient features conflict with efforts to create legal definitions of terrorism.

Efforts to transform academic definitions of terror into legal definitions are doomed under constitutional scrutiny. Law must go beyond the goals of empirical study, and decisions must be made regarding the social acceptability of an act, subsequently rendering empirical definitions unworkable. Consequently, *motive* or *political purpose* no longer become useful variables in legislating statutes in a system of justice where motive is not normally an essential element of an offense. Finding a universally accepted definition of terrorism has not met with much success in United States courts.

The conceptual difficulties are magnified when one attempts to write legislation that makes an act criminal because it was intended to invoke political change or influence an audience beyond the immediate victims, two widely accepted aspects of an acedemic definition of terrorism. The issue becomes one of requiring proof of motive as an element required in criminal liability. Typically, proof that the act occurred (*actus reus*) and that the particular act was accompanied by the required intent (*mens rea*) is sufficient for criminal liability. Normally, motive relates only to why a person might commit a given act to achieve a desired result. For example, A murders B to obtain money from B's wallet. A's intent was to kill, and it must be established in court to convict on a murder charge. A's motive was to steal, but it does not have be established in court as an essential element of the offense except for use as circumstantial evidence in establishing intent. Most academic definitions of terrorism, however, include as an element of the crime the motive of the perpetrator, i.e., to invoke political or social change.

Only one state, California, has attempted to criminalize terrorism explicitly. California's code specified that "to terrorize" means:

> to create a climate of fear and intimidation by means of threats or violent action causing sustained fear for personal safety *in order to achieve social or political goals.*[25]

Subsequently challenged because of its attempt to criminalize motive, a California Supreme Court decision, *People v. Mirmirani,* held that the phrase "to achieve social or political goals" was unconstitutionally vague.[26] In particular, the court raised the issue that whereas the "legislature did not intend to criminalize threats that were not made to achieve these goals," the entire statute must be declared void, since the phrase was vital to the statute.

California's attempt to make terrorism a criminal act represents the only effort to retain a definition of terrorism similar to that used in academe and generally believed by the American public to constitute terrorism. Although doomed by its purist approach, the statute reflects the enormous conceptual difficulty faced in specifically criminalizing acts of terrorism. Given the lack of deterrent power of the constitutionally acceptable but sanctionless terroristic-threat statutes and the constitutionally unacceptable criminalization of terrorism explicitly, what approach have prosecutors used to convict and incarcerate terrorists?

The strategy most widely used has been to portray terrorists as mere criminals—persons engaged in crime for purely personal, rather than social or political, goals. While it may at first appear that the restriction placed upon the American government by the elimination of the possibility of an explicitly identified crime of terrorism would be a major liability for federal prosecutors, in actuality it may have worked to its advantage. U.S. attorneys have been forced to rely upon traditional criminal statutes in the prosecution of terrorists. Obscuring the major reason for the high priority given to their apprehension and conviction, prosecution under traditional criminal statutes reinforces to the citizenry that these offenders are "mere criminals."

The terrorists unwittingly aid prosecutors in this endeavor by engaging in a wide variety of criminal conduct. Few terrorist groups have the external support necessary to fund a revolution for any length of time. Consequently, most groups turn to petty theft, counterfeiting, and armored car or bank robbery to support the cause. These activities give the government a wide range of prosecutorial choices. Few terrorists will be tried for an actual act of terrorism; instead, they are more likely to be indicted and prosecuted for crimes associated with efforts to obtain illegal weapons or funds or to conceal their identities. These behaviors can easily be subsumed under traditional criminal law. Terrorist leaders who try to circumvent this problem by seeking external support can expect severe sanctioning if prosecutions are successful. For example, Jeff Fort, the El Rukn leader convicted of forty-nine counts of a fifty-count indictment involving efforts to obtain financing from Libya, drew consecutive sentences on each count.

Table 8.2 is a list of the federal statutes most frequently used when prosecuting FBI officially labeled terrorists. More than a third of the counts lodged against terrorists in this country are for racketeering or RICO violations. In virtually all of these cases the prosecution sought to establish the existence of a criminal enterprise whose primary purpose was the procurement of financial gain for its members. The prosecution of members of the Order in Seattle in late 1985 typifies this approach. The primary purposes of the group were, according to the indictment, the "making and retaining (of) profits for the enterprise and for themselves" and "obtain(ing) money and other things of value for the enterprise and the defendants."[27] Although the white supremacist motives of the group were brought out frequently by the prosecution, these motives were not intrinsic elements of the rackeering charges brought against the defendants in this case. The fact that these defendants espoused a radical philosophy highly offensive to most persons was utilized by federal prosecutors as an extenuating circumstance that enhanced the probability of conviction and severe sentencing. Had it appeared to the prosecution that widespread public sympathy existed for the racist goals of the group, mention of these motives could have been minimized during the proceedings with little effect on the outcome of the trial.

A second major category of charges includes "presumed" or "inferred liability" statutes. Presumed liability statutes were created to enable prosecutors to obtain convictions for hard-to-prosecute crimes. Generally, they have been limited to minor felony status because they do not require proof of intent to obtain a conviction. Examples include possession of stolen property, illegal weapons, drugs, or explosive materials. Typically, the possession of these items is considered prima facie evidence of intent to possess. While not all of the counts charged under USC Title 18, Chapter 40 (Explosives), Chapter 44 (Firearms), Chapter 113 (Stolen Property), and USC Title 26, Chapter 53 (Machine Guns) involve presumed liability, clearly the majority require no proof of intent.

Table 8.2 Federal Statutes Most Frequently Used in the
Prosecution of American Terrorists: 1982–1989

U.S. CODE TITLE	CHAPTER	SUBJECT	NUMBER OF COUNTS	PERCENTAGE OF TOTAL
18	95	Racketeering	412	30.2
26	53	Machine guns, destructive devices, and certain other firearms	228	16.7
18	19	Conspiracy	127	9.3
18	96	Racketeer-Influenced and Corrupt Organizations (RICO)	91	6.7
18	44	Firearms	77	5.6
18	40	Explosive materials	74	5.4
18	113	Stolen property	64	4.7
18	103	Robbery and burglary	60	4.4
50	35	International Emergency Economic Powers	49	3.6
18	115	Treason, Sedition, and Subversive Activities	22	1.6
18	63	Mail Fraud	20	1.5
18	51	Homicide	19	1.4
18	47	Fraud/False Statements	18	1.3
		Other[a]	102	7.5
		TOTAL	1363	100.0%

a. These counts included violations contained in twenty-one different chapters of the U.S.C.

With the traditional establishment of intent not required for conviction, mention of terrorist motives is certainly unnecessary. Almost all of the terrorists in our study found themselves faced with one or more charges involving presumed liability.

Whether or not one is willing to conclude that the use of traditional criminal statutes to prosecute terrorists constitutes exceptional vagueness is largely a matter of one's personal beliefs regarding the motives of government. However, several things are clear from our discussion thus far of terrorist activities in America. First, those persons investigated for terrorism or terrorism-related activities in this country engaged in relatively few acts of actual terror. However, as part of their preparation, they committed a large number of other crimes along the way. Second, because of the wide variety of crimes committed by these persons, prosecutors have considerable latitude regarding the specific offenses from which they may choose to indict and pursue conviction. Finally, groups that might try to minimize traditional criminality and stick solely to terrorism by seeking funding from external sources probably will face the most severe governmental response. Although the El Rukn case may not be a good example because of the extensive criminal behavior committed by members of that organization, the severity of the sentences given members involved in the terrorism-for-hire scheme with Libya is suggestive (table 8.3).

Explicit Politicality

Of the offenses for which American terrorists were indicted, few immediately evoke images of political criminality. In particular, only charges involving treason, sedition, and subversive activities (USC Title 18, Chapter 115), "Extra-territorial Jurisdiction over Terrorist Acts Abroad Against U.S. Citizens" (USC Title 18, Chapter 113a), and the killing of foreign officials and internationally protected persons (USC Title 18, Chapter 51, Section 1116) explicitly label these offenders as either political terrorists or revolutionaries. The latter two of these statutes are apt to result in the offender being labeled as an international, rather than a domestic, terrorist. Tolerance among government officials for international terrorism seems to be substantially less than the latitude allowed domestic terrorists. However, the newness of the extraterritorial jurisdiction statute and the specificity of the assassination statute provide for few examples of their usage.

Thus far, the only utilization of the extraterritorial jurisdiction statute has involved Fawaz Younis, who was extradited from

Table 8.3 Outcomes of Ten Most Frequently Used Federal Statutes for Terrorism/Terrorism-related Activities

USC Chapter	OUTCOME[a]				
	Trial Conviction	Guilty Plea	Dismissed due to Plea[b]	Acquittal/ mistrial	Total
Racketeering	147 45.0%	2 .6%	78 23.9%	100 30.6%	327
Machine guns, etc.	86 40.8%	9 4.3%	95 45.0%	21 10.0%	211
Conspiracy	32 28.6%	42 37.5%	12 10.7%	26 23.2%	112
Racketeer-Influenced Corrupt Organizations	22 25.9%	20 23.5%	23 27.1%	20 23.5%	85
Firearms	22 29.7%	0 0.0%	17 23.0%	35 47.3%	74
Explosive materials	14 20.6%	5 7.4%	27 39.7%	22 32.4%	68
Stolen property	13 34.2%	0 0.0%	12 31.6%	13 34.2%	38
Robbery/burglary	4 33.3%	1 8.3%	3 25.0%	4 33.3%	12
Emergency Economic Powers	0 0.0%	1 4.8%	20 95.2%	0 0.0%	21
Mail Fraud	2 10.0%	0 0.0%	11 55.0%	7 35.0%	20
Treason, Sedition, Subversive Activities	4 18.2%	2 9.1%	0 0.0%	16 72.7%	22
TOTAL	346 34.9%	82 8.3%	298 30.1%	264 26.7%	990

a. Excludes cases pending and cases where outcome is unknown. Of 1,363 counts in the sample, case results were available for 1,117 of the counts. The remaining 127 count results for other federal statutes are not presented here.
b. Dismissed due to plea on this or other counts.

Beirut, Lebanon to be tried for his participation in the hijacking of Royal Jordanian Airlines flight 402 in June 1985. Convicted of conspiracy, hostage taking, and aircraft piracy, he was sentenced in October 1989 to thirty years imprisonment. Like Younis, members of Omega 7 found little sympathy in federal courts for their attempted assassination of Raul Roa, the Cuban Ambassador to the United Nations. Despite the similar positions held by Omega 7 leader Eduardo Arocena and the U.S. government regarding the legitimacy of Fidel Castro's Communist regime, Arocena was sentenced to one of the harshest sentences given the terrorists in our study.[28]

The remaining statutes that suggest explicit politicality involve crimes of treason or sedition. However, few of the terrorists in our study were charged with these offenses. Given the lack of successful prosecutions under these statutes, it is no wonder why. Trials relating to these charges have the highest acquittal or mistrial rate of the federal statutes used to prosecute terrorists (table 8.3). In the trials of nearly three-fourths of the persons charged with treason, sedition, or subversive activities, they were either acquitted of the charges, the jury was "hung," or the judge issued a directed verdict. Apparently, the American public finds it difficult to envision how a small band of revolutionaries could overthrow the government. While "impossibility" is not a defense, it certainly appears to affect jurors' as well as U.S. attorneys' willingness to pursue this line of prosecution.

The most famous terrorist case involving charges of seditious conspiracy occurred in Fort Smith, Arkansas in 1987–1988. Federal prosecutors brought together the unconvicted leaders of the white supremacy (Christian Identity) movement for trial on charges of sedition. Despite the testimony of numerous convicted leaders of smaller splinter groups, all nine persons (including Louis Beam, Robert Miles, and Richard Butler) who were charged with conspiracy to overthrow the government of the United States were acquitted.[29] The other six defendants charged with this offense were already in prison on other convictions. Sedition charges were dropped against a tenth person before the trial began. Sedition charges against members of the UFF resulted in similar outcomes in their trials during 1989 and 1990. The only terrorists in our sample successfully convicted of seditious conspiracy (18 U.S.C Section 2384) were four members of the FALN, tried in Chicago in 1983.[30]

In summary, statutes that explicitly politicize the criminal behaviors of the defendants tend to be used sparingly. The overwhelming majority of terrorists are never charged with these offenses. When terrorists do face indictment on these charges, the cases involve highly publicized groups that either have lengthy records of violent bombings (the FALN and the UFF) or those from which the government fears an outbreak of violence in the near future (the Christian Identity Movement). It was suggested earlier that these statutes were more likely to be used when the government believed there existed a high degree of public condemnation of the terrorist's actions. If this is true, federal prosecutors do not appear to have been very good judges of public sentiment based upon the low level of success they have had in prosecuting these cases. It may be, however, that additional factors influence the extent to which certain types of statutes are used.

Broadened Discretion in Law Enforcement

The American justice system requires that defendants be treated equally under the law: rights of search and seizure, due process, a jury trial if desired, and sentencing within the confines of regulated sanctioning are sacred to the American view of equal justice for all. Since terrorists generally are tried for the same types of offenses as traditional criminals and the government is mandated to grant terrorists the same judicial rights as other offenders, one might expect little variation in the treatment of those labeled as terrorists from those deemed "mere" criminals. However, as Howard Becker has suggested, selective enforcement becomes necessary when the number of crimes exceeds the capability of law enforcement to respond.[31] In the case of terrorists, this discretionary justice extends beyond the normal confines of selective enforcement to include an allocation of resources far greater than that given traditional crimes selected for enforcement.

This process begins with the FBI's decision to officially designate some crimes as terroristic. The identification of certain offenses as terroristic demands an increase in the efforts to protect the public against such crimes. The reallocation of FBI resources to domestic terrorism as well as the relaxation of restrictions on the collection of intelligence for domestic security investigations significantly increased the FBI's ability to provide evidence to federal prosecutors during the 1980s.[32] One approach to countering terrorism under the new guidelines involved the creation of task forces composed of local, state, and federal authorities sharing intelligence data. It is no coincidence that, within four months following the FBI's elevation of terrorism to a national priority program in October 1982, "the most intense manhunt in New England's history" took place.[33] Named BOSLUC—in reference to the Boston FBI office where the investigation originated and Raymond Luc Levasseur, the terrorist who officials sought to find—the task force created to find UFF members reflected the new strategies and energy injected into the FBI's counterterrorism efforts. There is little doubt that the FBI's efforts had significant impact. Left-wing terrorists who had hidden for nearly a decade were now sought with renewed vigor. By 1985 most of them had been apprehended. Right-wing terrorists organizing in 1983 and preparing for "War in '84" made their plans at a most inopportune time. The renewed emphasis on terrorism by the FBI in 1983 led to the rapid dissolution of white supremacy groups like the Order, the Order II, the CSA, and the White Patriot Party.

The expansion of intelligence-gathering and investigative activities by law enforcement agencies significantly affects the strategies used by federal prosecutors. As criminal activities occur, U.S. attorneys must choose whether to prosecute from a simple but effective list of traditional crimes (illegal possession of firearms, explosives, interstate shipment of firearms or explosives, and a host of other violations) or wait until all of the evidence is in and pursue prosecution under one of the more comprehensive statutes (racketeering, RICO, conspiracy, or sedition). One assistant U.S. attorney summarized her office's effort to prosecute a highly publicized right-wing group:

> When we received notice of the high priority to be given prosecution of the group, we tried to prosecute them on everything we could as fast as we could. Our intent was to get them off the streets and into jail before they could go underground. We made the conscious decision to prosecute the simple things first to give us time to develop the more complicated racketeering charges. We feared that if we waited to develop the full case, we would lose them.[34]

The decision described is the most common approach taken by federal prosecutors in terrorism cases. Some of the persons in our sample were named as defendants in as many as five different indictments. Generally, these indictments reflected a prosecutorial strategy typical of the one described above: the first indictments involved straightforward, traditional offenses, while latter indictments included more complex charges that summarized the racketeering or seditious activities of the person or group. To some extent conviction rates for offenses reflect the order in which the offenses were tried. Examples from trials of three of the most famous terrorism cases during the 1980s illustrate this point. Most of the thirteen defendants at the 1987–1988 trial of white supremacy leaders had already been convicted of crimes and were serving time in prison when brought to Fort Smith, Arkansas for their seditious conspiracy trial.[35] Bruce Carroll Pierce, for example, had already been convicted in Seattle for his role in Order robberies and counterfeiting and in Denver for his role in the murder of radio talk-show host Alan Berg. All of the members of the United Freedom Front brought to trial on conspiracy charges in 1989 in Massachusetts had been convicted of other charges stemming from their bombing spree during the previous decade.[36] Several had been convicted in three or four different trials in state and federal courts. Finally, the 1990 trials of M19CO members in Washington, DC, reflect an identical approach.[37] Marilyn Buck, Linda Evans, Susan Rosenberg, Timothy Blunk, and Alan Berkman were all in prison when finally tried for conspiracy to bomb federal buildings in the Washington, DC, area. Only Elizabeth Duke, a fugitive, and Laura Whitehorn were not in prison at the time of the trial.

Each of these cases had similar outcomes. The Fort Smith trial resulted in acquittal for all of the defendants. The trial against UFF members in Massachusetts resulted in acquittal on the major counts, and the judge declared a mistrial on the remaining counts when the jury was unable to reach a verdict. In Washington, Buck, Evans, and Whitehorn pled guilty to two counts each. To prosecutors the trial was a success: they had put Whitehorn, the only non-fugitive M19CO member involved in the bombings, behind bars for twenty years. Charges against other defendants were dropped after the judge ruled that the indictment was repetitious of charges for which they had been convicted previously.

While suggesting that our adversarial system works may sound trite, an important function of judges and juries in terrorism cases (in addition to determining guilt or innocence) is to serve as an effective system of checks and balances against excessive prosecution. Judges (and ultimately, jurors if the judge does not dismiss the case) are confronted with issues involving double jeopardy—not normally an issue in trials of traditional criminals. As one assistant U.S. attorney described the syndrome in a case against a terrorist organization:

> Part of our problem is that we have already convicted these
> defendants in previous trials. Some of the offenses described

as "overt acts" of the conspiracy for which they are currently
being tried were parts of previous trials. It becomes increasingly difficult to convince a jury who is asking, But haven't
they already been convicted of this before?[38]

Prosecutors have learned to regard these decisions by judges and
juries as indicators of an absence of public support for further prosecutorial efforts. However, even if defendants are not convicted of
the major charges in an indictment, federal prosecutors may be
able to convince a judge of the necessity for sentencing that exceeds that given traditional criminals convicted of similar offenses.

In summary, from the limited data available it is fairly clear
that terrorism cases are given higher priority than other cases involving similar offenses. In addition, the increase in expended resources probably results in significantly higher apprehension and
conviction rates for terrorists than for traditional criminals. Although table 8.3 does not provide a case-by-case analysis, it nonetheless demonstrates that a substantially larger number of terrorism cases go to trial than do traditional criminal cases. While
nearly 90 percent of all criminal trials result in a plea agreement,
a much smaller proportion of terrorists choose this option. The reason is not easily discerned: prosecutors may not have offered as
attractive plea agreements as those proffered to other offenders;
the terrorists may have preferred a public forum to politicize the
crime, or perhaps they simply were not guilty of the crimes charged.
The use of explicit politicality, which was supposed to be associated
with high levels of perceived social consensus, does not appear to
be widely used. When it was used, it was one of the least successful
prosecutorial strategies. However, it is important to recall that explicitly political statutes (i.e., treason, sedition) are usually evoked
late in the prosecutorial process. In summary, most terrorists are
convicted of traditional crimes, an approach distinctly intended to
magnify the personal profit motives of the defendant. While it is
debatable whether such an approach constitutes what Austin Turk
calls "exceptional vagueness," federal authorities in the 1980s
clearly made the decision to pursue prosecution of terrorist organizations as racketeering, money-making enterprises rather than as
radical political groups.

Chapter 9

Punishing Terrorists

Calls for more severe sanctions against persons convicted of terroristic violence frequently are heard from citizens on the street
and in congressional debates. Two major questions arise with re-
spect to these demands. First, does ideology or political orientation
affect the severity of sentences given terrorists? Are left-wing terrorists, for example, likely to receive more severe sanctioning than
right-wing terrorists? Similarly, are international terrorists, many
of whose ethnic and ideological backgrounds are different from
ours, likely to be treated more severely in American courts than
home-grown terrorists?

The second issue that merits consideration when examining
the punishment of terrorists is whether terrorists receive longer
sentences than traditional criminals convicted of similar offenses
in an effort to deter terrorist acts. If two defendants are convicted
of almost identical crimes but one's action was politically motivated
while the other was not, are they sentenced differently in American
courts? These issues have never been addressed empirically, and attempting to find answers has been anything but routine.

Differential Treatment: Leftists, Rightists,
and International Terrorists

It is not uncommon for members of legitimate political or special
interest groups to claim that criminal indictments against their
members are politically motivated. The Keating Five, participants
in the Iran-Contra scandal, and both sides in the Clarence Thomas
confirmation hearings (although in that case no criminal charges

171

were involved), produced claims and countercharges regarding the
political motivations of the accusers. Trials involving terrorists
produce similar claims. The typical trial scenario depicts government prosecutors trying to keep the trial within the confines of
traditional criminality while defendants attempt to evoke the spec-
ter of political prosecution and persecution.

Are defendants who raise these issues correct in their asser-
tions? A review of cases in our sample revealed that left-wing defendants were much more likely to wave the banner of political
oppression than were right-wing defendants. Members of the New
African Freedom Fighters, the UFF, and M19CO intentionally focused attention during their trials on supposed government oppression of opposition groups such as theirs.[1] Similarly, left-wing defendants were more likely to proudly proclaim their affiliation with
these terrorist groups. In contrast, right-wing defendants frequently attempted to prevent federal prosecutors from using the
names of groups they associated with, fearing it would prejudice
juries. For example, SPC members in Minnesota successfully
blocked prosecutors from mentioning the names of anti-tax groups
with which the defendants were affiliated.[2]

Prosecutors also demonstrate different behaviors when dealing with left-wing, right-wing, and international terrorists. The
punishment process begins long before a judge signs the Judgment
and Probation/Commitment Order.[3] Early in the development of a
criminal trial, particularly one that involves multiple defendants,
prosecutors begin to prioritize punishment strategies. Most importantly, during these sessions the prosecution identifies defendants
it wants to convict and be given maximum punishment. In contrast, other defendants of lesser importance in the same case are
identified and allowed to return to the streets as a result of a plea
bargain that gives them a minimal sentence in return for their
testimony against other defendants. These defendants, as wit-
nesses for the state, are central to establishing the prosecution's
case and are unlikely to lead the terrorist organization to its former glory. Although it is not possible to quantify fully the interactions that take place between prosecutors and defendants in terrorism cases, some general findings can be quantified that are
suggestive of this process.

Variations in Case Outcomes

Although our primary intent in this section is to examine differences within groups, some of the overall totals are striking. Tables

Table 9.1 Count Results by Type of Terrorist Group

TYPE OF TERRORIST GROUP	JURY CONVICTION	PLED GUILTY	DISMISSED DUE TO PLEA ON OTHER COUNTS	DISMISSED DUE TO MISTRIAL OR ACQUITTAL
Domestic				
Left-wing[a]	244 (43.6%)	17 (3.0%)	64 (11.4%)	234 (41.9%)
Right-wing[b]	89 (25.9%)	53 (15.5%)	146 (42.6%)	55 (16.0%)
International[c]	55 (25.6%)	37 (17.2%)	115 (53.5%)	8 (3.7%)
Total	388 (34.7%)	107 (9.6%)	325 (29.1%)	297 (26.6%)

a. "Left-wing" includes members of FALN, el Rukn, May 19 Communist Organization, United Freedom Front, Provisional Party of Communists, New African Freedom Front, and the Macheteros.
b. "Right-wing" includes members of Aryan Nations; Arizona Patriots; Covenant, Sword, and Arm of the Lord; the Order; the Order II; Posse Comitatus; Ku Klux Klan; and White Patriot party.
c. "International" includes members of the Provisional IRA, Omega 7, Japanese Red Army, Libyans, and Palestinian/Syrians.

9.1 and 9.2 emphasize the extremely low guilty-plea rate among extremists. American terrorists pled guilty to fewer than 10 percent (9.6 percent) of the federal charges they faced. This small percentage of guilty pleas was distributed among approximately two-fifths (41.7 percent) of the defendants, significantly lower than in non-terrorism trials. Nationally, 85 percent of convictions obtained in federal trials result from plea bargains.[4] Possible reasons for this disparity were discussed in Chapters 7 and 8.

In addition to these general findings, more important are the differences between the outcomes of left-wing and right-wing cases. The most striking feature of table 9.1 is the difference between these two groups regarding the percentage of counts that resulted in mistrial or acquittal. Only 16 percent of the counts against right-wing defendants resulted in either a dismissal due to mistrial or acquittal, while over 40 percent (41.9 percent) of the counts against left-wing defendants were closed in this manner. Nearly a

Table 9.2   Case Outcomes by Type of Terrorist Group

TYPE OF TERRORIST GROUP	JURY CONVICTION	PLED GUILTY	DISMISSED DUE TO MISTRIAL OR GOVERNMENT MOTION	DISMISSED DUE TO ACQUITTAL
Domestic				
Left-wing[a]	26	11	9	2
	(54.2%)	(22.9%)	(18.8%)	(4.2%)
Right-wing[b]	26	42	12	17
	(26.8%)	(43.3%)	(12.4%)	(17.5%)
International[c]	9	22	4	0
	(25.7%)	(62.9%)	(11.4%)	(0.0%)
Total[d]	61	75	25	19
	(33.9%)	(41.7%)	(13.9%)	(10.6%)

a. "Left-wing" includes members of FALN, el Rukn, May 19 Communist Organization, United Freedom Front, Provisional Party of Communists, New African Freedom Front, and the Macheteros.
b. "Right-wing" includes members of Aryan Nations; Arizona Patriots; Covenant, Sword, and Arm of the Lord; the Order; the Order II; Posse Comitatus; Ku Klux Klan; and White Patriot party.
c. "International" includes members of the Provisional IRA, Omega 7, Japanese Red Army, Libyans, and Palestinian/Syrians.
d. N = 180 defendants in 60 criminal trials. The remaining 32 defendants in our sample were either awaiting trial (e.g., the Macheteros trial in Hartford, Connecticut) or they were fugitives.

third of the dismissals due to acquittal against right-wing defendants occurred during the 1987–1988 trial of right-wing extremists in Fort Smith, Arkansas.[5] With the exception of this trial, dismissals due to hung juries or acquittals have been rare for right-wing defendants. The 42 percent acquittal or mistrial rate for left-wing defendants is in stark contrast to the results of right-wing trials.

Table 9.2 reveals additional differences in left-wing and right-wing terrorist defendants' experiences. Left-wing defendants were significantly more likely to go to *trial*, while right-wing defendants were significantly more likely to *plead guilty* than left-wing defendants. The percentage of counts (table 9.1) dismissed due to guilty pleas is nearly four times greater for right-wing (42.6 percent) than for left-wing (11.4 percent) defendants. Likewise, the proportion of defendants who pled guilty (table 9.1) was almost twice as great for right-wing (43.3 percent) as for left-wing (22.9 percent) defendants.

How does one account for these differences? We have already noted the greater tendency on the part of left-wing defendants to attempt to politicize their trials. While this effort to create a public forum for their cause may account for part of the difference in the percentage of cases going to trial, it would not account for the differences in the acquittal or mistrial rates for the two groups. The tendency on the part of left-wing defendants to go to trial, when combined with the relatively high acquittal rate for this group, *should* simply reflect that these defendants were not guilty of the crimes charged. However, this simple notion of guilt or innocence may mask at least two underlying factors that are important to address. First, could the higher acquittal rates of left-wing defendants be the result of differences in the quality of trial counsel provided the two groups? Second, if the differences merely suggest that a much larger proportion of left-wing defendants were not guilty of the crimes charged, why were they indicted for these offenses in the first place? This study's qualitative analysis of these differences reflects support for both possibilities: overbooking by federal prosecutors when charging left-wing defendants *and* better trial counsel for leftists than for rightists.

Few persons would dispute the argument that good counsel can influence the outcome of a case. Likewise, some attorneys in the United States specialize in politicized crimes. While right-wing terrorists typically retained local attorneys for their defense, left-wing terrorists were much more likely to complement the use of local attorneys with the expertise of nationally known lawyers specializing in political crime. William Kunstler and Leonard Weinglass, perhaps the most noted attorneys identified with leftist causes who specialize in politicized crimes, were involved in the defense of several of the left-wing terrorists in our sample. Kunstler, for example, was an ardent defender of members of the UFF at their 1990 trial, a case that resulted in acquittal and mistrial for all of the defendants who went to trial.[6] His skill and the skills of other lawyers in politicized crimes may account for part of the difference in the acquittal rates for left-wing and right-wing defendants.

But such an explanation cannot account for all of the variation in these rates. It does appear that federal prosecutors have been more likely to excessively charge left-wing defendants than right-wing defendants. As a prosecutorial strategy, overbooking is commonly used to elicit a guilty plea on some counts in exchange for dropping numerous extraneous counts. If the defendant refuses to plead guilty, however, the prosecution finds itself going to trial with a large number of counts for which the prosecution may have probable cause but insufficient evidence with which to convince a jury of guilt beyond a reasonable doubt. Several findings in our data point to such a prosecutorial approach. Left-wing defendants were significantly less likely to plead guilty, suggesting that these defendants were not offered plea bargains that were as attractive as those offered to right-wing defendants. If this is true, it would explain why left-wing defendants go to trial more. In addition, prosecutors recognize that conviction is sometimes a matter of probability—the greater the number of charges, the greater the probability of conviction on at least some counts. As a result of overcharging these defendants, prosecutors are significantly more likely to encounter high acquittal rates for overcharged counts. Our data suggest this is precisely what happens to left-wing terrorists. Almost as many counts against left-wing extremists resulted in mistrial or acquittal (table 9.1) as resulted in conviction (244, table 9.1). Despite the high acquittal rates per count for left-wing defendants, prosecutors obtained higher conviction rates (table 9.2) for left-wing (77.1 percent) than for right-wing (70.1 percent) defendants.

In contrast to the circumstances of domestic terrorists, international terrorists indicted for crimes in U.S. federal courts appear substantially different in three areas. International terrorists, perhaps fearful of the uncertainty of American justice, have the highest guilty plea rate (62.9 percent) of the three groups (table 9.2), the highest overall conviction rate (88.6 percent) (table 9.2), and the lowest acquittal or mistrial rate (3.7 percent) by count (table 9.1). The most striking difference is the guilty plea rate for international terrorists. The percentage of international terrorists who pled guilty (62.9 percent) is nearly twenty percentage points higher than the rate for right-wing terrorists (43.3 percent) and is nearly three times higher than the rate at which left-wing terrorists entered guilty pleas (22.9 percent).

The notion of international terrorists conjures up images of masked airline hijackers or suicide bombers. The types of behavior exhibited by persons linked to international terrorism in this country, however, typically have not involved the actual commission of violent acts. Over half of the international terrorists in our study were members of the Provisional IRA, almost all of whom were convicted of illegal gun smuggling.[7] Even the Libyans accused of plotting the deaths of Oliver North and other officials associated with the 1986 bombing of Kaddafi's Bab al Azzizia barracks accepted plea bargains.[8] In several cases, the federal government found it to its advantage to offer defendants the choice of deportation rather than imprisonment in a federal penitentiary. Needless to say, the former was a much more attractive alternative than going to trial. Other than some members of Omega 7 (who did commit acts of violence)[9] and the more recent acclaimed cases of international terrorism involving Fawaz Yonis[10] and Yu Kikumura,[11] few international terrorists chose to stand trial in federal courts.

Variations in Sentencing

Although significant differences were noted in the way left-wing, right-wing, and international terrorists were prosecuted, were these differences also reflected in harsher sentences for left-wing terrorists? Efforts to measure these differences are considerably more difficult than it might be assumed. The most common method of measuring sentencing differences involves simply comparing the average sentences given to different groups of defendants. However, problems in using this approach are complicated by changes that took place in federal sentencing procedures during the 1980s.[12] In general, these changes reflected efforts to restrict the discretionary power of judges to ensure that defendants convicted of similar offenses received similar sentences. These changes in federal sentencing guidelines became effective in 1987. Although a majority of our terrorists were tried prior to that time, a substantial portion went to trial after these changes took effect. These cases, particularly, when averaged with the sentences given defendants under the earlier guidelines, probably have the effect of reducing overall variations in sentencing.

In addition to the ideological beliefs of defendants, what other considerations did judges use in determining sentences for American extremists involved in terrorism? Were female terrorists treated differently than male terrorists? Were black and Hispanic extremists somehow perceived as more dangerous to the polity and apt to elicit more severe sentencing from federal judges than white defendants? Was the extent of involvement as leader within the group a major consideration for sentencing? (table 9.3).

Females received sentences that, on average, were approximately three-fourths as long as the sentences given male terror-

Table 9.3 Total Sentence Length by Defendant Characteristics

CHARACTERISTIC[a]	TOTAL SENTENCE LENGTH IN MONTHS					
	Number	Mean	Minimum	Maximum	Standard Deviation	Statistical Significance[b]
Sex						
Male	110	201.01	0	1800	334.69	NS
Female	19	157.42	0	696	208.18	
Total	129	194.59	0	1800	318.94	
Race						
White	97	192.44	0	1800	333.01	NS
Non-white	32	201.09	0	960	276.68	
Total	129	194.59	0	1800	320.18	
Group Type						
Right-Wing	66	224.61	0	1800	380.10	NS
Left-Wing	36	222.42	0	960	291.09	NS
International	27	84.11	0	360	97.53	NS
Total	129	194.59	0	1800	316.28	

Role in Group						
Leader	37	327.59	0	1800	431.06	**
Cadre	92	141.10	0	1800	243.91	
Total	129	194.59	0	1800	308.71	

a. Excludes four international terrorists (three who were deported and one who received a life sentence) and five single-issue terrorists (members of EMETIC, also known as Earth First, convicted in Phoenix, AZ in 1991).

b. Statistics were generated using one-way analysis of variance. Since the distribution of sentence lengths was not normal (i.e., 28 defendants were given probation), the Mann-Whitney U-Wilcoxon test was used to verify statistical significance. Non-parametric tests such as the Mann-Whitney are generally not as powerful in identifying statistical differences; consequently, the failure of these tests to reveal statistical significance should not be used as ultimate indicators that statistical differences are not important.

**Mann Whitney U-Wilcoxon rank sum test, $Z = -2.89$, $p = .004$. One-way analysis of variance, $DF = 128$, $F = 9.63$, $p = .002$.

ists. Females received sentences that averaged approximately thirteen years, while males reaped an average of seventeen years for their indiscretions. The small number of convicted females in the sample prevents conclusive statements, but additional findings related to gender are worthy of note. First, female members of right-wing groups were much less likely to be arrested, indicted, and convicted. Those who were convicted received less severe sentences than left-wing female terrorists. These differences, as discussed earlier, reflect the variations in involvement between females in left-wing and right-wing groups. The shorter sentences given right-wing females reflect the overall lower sentences given females in general, whereas left-wing female terrorists received sentences equal to those given male terrorists.

Given America's past record of racial discrimination, its disdain for communism and Marxism, and the general conservative political climate of the 1980s, one might be led to predict that convicted leftist and minority terrorists would be treated more harshly than right-wing terrorists by federal judges at sentencing. However, there is little variation in the sentences given white and non-white terrorists. The average sentences given these two groups differed by less than one year. Similarly, left- and right-wing terrorists, on average, received almost identical sentences (222 months and 224 months, respectively). Although our earlier discussion regarding strategies used to prosecute leftists and rightists suggested the possibility that prosecutors adopted a harder line against left-wing terrorists, the differences in *sentencings* were negligible. In contrast, our suggestion that the high rate of international terrorists who pled guilty may have occurred as a result of more favorable plea agreements appears to be well founded. The average length of sentence given to international terrorists was only about one-third the sentence given to either left-wing or right-wing domestic terrorists.

Of the traits or characteristics that affected length of sentences presented in table 9.3, the terrorist's role in the organization appears to be most important. The most severe punishments were reserved for the leaders[13] of terrorist organizations in America. The average sentence given to the leaders of these groups exceeds twenty-seven years. Cadre members received punishments that averaged less than half the sentence lengths given to their leaders.

The sentencing of terrorist leaders and cadre members is clearly determined by prosecutorial and plea bargaining strategies. Over one-fifth of the convicted terrorists in our study received no

Table 9.4 Terrorists Convicted But Sentenced to Probation or Time Served

GROUP TYPE/NAME	NUMBER	PERCENTAGE
Right-wing		
Arizona Patriots	4	14.5%
Covenant, Sword, Arm of the Lord	3	10.7%
The Order	5	17.9%
The Order II	2	7.1%
White Patriot Party	1	3.6%
Subtotal	15	53.6%
Left-wing		
FALN	1	3.6%
El Rukn	1	3.6%
New African Freedom Front	7	25.0%
Provisional Party of Communists	1	3.6%
Subtotal	10	35.7%
International		
Omega 7	1	3.6%
Libyan[a]	2	7.1%
Subtotal	3	10.7%
TOTALS	28	100.0%

a. Does not include three Libyans who were deported.

additional incarceration time after sentencing—that is, they were frequently sentenced to a particular length of time, given credit for the amount of time they had served while awaiting trial, then were placed on probation for the duration of the sentence. In an overwhelming majority of cases, the use of probationary sentences involved plea bargains in exchange for testimony against other defendants. Oddly, this approach was widely used against right-wing terrorists but rarely against left-wing terrorists (table 9.4).

This strategy was seen in the convictions of the leaders of right-wing groups associated with the Christian Identity Movement. Numerous members of the Order and CSA received probation and the safety of the Federal Witness Protection Program in exchange for testimony: Mark Jones, an Order member present at the Whidbey Island signing of the 1983 "Declaration of War";[14] Thomas Martinez, friend of Order leader Robert Mathews, who helped launder counterfeit money for the group;[15] Randall Rader, active member of both the Order and CSA; and even James Ellison, leader of CSA who agreed to testify against Butler, Miles, and Beam at the 1987–1988 trial in Fort Smith,[16] were just a few of the famous right-wing extremists who were placed on probation and who also entered the witness protection program.

Left-wing terrorists in our study were noticeably absent from the Federal Witness Protection Program. Virtually no members of leftist groups in our sample received probationary sentences in exchange for testimony. The seven members of the New African Freedom Fighters who received probation did not plead guilty, preferring instead to go to trial.[17] This highly politicized case involving black revolutionaries resulted in felony convictions for all seven defendants. The judge, however, chose to place the seven on probation after jurors failed to convict on the most important charge—a conspiracy charge involving planned robberies. Their case was typical of left-wing terrorists in 1980s America. Highly committed ideologically and belonging to groups whose egalitarian organizational structure produced greater involvement by all of the members, left-wing terrorists appeared to have greater allegiance to their cause than right-wing terrorists. Despite that data provide no evidence that leftists were less likely than rightists to be offered plea bargain opportunities in exchange for testimony and the possibility of probation, leftists preferred to take their chances with juries and judges.

Some general conclusions regarding the variations in treatment and sentencing of international and left- and right-wing terrorists: First, although there is substantial evidence that federal prosecutors have used different strategies when trying left- and right-wing extremists, the overall outcomes of these cases were unusually similar. The conviction rate for leftists (77 percent) was slightly higher than for rightists (70 percent), but the average sentences given members of these groups were almost identical. While some prosecutorial patterns suggest different treatment of the two groups, the overall picture is not one of a government that was more tolerant of rightist violence than leftist violence (or vice versa). Although our study does not empirically examine the discretion that determines which acts will be labeled as terroristic and set in motion the federal investigations that follow, we conclude that once they are labeled the federal government pursues the conviction and punishment of left- and right-wing terrorists with equal vigor.

Second, the Department of Justice's decision to focus its efforts on the prosecution of terrorist groups, rather than individual acts of terror, significantly affects prosecutorial strategies. Efforts were concentrated on breaking up the organizational structure and leadership of the terrorist group. Consequently, an individual's role in the organization (as leader or cadre) was the most significant factor associated with prosecutorial and sentencing decisions. While the FBI and the U.S. Attorney's Office investigated and sought indictments against the perpetrators of officially labeled acts of terrorism, prosecution of these individuals was secondary to dismantling the organization that committed such acts.

Differential Sentencing Patterns: Terrorists and Traditional Criminals

In another sense, we are confronted with a major irony in the treatment of terrorists convicted in federal courts. Prosecutorial efforts before and during the trials of these defendants attempted to limit the scope of discussion of the crimes to the essential elements of the offense; i.e., that these offenders were no different from traditional criminals. If they were convicted, however, the focus of prosecutorial documents shifted markedly. Pre-sentence reports and pre-sentence memoranda tended to emphasize the *political* nature of the defendant's behavior and activities, to include behaviors and associations that in and of themselves were not criminal. In the previous chapter, we discussed Austin Turk's hypothesis that 'explicit politicality' was a primary characteristic of government prosecution of terrorists. In contrast, we found that prosecutors rarely used this tactic to *prosecute* terrorists, but widely used the tactic in the *sentencing* process.

Legal Traditions in Federal Sentencing

Federal courts have a long tradition of allowing consideration of "uncharged and unconvicted conduct at sentencing."[18] Terrorists, as well as other criminals convicted in federal courts in the 1980s, found that extra-legal factors could be used to affect their sentencing. Defendants were given the opportunity to establish the existence of mitigating factors that might lessen sentence severity, while the government was required to establish the existence of aggravating factors if more severe sentencing than normal was desired.[19] Consequently, three important differences set these procedures apart from judicial proceedings during the sentencing phase: (1) the absence of a jury; (2) a reduction in the standard of proof from 'beyond a reasonable doubt' to the standard used in civil suits—'preponderance of the evidence';[20] and (3) the allowance of 'uncharged and unconvicted conduct' as evidence.[21]

The introduction of new federal sentencing guidelines in 1987 did not substantially alter these procedures. While the guidelines created a new formula for sentence computation that restricted the range of sentences, the use of 'uncharged and unconvicted conduct' still could be raised at sentencing; the standard of proof continued to be the lesser 'preponderance of the evidence'; and sentencing remained under the authority of the judge rather than a jury of one's peers. Consequently, federal courts have allowed upward adjustments under the new sentencing guidelines for a variety of behaviors relevant to terrorism: cases in which the defendant made threats against the President of the United States;[22] took hostages;[23] was an organizer, leader, or supervisor in criminal activities involving five or more persons;[24] and, most importantly, where "reliable information indicates that the criminal history category does not adequately reflect the seriousness of the defendant's past criminal conduct or the likelihood the defendant will commit future crimes."[25]

Information regarding the political motives of the person and groups to which the defendant belongs as well as other 'uncharged and unconvicted conduct' is frequently part of the pre-sentence report presented by the government to a federal judge. Right-wing defendants in our sample regularly and frequently objected to the political nature of the pre-sentence report. For example, Jack Oliphant, a member of the Arizona Patriots, objected to the "PSI (pre-sentence investigation) making reference to the Arizona Patriots' planning to overthrow the government as being relevant to the defendant Jack Oliphant."[26] While the government in some cases has been prevented from making reference to the political ideology of some right-wing defendants during trial,[27] such objections are generally overruled during the sentencing phase. Prosecutors are normally free to address such issues as being relevant to sentencing.

In contrast, left-wing defendants seldom objected to the use of group names with which they were associated. In fact, the defendants themselves often used them in motions and in testimony. What left-wing defendants objected to most strenuously was the *manner* in which the names of these groups were used. They frequently argued that pre-sentence reports, in reciting the activities of these revolutionary groups, frequently *implied* that the defendant was involved in activities the group committed without evidence to verify such associations. Attorneys for Linda Evans, of M19CO fame, made such an argument at her 1990 sentencing. She argued that her sentencing was going to be determined less by *her actions* than by her *associations* with Marilyn Buck and other M19CO members.[28]

While prosecutors have used arguments involving explicit politicality as justifications for upward departures (an aggravating circumstance that warrants more severe sentencing), federal judges also received motions from defendants countering those claims. Defendants' motions frequently identified mitigating circumstances that might warrant downward departures from normal sentencing. The question that warrants answering is: Do the actions of prosecutors that politicize the criminality of these defendants impact sentencing decisions?

Sentencing Patterns: Terrorists and Traditional Criminals

To attempt to compare or contrast the sentences received by terrorists and common criminals is difficult at best. No two cases appearing before federal courts are identical. Defendants may be convicted of hundreds of different statutes, each of which may have several subsections that carry different penalties. The issue is complicated further by the fact that a defendant being sentenced in a single case may have been convicted of several counts involving different statutes. To simplify matters the Administrative Office of U.S. Courts records convictions and sentences according to the most serious offense for which the defendant was convicted. Convictions for specific statutes (i.e., conspiracy) are then divided into offense categories[29] that identify the specific nature of the offense (conspiracy to murder a foreign official, for example). It is therefore possible to create only a crude comparison of the sentences received by terrorists using national averages with non-terrorists convicted of the same statutes.[30] The terrorists in our sample were compared with national averages on three issues: (1) the percentage of sentenced defendants who received probation; (2) the average sentences of terrorists per specific statute; and (3) the sentences of each terrorist per statute. If terrorists were being treated more harshly in the federal court system, we would predict that they were less likely to receive probation than other felons, that their average sentences per statute were higher than national averages for similar offenses, and that a disproportionate number of terrorists received higher than average sentences.

The terrorists in our study were sentenced under twenty-nine different offense codes. In some instances, defendants were convicted of different sections or subsections of the U.S. Code for the same offense code. Since different penalties applied, these defendants were compared separately to national averages for those specific subsections. Comparisons were made for thirty-six different combinations of statute section or subsection and offense code. Four of the federal statutes were applied almost exclusively to terrorists during the period examined: murder, manslaughter, sedition, and a miscellaneous category of "national defense." Comparisons with national averages for these statutes were relatively meaningless since the national averages reflected the same cases as those in the terrorism sample (table 9.5).

By far the statute most frequently used against terrorists involved racketeering charges under subsections C and D of U.S.C. Title 18, Section 1962. Nationally, persons convicted of those subsections have been subjected to rather harsh punishments: only eight percent of defendants were sentenced to probation, while the remainder received an average sentence of 158 months. The terrorists in our study, many of whom were members of the Order, received even more severe sanctioning: none received probation, and the nineteen terrorists received an average sentence of 506 months. The second most frequently used statute involved violations of Title 18, Section 844 D (Explosives). A similar trend emerged regarding punishment for conviction of this offense. Nationally, probation was used sparingly (8 percent), and defendants received rather severe sentences (125 months on average). Terrorists fared even worse: no one was sentenced to probation and the average sentence per terrorist defendant (530 months) far exceeded the national average (table 9.6).

In general, convicted terrorists found few opportunities for probationary sentences.[31] Of the thirty-six statutes for which terrorists were convicted, the percentage of terrorists receiving probation was lower than the national average for nearly two-thirds (63.9 percent) of the statutes. Under only seven statutes did terrorists beat the odds and receive probation at rates higher than the national average.

A similar comparison was made regarding the average sentences of terrorists per statute. Terrorists received higher than average sentences under nearly twice as many federal statutes as lower than average sentences (21 to 12 months). Finally, of the

Table 9.5 Percent Receiving Probation and Average Sentence Lengths in Months for all Federally Convicted Defendants and for Terrorists by Offense Type

A.O. Code	Offense Type	USC Title Section	ALL DEFENDANTS		TERRORISTS		
			% Receiving Probation	Average Sentence	% Receiving Probation	Average Sentence	N
0100	Murder, 1st	18 1116	0%	540	0%	540	1[a]
0101	Murder, 1st Conspiracy	18 371	NA	NA	0%	120	1
0300	Manslaughter	18 1116	0%	120	0%	120	1[a]
1100	Robbery, Bank	18 2113 A	9%	130	0%	300	3
1400	Robbery, Conspiracy	18 371	22%	42	25%	48	4
3100	Theft, Bank	18 2113 C	57%	8[b]	0%	12	1
3400	Theft, U.S. Property; Conspiracy	18 371	44%	29[b]	0%	44	2
3600	Theft, Transportation; Conspiracy	18 2315	33%	57[b]	0%	12	1
	Theft, Transportation; Accessory	18 3	40%	57[b]	0%	60	1
4700	Embezzlement, Postal/Wire	18 1343	40%	44[b]	0%	60	1
4900	Embezzlement, Bankruptcy	18 1962	0%	144	100%	0	1
4991	Embezzlement, False Claims	18 1001	60%	38[b]	67%	6	3
4999	Embezzlement, Other	18 2314	21%	58[b]	0%	120	2
5100	Auto Theft, Transporting	18 2312	26%	52[b]	0%	48	1

Table 9.5 *Continued*

A.O. Code	Offense Type	USC Title Section	ALL DEFENDANTS		TERRORISTS		
			% Receiving Probation	Average Sentence	% Receiving Probation	Average Sentence	N
5800	Counterfeit	18 1962	NA	NA	0%	96	1
6501	Drugs, Dist. Marijuana	21 963	20%	13	0%	78	2
6701	Drugs, Poss. Cocaine	21 841	0%	57	0%	156	1
7312	Escape	18 3150	14%	29[b]	0%	36	1
7320	Aiding Escapee	18 1071	72%	40[b]	0%	36	1
7400	Racketeering	18 876	40%	53[b]	0%	60	1
	Racketeering	18 1951	17%	97[b]	0%	240	1
	Racketeering	18 1962 C&D	8%	158[b]	0%	506	19
7410	Racketeering; Arson; Conspiracy	18 371	0%	50	0%	24	1
7611	Kidnapping, Hostage	18 1203	NA	NA	0%	360	1
7800	Firearms, Conspiracy	18 371	50%	47	33%	78	9
	Firearms, Machine guns	26 5861 D	34%	62[b]	37%	104	16
7820	Firearms, Possession	18 1202 A1	30%	21[b]	100%	0	1
7830	Firearms	18 922 A	41%	38[b]	100%	0	2
	Firearms	18 924 C	11%	74[b]	0%	360	1

9754	Treason, Sedition	18 2384	20%	480	20%	330	5[a]
9790	National Defense	18 371	44%	33	0%	18	6
	National Defense	50 1702	0%	60	0%	60	1[a]
9921	Contempt	18 401	18%	56	33%	54	3
9994	Explosives, Conspiracy	18 371	33%	39[b]	0%	96	1
	Explosives	18 842 A	48%	166[b]	0%	192	2
	Explosives	18 844 A	8%	54	0%	360	1
	Explosives	18 844 D	8%	125	0%	530	6
	Explosives	18 844 F	29%	288	0%	696	2
9999	Other, Conspiracy	18 371	48%	26[b]	0%	6	1

a. Statute used almost exclusively for terrorists.
b. 1985–1986 averages. 1985–1986 averages were used when at least fifty defendants were sentenced under the particular statute during those years and the average did not differ significantly from previous years. If the 1985–1986 averages differed substantially from previous years or only a small number of defendants were sentenced under that statute, the figures reflect a recomputed average that includes defendants sentenced from 1981–1986.

Table 9.6 Distribution of Sentences Received by Terrorists
Relative to National Averages

	PERCENTAGE OR SENTENCE			
	Higher than Average	Same as Average	Lower than Average	Total
Number of statutes in which the percentage of terrorists receiving probation was:	7 19.4%	6 16.7%	23 63.9%	36 100.0%
Number of statutes in which the average sentence of terrorists was:	21 58.4%	3 8.3%	12 33.3%	36 100.0%
Number of terrorists whose sentences were:	53 66.3%	3 3.7%	24 30.0%	80 100.0%

eighty terrorists sentenced to terms of imprisonment for whom
data were available, exactly two-thirds (66.67 percent) received
sentences that were higher than the average sentences given
felons sentenced under the same statutes. Only 30 percent received
lower than average sentence lengths.

As crude as these indicators may be, they all suggested a similar pattern—that persons convicted of crimes relating to officially
designated acts or suspected acts of terrorism were punished more
severely than persons committing similar acts that were devoid of
political motives. To some extent, comparing sentencing patterns
by using 'most serious offense' criteria, as recorded by the Administrative Office of U.S. Courts, helps control the effects that consecutive (as opposed to concurrent) sentencing might have on total
sentence length. It does not, however, measure the effect of consecutive sentences given to defendants when convicted in two, three,
or four separate cases. While not all terrorists were tried in multiple cases, the leaders of terrorist groups in our survey did tend to
be tried repeatedly. To the extent that this phenomenon existed,
the greater severity of sentencing received by terrorists compared

to common criminals may be even greater than is suggested by the data in tables 9.5 and 9.6. The issue has been raised on several occasions by attorneys for terrorist leaders. In a pre-sentencing memorandum for M19CO member Linda Evans, her attorneys charged that:

> no court of which we are aware had imposed such a lengthy sentence for the offenses with which she was charged. Moreover, data . . . indicates that for pre-guideline sentences from 1980 to 1986 for the offenses which Ms. Evans was convicted, her initial sentence . . . far exceeded the average sentence imposed.[32]

Conclusions

Are the more severe penalties imposed on terrorists justified? Is a deterrent effect achieved by punishing these persons more harshly than other, non-political criminals? Although we are not able to provide definitive answers to these questions, clearly the results presented in this chapter warrant comment on these issues. First, if public opinion regarding severity of offense is considered an important criterion for sentencing, then terrorists may not have been punished as harshly as the American public would like. Terrorism ranks high on the public's list of heinous offenses.[33] Since most terrorists are convicted of traditional crimes that resulted from an investigation of the activities of terrorist organizations, these defendants found at sentencing that the activities of the entire group were being used as indicators of the defendant's proclivity for future criminal conduct. Federal court rulings that allowed consideration of uncharged and unconvicted conduct clearly worked to the disadvantage of terrorists at sentencing.

Since the overwhelming majority of our terrorists were sentenced under pre-1987 guideline standards, the comparisons made in tables 9.5 and 9.6 involved national averages for federal sentences prior to the effect of the new sentencing guidelines.[34] It is not yet possible to determine if the new sentencing guidelines have decreased the disparity between the sentences of terrorists and non-terrorists convicted of similar offenses. Too few terrorism cases have been sentenced under the new guidelines to provide statistical comparisons. In all probability, however, the new guidelines may not have as great an effect on the sentencing of terrorists as might be supposed.

The new guidelines clearly allow for upward departures in sentencing (as terrorists typically receive), for a variety of reasons. The ideological commitment of many terrorist group members make them ideal candidates for upward departures on several legally acceptable criteria. "Obstruction of administration of justice," lack of "acceptance of responsibility," and "participation as a leader in organized criminal activities involving five or more persons" have all been recognized as justifications for upward departures under the new sentencing guidelines.[35] Most importantly, one section of the guidelines permits a departure if the court finds that "reliable information indicates that the criminal history category does not adequately reflect the seriousness of the defendant's past criminal conduct or the likelihood the defendant will commit future crimes."[36] Terrorists who believe that future convictions under the new guidelines might not result in their being singled out for more severe sanctioning probably are mistaken. The structure of sentencing guidelines for federally convicted offenders clearly allows sufficient discretion for federal judges to sanction terrorists more harshly than other defendants.

Chapter 10

Dream On: Facts and Fantasies about American Terrorism

This study reveals a great deal about the characteristics and motivations of political extremists who are willing to use violence to further their goals, about terrorist organizations in the United States, and about how their actions came to be called "terroristic." In addition, we have made some rather surprising discoveries about our government's response to terrorism and about the attitudes of American citizens who serve as jurors in terrorism cases. An overview of this information may be useful to predict the future behavior of terrorists in America as well as the behavior of those who attempt to control and restrict those activities.

Some Conclusions about American Terrorism and American Terrorists

The Characteristics of Terrorists

While commonly accepted characterizations typify the terrorist as universally leftist, Marxist, and Communist, the American terrorist defies such stereotypes. Although leftist terrorist groups have committed their share of terrorism in America, right-wing, Jewish, and single-issue terrorists played major roles in the terrorism of the 1980s. The number of right-wing and left-wing groups that attracted the attention of federal authorities for terrorism-related activities was approximately the same. In addition, the number of right-wing extremists indicted for terrorism-related activities far

193

exceeds the number of left-wing extremists indicted, even when Puerto Rican extremists are included in the left-wing category.

Given these disparities in traditional thinking about terrorists, it is not surprising that the demographic traits of these persons do not coincide with previous descriptions of the typical terrorist either. Although leftist groups in the 1980s were more likely to be egalitarian (having large numbers of male and female active members as well as racial integration within some groups), more than half of the domestic terrorist groups in America, particularly right-wing groups, were virtually all white and all male. Nor did American terrorist organizations fit the stereotype that suggests terrorists are largely drawn from the middle and upper classes. Although the leaders of many of the organizations fit that description, an equal number of extremist group leaders had lower-income backgrounds with little education or social status. The cadre members in our sample were almost exclusively from lower-income families with little college education. Only among the Puerto Rican Macheteros and the central core of the M19CO did we find terrorist cadre members that represented the intelligentsia.

Of equal importance were our findings regarding age. Typically, terrorists are believed to be young idealists. Our study revealed that they may indeed be idealists, but they certainly were not as young as most scholars have depicted them. This finding is of tremendous importance to criminological theory, for virtually all perspectives of delinquent behavior maintain that criminality peaks no later than the early twenties and declines sharply thereafter.[1] Although many of the left-wing terrorists in our sample had been involved in extremist violence since their teenage years, the maturation process had little effect on reducing the violent nature of their behavior. The typical leftist terrorists continued bombing until their mid-thirties, interrupted only by their arrest and incarceration. Right-wing extremists started later in life as terrorists but tended to be even older at arrest than left-wing extremists. While age has been the single, most consistent explanatory variable in the criminological literature, the age differences (and patterns of continuing criminality) revealed in our study suggest fundamental differences between the causes of terrorism and the causes of traditional crime.

The Process of Becoming a Terrorist

In addition to these differences among the characteristics of persons who turn to violence for political reasons, we noted that the process of becoming a terrorist is incomplete without the official stamp of governmental labeling. Although we know a great deal about the official definition of terrorism followed by the federal government, about the requirements for investigations of terrorist groups, and about the types of behaviors that warrant the official governmental designation of "terroristic"; the decision-making process in labeling specific cases remains vague. We also noted that terrorists were arrested and prosecuted primarily for the violation of traditional criminal offenses, and we saw little evidence[2] in the case files that the basic constitutional rights of these defendants had been violated. Despite efforts to focus upon the traditional criminal behaviors of defendants in terrorism cases, the political nature of an accused's behavior was the central element in the government's decision to unleash the full scope of its investigative and prosecutorial authority.

Investigative and Prosecutorial Discretion

Despite the common protection afforded all defendants, the justice system allows considerable latitude in the differential treatment of alleged offenders. While certain constitutional safeguards are available to all offenders, terrorists appear to be treated differently than traditional offenders in both the *intensity* with which investigations are pursued and in the *strategy* taken in prosecution. First, the intensity with which terrorist groups were investigated during the mid-1980s and the consequent arrests and prosecution of large numbers of terrorists during that period is a stark contrast to the limited expenditures and substantially fewer prosecutions that occurred during the late 1970s and early 1980s.[3] Although most studies of the relationship between law enforcement expenditures and reductions in the crime rate have provided mixed results at best, increased expenditures for fighting terrorism by the FBI after 1983 brought impressive results. The decrease in terroristic activity after 1985 must be attributed, in all fairness, primarily to the intensity with which the Federal Bureau of Invesitigation and the Attorney General focused their attention on terrorism. While the effort expended in bringing these defendants to trial is considerably higher than for traditional crimes, the dominant prosecutorial strategy used in terrorism cases involved *minimizing* the political motivations of the terrorists. Terrorists were to be seen as common criminals; to do otherwise glorified their cause. Like a duck who appears calm on the surface while it paddles feverishly underwater, prosecutorial efforts against terrorists attempted to appear "normal" and not significantly different from other trials, while in reality frenzied efforts were being made to bring such offenders to justice.

Were these practices, then, deceptive and inappropriate? Not necessarily. On both counts (intensity and strategy), the government had legitimate reasons for its conduct. Certainly, the disproportionate level of federal expenditures in the war on terrorism reflected the sentiments of the American public and its elected representatives.[4] Secondly, as we discussed in Chapter 8, efforts to introduce political motivation as part of the essential elements of prosecuting the crime raised constitutional questions.

We also noted, however, two practices that appeared to be questionable despite their clear constitutionality: (1) the use of political motivation in the pre-sentencing report and (2) the tendency to try terrorists repeatedly. Prosecutorial efforts to limit jurors' access to the political motivation of the defendant seems particularly ironic when they are later used extensively (once a conviction has been obtained) to justify upward departures for sentencing. Similarly, trying a terrorist for violating presumed-liability statutes to get him or her off the streets while preparing a more complex conspiracy case against the defendant may have its practical benefits, but the strategy also raises issues of judicial fairness. Certainly, federal judges must carefully monitor previous prosecutorial efforts used against a defendant as well as previous sentences the terrorist may have received.

The Function of Juries and Judges in Terrorism Trials

Although the American public considers terrorism among the most serious offenses, juries have not automatically responded to prosecutorial desires to convict and severely punish suspected terrorists. When the trials of terrorists result in acquittal or dismissal of nearly half the counts against the defendants, as our study revealed,[5] either the prosecution has overbooked or wrongfully accused the defendants or has been poorly prepared for trial. Most of the dismissals or acquittals not due to pleas on other counts reflect the unwillingness of juries (and in some cases, judges)[6] to allow repeated prosecution on conspiracy charges after the defendant has already been convicted for the individual acts in previous trials. The acquittal of thirteen white supremacists in Arkansas in 1988 should not be viewed as an indicator of America's tolerance for right-wing extremism. Instead it should be seen as the result of the reasoned judgment of rational jurors who determined that most of these men had already been tried and convicted in previous trials for most of the crimes charged in the current indictment. The behavior of juries and judges in terrorism cases provides an important function not normally performed in the average criminal trial: they serve as a reflection of public opinion informing prosecutors of the extent to which society is willing to allow further prosecution.

The Severity of Punishment for Terrorists

We found that terrorists received, on average, substantially longer sentences than traditional offenders and that far fewer terrorists than non-terrorists were given probation instead of incarceration. Did these longer sentences have a deterrent effect? To answer that question one must recall the polity's stated goal in dealing with terrorism—dismantling terrorist organizations rather than punishing offenders for specific acts of terror. While convicting terrorists for officially designated acts of terror was desired by the state, it was regarded as a bonus. Consequently, the overwhelming majority of terrorists were convicted and sentenced for terrorist-*related* activities.

The government's strategy was reflected in the different sentences received by leaders of terrorist groups. Neither political ideology, sex, nor race were relevant to the severity of terrorists' sentences. A terrorist's role in the group as leader or cadre member was the single best predictor of sentence length. Was the strategy to sentence terrorist leaders to longer terms successful? One would have to say unequivocally yes. The arrests and convictions of Eduardo Arocena, Marilyn Buck, Raymond Levasseur, Glenn Miller, Filiberto Ojedo Rios, and James Ellison left the members of many terrorist groups dismayed, disorganized, and fearful that arrested leaders would turn state's evidence, thereby implicating remaining members. While some of these groups may recover and others may take their place, the small size of most terrorist organizations limits their ability to regroup and reorganize. Organizational size presents a fundamental dilemma for terrorist groups. Attempts to expand or to recruit large numbers invites infiltration by law enforcement authorities, while the retention of small, secret cells brings with it the risk of complete eradication if members are caught or if they defect. In the 1980s most American terrorist groups experienced the shock effect of arrest. Some of these groups will survive. Other violent extremist groups may arise in new or modified form from the ashes of decimated organizations like the Order and the Covenant, Sword, and Arm of the Lord.

Prospects for the Future

Predicting terrorism is a risky business. Because levels of terrorism can be dramatically altered by extremely small groups of people, all predictive efforts are tenuous at best. Yet despite the high probability of error, some general predictions can be made based on the presence or absence of the causal elements of terrorism. Since these causal elements vary for different groups, blanket statements about increases in American terrorism are probably neither possible nor useful. A better approach is to examine the prominent types of American terrorist groups separately (table 10.1).

The decline of the Soviet Union and the Warsaw Pact Alliance countries as supporters of communist insurrections around the world should have a major impact on international terrorism. The financial and psychological support provided by eastern bloc countries was a major stimulant of the anti-American terrorist movement in the 1970s and 1980s. Libya, Syria, and Cuba, the three countries most heavily linked to anti-American terrorism around the world, were all heavily supported militarily and financially by the Soviet Union. The dissolution of the Soviet Union and its movement toward democracy has had a tremendous impact on the political perspectives of these three nations. While Libya and Syria look for ways to accomodate these new realities in world politics, Fidel Castro seems determined to continue the revolutionary work of communism. Without the financial support of the Soviet Union, he is forced to focus on internal problems, thus restricting his ability to concentrate on the exportation of terrorism.

Although the decline of communism and the demise of the Soviet Union may reduce international terrorism, other forces are at work that may increase it. The rise of Moslem fundamentalism and the Shiites' willingness to use random violence for political purposes has already been clearly etched in the minds of most Americans. The February 1993 bombing of the World Trade Center[7] in New York and the March 1993 arrests in St. Louis of four alleged members of the Abu Nidal terrorist group for conspiring to blow up the Israeli Embassy[8] have finally convinced most Americans that international terrorism of the magnitude well known to Europeans has finally arrived in the United States.

Table 10.1   Predicted Changes in American Terrorist Activity

TYPE OF TERRORISM/GROUP	PREDICTION	MAJOR CAUSAL ISSUES
International	Mixed	Decline of communism Increasing influence of Moslem fundamentalism
Domestic Left-Wing	Significant decreases	Decline of communism/reduced Cuban involvement
Right-Wing	Increases	Affirmative action/immigration/increased perception of minorities as burdens on society and causes of high crime rates
Puerto Rican	Increases, then declines after final determination of Puerto Rico's future	The uncertainty of Puerto Rico's political relations with the United States
Environmental	Significant increases	Environmental issues will become a major political issue

Left-wing domestic terror in the United States will most likely suffer a similar fate. While extremists of the Left struggle to reassess their ideological goals, their most extreme expression, terrorism, will also abate. On the practical level, the domestic political and economic problems faced by Castro will have a dramatic effect on leftist terror in America. Fidel Castro's long history of support for the leftist student movement in America will have to take a back seat to more pressing domestic issues. Although Cuba has been a safe haven for extremists like JoAnne Chesimard and William Morales in the past, it is unlikely that Cuba will continue to provide sanctuary for American fugitives in the future. Nor will American lefists look to Cuba as an example of a working communist paradise. The days of the Vinceremos Brigades are past.

Despite the continuing activity of Puerto Rican terrorists, a

decline in Puerto Rican terrorism is also probable. Political violence in Puerto Rico has been a thorn in Washington's side for
nearly forty years. Since Puerto Rican nationalists opened fire on
the floor of the United States House of Representatives in 1954,
the U.S. government has been constantly reminded that some
Puerto Ricans disapprove of the American presence on the island.
Congress has come closer than ever to resolving Puerto Rico's awk-
ward commonwealth status. In October 1991, the House of Representatives passed a bill calling for a referendum to allow the people
of Puerto Rico to choose statehood, independence, or continuation
of their commonwealth status.[9] It marked the first time either
house of Congress has voted for such a measure. Although an increase in terrorism during the interim is likely, once a final decision regarding Puerto Rico's status is reached opposing groups may
accept the vote of the island's residents as conclusive.

    In contrast, right-wing and environmental terrorists show
distinct promise of increasing in number and activity before the
close of the twentieth century. Outbreaks of terrorist activity are
frequently preceded by increases in demonstrations and minor
criminal incidents associated with a political or social movement.
For example, many of the leftist terrorist groups of the 1970s and
1980s emerged from the student demonstrations and racial unrest
of the late 1960s. An increase in the number of right-wing demonstrations, strong political support for extremist candidates like former neo-Nazi David Duke, and expansion of the skinhead movement all signal the possibility of an increase in right-wing terror.
Frustration over the election of Bill Clinton in the 1992 presiden-
tial election, a narrowing job market, and slower economic growth
in America will severely aggravate the extreme Right's perception
of minorities as parasitic. Under such conditions, one can only sur-
mise that groups like the Order, the Ku Klux Klan, and the White
Patriot Party will emerge with renewed vigor. Some of these
groups almost certainly will turn to terror to express their frustration with social conditions.

    Equally ominous are the signs that violent environmental ex-
tremism is alive and well. Despite the convictions of David Foreman, the founder of Earth First, and other members of EMETIC,
violent expresions of environmental extremism will probably be
the most prominent form of American terrorism in the near future.
Foreman, who has split with the Earth First movement over ideological differences, has claimed that the environmental movement
has been co-opted by leftist radicals and that he "was driven out of
Earth First by the flag burning and left-wing politics of the group's

California wing."[10] Environmental extremists not allied with the far Left may form their own splinter groups.

Foreman's claims are particularly disturbing given the ideology and callous, business-like perspective of the leaders of the California wing of Earth First. As Foreman acknowledged, Earth First is now marked by "a lot of class-struggle rhetoric and focusing on evil corporations and that sort of thing, pulling in a lot of social justice issues . . . (the movement has become) a class struggle sort of group."[11] As the environmental movement has become more sophisticated it has also become more concerned about the possible adverse effects of using terrorism. The current leaders of Earth First still view monkey wrenching as an effective strategy, although they advocate that it should be used with restraint and only after analyzing its impact on public opinion. As California Earth First leader Mike Rosell put it: "Our position is not a sweeping condemnation of monkey wrenching, but you can only go so far without destroying public opinion."[12] This willingness to use environmental terrorism reflects not a moral shift away from the use of violence, but merely a change in strategy—and a particularly dark and foreboding one at that. Although the use of terrorism has not significantly altered the course of human history, the possibility that a single, violent act can shatter the fragile balance of human society demands vigilance on the part of the polity as they attempt to control this unique form of criminal expression.

Appendix

Federal Criminal Cases Resulting From FBI Investigations of Terrorism or Terrorism-related Activities

CASE NAME	CASE NUMBER	JURISDICTION	NAME OF ORGANIZATION	NUMBER OF DEFENDANTS
United States v. --				
Walter Wolfgang Droege	CR–84–C–301–NE	Alabama Northeast	Ku Klux Klan	1
David Foreman et al.	CR–89–192–PHX	Arizona	EMETIC	5
Jack Oliphant et al.	CR–86–336–PCT	Arizona	Arizona Patriots	4
Rita Schlect	CR–86–337–PCT	Arizona	Arizona Patriots	1
Foster Hoover	CR–86–338–PCT	Arizona	Arizona Patriots	1
J. R. Hagen and Tom Palmer	CR–86–292–TUC	Arizona	Arizona Patriots	2
James Ellison and William Thomas	CR–85–20006	Arkansas Western	Covenant, Sword, Arm of the Lord	2
Robert Smalley and William Brugle	CR–85–20007	Arkansas Western	CSA	2
James Wallington	CR–85–1583M	Arkansas Western	CSA	1

Name	Case Number	District	Group	Count
Stephen Scott	CR–85–20014	Arkansas Western	CSA	1
James Ellison and Kerry Noble	CR–85–20015	Arkansas Western	CSA	2
James Ellison et al.	CR–85–20016	Arkansas Western	CSA	3
James Ellison et al.	CR–85–20017	Arkansas Western	CSA	6
Robert Edward Miles et al.	CR–87–20008	Arkansas Western	CSA	14
Ronald King et al.	CR–85–0102–WHO	California Northern	Order	3
Frank Scutari	CR–85–0291–JPV	California Northern	Order	1
transferred to:	CR–85–0291	Florida Southern		
Bruce Carroll Pierce et al.	CR–85–0476	California	Order	7
David Gumaer and Steven Christensen	86–CR–354	Colorado	Arizona Patriots	2
David Eden Lane et al.	87–CR–114	Colorado	Order	4
Victor Manuel Gerena et al.	H–85–50(TEC)	Connecticut	Macheteros	19
Eduardo Arocena	83–1015–CR	Florida Southern	Omega 7	1
David R. Dorr et al.	CR–88–30004	Idaho	Order II	5
Alejandria Torres et al.	83–CR–0494	Illinois Northern	FALN	4

Appendix (*Continued*)

CASE NAME	CASE NUMBER	JURISDICTION	NAME OF ORGANIZATION	NUMBER OF DEFENDANTS
Jeff Fort et al.	86–CR–572	Illinois Northern	El Rukns	7
Linda Sue Evans	CR–85–337	Louisiana Eastern	M19CO	1
Noel Murphy et al.	CR–86–184–MA	Massachusetts	IRA	8
Joseph P. Murray et al.	CR–86–118–T	Massachusetts	IRA	7
Raymond Luc Levasseur et al.	CR–86–00180	Massachusetts	United Freedom Front	8
Joseph P. Murray et al.	CR–87–181–T	Massachusetts	IRA	3
Joseph P. Murray and Robert Andersen	CR–87–225–T	Massachusetts	IRA	2
Wilhelm Ernst Schmitt et al.	CR–6–84–124	Minnesota Third Div.	Sheriff's Posse Comitatus	3
Wilhelm Ernst Schmitt and Harry Mott	CR–6–84–185	Minnesota Third Div.	SPC	2
Susan Lisa Rosenberg and Timothy Blunk	CR–84–360	New Jersey	M19CO	2
Yu Kikumura	CR–88–166	New Jersey	Japanese Red Army	1
Eduardo Arocena	83–CR–821 (RJW)	New York Southern	Omega 7	1
Coltrane Chimurenga	84–CR–818 (RLC)	New York Southern	New African Freedom Fighters	9

Eduardo Losado Fernandez	84–CR–1134 (WK)	New York Southern	Omega 7	1
Jose V. Lopez	84–CR–880 (RJW)	New York Southern	Omega 7	1
Pedro Remon	84–CR–282 (ADS)	New York Southern	Omega 7	1
Linda Sue Evans	85–CR–450 (VLB)	New York Southern	M19CO	1
Pedro Remon et al.	85–CR–830 (RJW)	New York Southern	Omega 7	3
Amanda Reid	CR–85–26 (WS)	North Carolina Middle Dist. Winston Div.	Provisional Party of Communists	1
Stephen Samuel Miller et al.	87–2–01 thru 05–CR–3	North Carolina Eastern Dist. Fayetteville Div.	White Patriot party	5
Glenn Frazier Miller	87–31–01–CR–5	North Carolina Eastern Dist. Raleigh Div.	WPP	1
Robert Eugene Jackson et al.	87–03247–01/03 03–CR–S–4	Missouri Western Dist. Southern Div.	WPP	3
Patricia Gros	CR–84–222	Ohio Northern Dist. Eastern Div.	UFF	1
James Barr	CR–84–00272	Pennsylvania Eastern Dist.	IRA	1

Appendix (*Continued*)

CASE NAME	CASE NUMBER	JURISDICTION	NAME OF ORGANIZATION	NUMBER OF DEFENDANTS
Carlos Rodriguez-Rodriguez	CR–84–169 (JP)	Puerto Rico	FALN	1
Mark Frank Jones and Michael Norris	CR–85–00010 (W) transferred to: CR–85–HM–80–S	Utah Central Div. Alabama Northern	Order	2
Walid Nicolas Kabbani et al.	CR–87–78–1 thru 3	Vermont	Syrian Social Nationalist party	3
Mousa Hawamda et al.	CR–88–00168	Virginia Eastern Dist. Alexandria Div.	Libyan	8
Bruce Carroll Pierce et al.	CR–85–001M	Washington Western Dist. Seattle Div.	Order	23
Richard Joseph Scutari	CR–86–116M	Washington Western Dist. Seattle Div.	Order	1
Laura Whitehorn et al.	CR–88–145 (HHG)	District of Columbia	M19CO	7
Fawaz Yunis (Also spelled Younis)	CR–87–0377	District of Columbia	Amal	1

Notes

Introduction

1. Frank Tannenbaum, *Crime and the Community* (New York: Columbia University Press, 1938).

2. Howard S. Becker, *Outsiders: Studies in the Sociology of Deviance* (New York: Free Press, 1963), pp. 8–9.

Chapter 1

Terrorism in the Criminal Justice System: Political and Conceptual Problems

1. The problem is reminiscent of the famous 1940s dispute between noted American criminologists Edwin Sutherland and Paul Tappan regarding the study of white collar crime. While Sutherland advocated expanding the definition of white collar crime to include violations of regulations that were handled administratively by federal agencies through fines and other punishment not involving incarceration, Tappan argued that allowing academics and researchers to define what constitutes criminal behavior was inappropriate and irresponsible. Instead, he argued that the subject matter of criminologists is defined for them by criminal law. Edwin Sutherland, "Is 'White Collar Crime' Crime?" *American Sociological Review* (1945), 10:132–139; and Paul Tappan's "Who is the Criminal?" *American Sociological Review* (1947), 12:96–102.

2. Criticisms about definitions of terrorism are identical to those leveled by Tappan over forty years ago regarding white collar crime: "A special hazard exists in the employment of the term, "white collar criminal," in that it invites individual systems of private values to run riot in an area where gross variation exists among criminologists as well as

others." Paul Tappan, "Who is the Criminal?" *American Sociological Review* (1947), 12:96–102. p. 99.

3. See Grant Wardlaw, *Political Terrorism* (New York: Cambridge University Press, 1989) for a good review of conceptual difficulties regarding terrorism.

4. See FBI Terrorist Research and Analytical Center, *Terrorism in the United States: 1990* (Washington, DC: U.S. Department of Justice, 1991); and FBI Terrorist Research and Analytical Center, *FBI Analysis of Terrorist Incidents in the United States: 1982* (Washington, DC: Federal Bureau of Investigation, 1983).

5. FBI Terrorist Research and Analytical Center, *Terrorism in the United States: 1990* (Washington, DC: U.S. Department of Justice, 1991), p. 25.

6. U.S. House of Representatives, *Hearings Before the Sub-committee on Civil and Constitutional Rights on Dissemination of FBI Arrest Records.* 100th Cong., 1st sess., Oct. 14 and 21, 1987. (Washington, DC: U.S. Government Printing Office, 1987), p. 122.

7. See Chapter 7 for a more thorough discussion of this issue. Terroristic-threatening statutes have seldom been used to prosecute crimes that would meet any reasonable definition of terrorism. Instead, they have been used to criminalize verbal threats. See also Brent L. Smith, "Antiterrorism Legislation in the United States: Problems and Implications," *Terrorism: An International Journal* (1984), 7(2): 213–231.

8. *Attorney General's Guidelines on Domestic Security/ Terrorism Investigations,* (Washington, DC: Office of the Attorney General, March 7, 1983), p. 1–19.

9. See Tony Poveda's *Lawlessness and Reform: The FBI in Transition* (Pacific Grove, CA: Brooks/Cole, 1990) for an excellent discussion of the impact of the Watergate hearings on FBI reform efforts. I am indebted to Poveda's discussion of terrorism and the FBI for providing a useful framework from which to analyze the FBI's response to terrorism in the early 1980s.

10. Ibid., pp. 73–78.

11. John T. Elliff, *The Reform of FBI Intelligence Operations* (Princeton, NJ: Princeton University Press), p. 79.

12. *Hearings Before the Subcommittee on Administrative Practice and Procedure of the Committee of the Judiciary on FBI Statutory Charter.* 95th Cong., 2d sess., June–Sept. (Washington, DC: U.S. Government Printing Office, 1978), pp. 98–99.

13. Clarence M. Kelley and James K. Davis, *Kelley: The Story of an FBI Director* (Kansas City, MO: Andrews, McMeel, and Parker, 1987).

14. Tony Poveda, *Lawlessness and Reform: The FBI in Transition* (Pacific Grove, CA: Brooks/Cole, 1990), pp. 76.

15. Ibid., pp. 128–130.

16. *Hearings on FBI Oversight Before the Subcommittee on Civil and Constitutional Rights of the Committee of the Judiciary.* 96th Cong., 1st and 2d sessions, Mar. 1979 and Mar. 1980. (Washington, DC: U.S. Government Printing Office, 1980), p. 5.

17. Tony Poveda, *Lawlessness and Reform: The FBI in Transition* (Pacific Grove, CA: Brooks/Cole, 1990), pp. 128.

18. *Hearings on FBI Oversight Before the Subcommittee on Security and Terrorism of the Committee on the Judiciary.* 97th Cong., 2d sess. (Feb. 4). (Washington, DC: U.S. Government Printing Office, 1982), p. 10.

19. Kevin Cullen, "Search for 'Cop-Killers' Comes to an End," *Boston Globe,* 5 November 1984, p. 4.

20. Tony Poveda, *Lawlessness and Reform: The FBI in Transition* (Pacific Grove, CA: Brooks/Cole, 1990), p. 128.

21. *Attorney General's Guidelines on Domestic Security/ Terrorism Investigations,* (Washington, DC: Office of the Attorney General, March 7, 1983), pp. 1–19.

22. Henry Hurt, "Search for a Terrorist Gang," *Reader's Digest,* December 1985, pp. 167–180. For a different opinion, see Terry Bisson and Sally O'Brien, "Young Hostages," *The Nation,* 3 December 1985, p. 69.

23. L. J. Davis, "Ballad of an American Terrorist," *Harper's Magazine,* July 1986 (Vol. 273), p. 60.

24. FBI Terrorist Research and Analytical Center, *Terrorism in the United States: 1990* (Washington, DC: U.S. Department of Justice, 1991), p. 25.

25. Ibid., p. 25.

26. *The Attorney General's Guidelines on General Crimes, Racketeering Enterprise and Domestic Security/Terrorism Investigations* (Washington, DC: Office of the Attorney General, March 7, 1983), pp. 1–19.

27. Ibid., p. 13.

28. Ibid., p. 16.

29. Ibid., p. 13.

30. Ibid., p. 13.

31. *Oversight Hearing on FBI Domestic Security Guidelines Before the Subcommittee on Civil and Constitutional Rights of the Committee of the Judiciary.* 98th Cong., 1st sess., Apr. 27, 1983. (Washington, DC: U.S. Government Printing Office, 1987, p. 25.

32. Neil Gallagher, Chief of the Counter-terrorism Section, Criminal Investigation Division, FBI Terrorist Research and Analytical Center, commented in a letter that accompanied release of the data, "enclosed is a list of persons indicted or arrested within the Counterterrorism Program since 1980; however, this list should not be considered all inclusive." Letter dated 29 March 1989.

33. Information on each case was obtained in one of three ways. First, each of the major trial sites (federal district courts) was visited. Copies of the indictment, judgment/ commitment orders, and anecdotal information related to each available case were obtained for analysis. Second, cases that had been completed for several months or years (depending on the storage space of the district court) were traced to the receiving federal records center (national archives). Documentation necessary to retrieve these case files was obtained from the district courts, and these case files were examined at the various federal records centers throughout the United States. Third, for isolated cases, copies of the indictment, court docket, and judgment/commitment orders were obtained from some federal district courts by mail. Missing demographic and sentencing information was provided by the Administrative Office of U.S. Courts.

Chapter 2

The Extent of Terrorism in America

1. The data in this chapter were derived from information provided in the annual reports of the FBI's Terrorist Research and Analytical Center. The title of the reports has changed slightly over the years. Initially it was called *FBI Analysis of Terrorist Incidents in the United States*. In 1984, the title was changed to *FBI Analysis of Terrorist Incidents and Terrorist Related Activities in the United States*. The 1986 report reverted to the pre-1984 title. In 1987, the FBI adopted the current title: *Terrorism in the United States*.

2. FBI Terrorist Research and Analytical Center, *FBI Analysis of Terrorist Incidents in the United States: 1982* (Washington, DC: Federal Bureau of Investigation, 1983).

3. FBI Terrorist Research and Analytical Center, *FBI Analysis of Terrorist Incidents and Terrorist Related Activities in the United States: 1985* (Washington, DC: Federal Bureau of Investigation, 1986).

4. FBI Terrorist Research and Analytical Center, *FBI Analysis of Terrorist Incidents in the United States: 1986* (Washington, DC: U.S. Government Printing Office, 1987).

5. Indictment, United States v. Victor Manuel Gerena et al. (H–85–50), United States District Court, (District of Connecticut).

6. FBI Terrorist Research and Analytical Center, *Terrorism in the United States: 1989* (Washington, DC: U.S. Government Printing Office, 1990).

7. FBI Terrorist Research and Analytical Center, *Terrorism in the United States: 1990* (Washington, DC: U.S. Government Printing Office, 1991).

8. United States v. Mousa Hawamda et al. (CR–88–00168), United States District Court, Eastern District of Virginia, Alexandria Division.

9. United States v. Walid Nicolas Kabbani et al. (CR–87–78), U.S. District Court, District of Vermont.

10. United States v. Yu Kikumura (CR–88–166), U.S. District Court, District of New Jersey.

11. See, for example, United States v. Alejandrina Torres et al. (83–CR–0494), U.S. District Court, Northern District of Illinois.

12. FBI Terrorist Research and Analytical Center, *FBI Analysis of Terrorist Incidents in the United States: 1983* (Washington, DC: Federal Bureau of Investigation, 1984), p. 17.

13. FBI Terrorist Research and Analytical Center, *FBI Analysis of Terrorist Incidents in the United States: 1986* (Washington, DC: U.S. Government Printing Office, 1987), p. 21.

14. FBI Terrorist Research and Analytical Center, *Terrorism in the United States: 1987* (Washington, DC: U.S. Government Printing Office, 1988), p. 11.

15. The May 19th Communist Organization used at least three different names during its bombing spree in the early 1980s. Its crimes are officially recorded under the names "Red Guerrilla Resistance," "Revolutionary Fighting Group," and "Armed Resistance Unit."

16. Andrew MacDonald, *The Turner Diaries* (Arlington, VA: National Alliance, 1978).

17. FBI Terrorist Research and Analytical Center, *Terrorism in the United States: 1988* (Washington, DC: U.S. Government Printing Office, 1989), p. 37.

Chapter 3

Extremists Right and Left

1. Charles Russell and Bowman Miller, "Profile of a Terrorist," *Terrorism: An International Journal*, (1977) 1(1):17–34.

2. Richard L. Clutterbuck, *Guerrillas and Terrorists* (Chicago: Ohio State University Press, 1980).

3. Richard Rubenstein, *Alchemists of Revolution: Terrorism in the Modern World* (New York: Basic Books, 1987).

4. Russell and Miller, "Profile of a Terrorist"; Jillian Becker, *Hitler's Children: The Story of the Baader-Meinhoff Terrorist Gang* (Philadelphia: J. B. Lippencott, 1977).

5. Paul Wilkinson, "Support Mechanisms for International Terrorism," in *Current Perspectives on International Terrorism,* eds. Robert Slater and Michael Stohl (New York: St. Martin's, 1987).

6. Peter Flemming and Michael Stohl, "The Theoretical Utility of Typologies of Terrorism: Lessons and Opportunities," in *The Politics of Terrorism,* 3rd Ed., ed. Michael Stohl (New York: Marcel Dekker, 1988).

7. Russell and Miller, "Profile of a Terrorist," p. 32.

8. Claire Sterling, *The Terror Network* (New York: Holt, Rinehart, Winston, 1981).

9. Carlos Marighella, "Mini-manual of the Urban Guerrilla." Revised and published as "Handbook of Urban Guerrilla Warfare" in *For the Liberation of Brazil* (Baltimore: Penguin Books, 1971).

10. Steven Emerson, "Taking on Terrorists," *U.S. News & World Report,* 12 September 1988, pp. 26–34.

11. Peter Flemming and Michael Stohl, "The Theoretical Utility of Typologies of Terrorism: Lessons and Opportunities."

12. Ibid., p. 156.

13. Ibid., pp. 157–170.

14. Paul Wilkinson, unpublished manuscript, quoted in Peter Flemming and Michael Stohl, "The Theoretical Utility of Typologies of Terrorism: Lessons and Opportunities."

15. Ibid., p. 177.

16. Bruce Hoffman, *The Contrasting Ethical Foundations of Terrorism in the 1980s* (Santa Monica, California: The Rand Corporation, 1988).

17. Karl Marx and Frederick Engels, *The German Ideology,* ed. C. J. Arthur (New York: International Publishers, 1970).

18. Indictment, United States v. Fort et al., filed September 1986 (86–CR–572) U.S. District Court, Northern District of Illinois, Eastern Division.

19. Indictment, United States v. Hawamda et al., filed 13 September

1988 (CR–88–00168) U.S. District Court, Eastern District of Virginia, Alexandria Division.

20. Richard Rubenstein, *Alchemists of Revolution: Terrorism in the Modern World,* p. 141.

21. Ibid., p. 10.

22. George Homans, *Social Behavior: Its Elementary Forms,* Revised Edition (New York: Harcourt Brace Jovanovich, 1974).

23. Max Weber, *The Protestant Ethic and the Spirit of Capitalism* (New York: Charles Scribner's Sons, 1976).

24. See Anti-Defamation League of B'nai B'rith's *Hate Groups in America: A Record of Bigotry and Violence* (New York: Anti-Defamation League of B'nai B'rith, 1982), p. 52; Read also Aryan Nations member Louis Beam's "Common Sense," in *Freedom's Echo,* Winter, 1987, 1(1), an Aryan Nations publication.

25. Karl Marx, *Karl Marx: Selected Writings in Sociology and Social Psychology,* tr., T. B. Bottomore (New York: McGraw-Hill, 1956), p. 258.

26. See for example, Ronald Fernandez, *Los Macheteros: The Wells Fargo Robbery and the Violent Struggle for Puerto Rican Independence* (New York: Prentice Hall, 1987). For an interesting discussion of the motives of the United Freedom Front, see Kevin Cullen's "Search for 'Cop-killers' Comes to an End," *The Boston Globe,* 5 November 1984.

27. Leon Trotsky, *Against Individual Terrorism* (New York: Pathfinder, 1974), p. 8.

28. Peter Janke, *Guerrilla and Terrorist Organisations: A World Directory and Bibliography* (New York: Macmillan, 1983) p. 433.

29. Carlos Marighella, "Mini-manual of the Urban Guerrilla"; see also Abraham Guillen, *Philosophy of the Urban Guerrilla,* trans. Donald Hodges (New York: William Morrow, 1973).

30. Viewing themselves as the true people of God, Identity Christians utilize specific end-of-time prophetic scriptures as proof of their activities, e.g.: "then let them which be in Judaea flee into the *mountains*" (Matthew 24:16, KJV); "and to the woman were given two wings of a great eagle, that she might fly into the *wilderness*. . . . where she is nourished for a time" (Revelation 12:14, KJV). Emphasis added.

31. Louis Ray Beam, "Common Sense."

32. Walter Laqueur, *Terrorism: A Study of National and International Political Violence* (Boston: Little, Brown, 1977), pp. 184–185.

33. Kevin Cullen, "Search for 'Cop-Killers' Comes to an End," *Boston Globe,* 5 November 1984, p. 4.

34. Walter Laqueur, *Terrorism: A Study of National and International Political Violence,* p. 184.

35. From FBI interview dated 10 May 1985, p. 5–6, submitted as evidence in United States v. Hoover (CR–86–338), U.S. District Court, Arizona.

36. United States v. Miles et al. (CR–87–20008), U.S. District Court, Western District of Arkansas, Fort Smith Division.

37. Carlos Marighela, *For the Liberation of Brazil,* p. 66.

38. United States v. Fort (86–CR–572), U.S. District Court, Northern District of Illinois, Eastern Division.

39. "FBI Says Two Men Planned Bomb Attack on Homosexual Bar," *Birmingham News,* 15 May 1990, p. 3a.

40. See Response of United States of America to James D. Ellison's Motion for Reduction of Sentence, 11 May 1988, United States v. Ellison et al. (CR–85–20006), and United States v. Ellison (CR–85–200017), U.S. District Court, Western District of Arkansas, Fort Smith Division.

41. "Group Weighed Cyanide Assault, Witness Testifies," *Birmingham News,* 23 February 1988, p. 6b.

42. "Mail-bomb Probers Still Puzzled by Letter," *Birmingham News,* 31 December 1989, p. 32a.

43. Indictment filed 28 May 1986, United States v. Levasseur et al. (CR–86–00180), U.S. District Court, District of Massachusetts.

44. Indictment filed 6 July 1983, United States v. Torres et al. (83–CR–494), U.S. District Court, Northern District of Illinois, Eastern Division.

45. See, for example, Russell and Miller, "Profile of a Terrorist"; Rubenstein, *Alchemists of Revolution;* and National Governors Association, *Domestic Terrorism.*

46. National Governor's Association, *Domestic Terrorism,* p. 5.

47. For additional reading on female involvement in terrorism, see Daniel E. Georges-Abeyie's "Women as Terrorists," in *The Terrorism Reader,* ed. Walter Laqueur and Yonah Alexander (New York: Meridian, 1987) pp. 260–266; and Carolsue Holland and B. Mark Cato, "Are Women Terrorists Different? An Analysis of Current Social Science Scholarship," Washington, DC: Academy of Criminal Justice Sciences, 1989.

48. National Governors Association, *Domestic Terrorism,* pp. 5–6.

49. Sentencing at 46–47, United States v. Schmitt et al. (CR–6–84–125–1), District of Minnesota, Third Division.

50. FBI Interview, United States v. Miles et al. (CR–87–20008), U.S. District Court, Western District of Arkansas, Fort Smith Division.

Chapter 4

The Righteous and the Extremists of the Right

1. John Turner, *The Ku Klux Klan: A History of Racism and Violence* (Montgomery, AL: The Southern Poverty Law Center), pp. 6–11.

2. L. J. Davis, "Ballad of an American Terrorist," *Harper's Magazine*, July 1986 (Vol. 273), p. 57.

3. L. J. Davis, p. 57.

4. *The International Jew* was originally published by "The Dearborn Independent," Ford Motor Company's periodical. It is considered must reading for those believing in a Jewish conspiracy to dominate the world economically. Although no longer published by major publishing firms, smaller publishers, such as neo-Nazi William Pierce's National Alliance, publish it and a variety of other anti-semitic works, including Pierce's *The Turner Diaries*.

5. In testimony given by Bruce Pierce to FBI agents and presented as evidence in United States v. Pierce et al. (CR–85–001M), U.S. District Court, Western District of Washington, Seattle Division.

6. Internal Revenue Service document introduced as evidence in United States v. Miles et al. (CR–87–200008), U.S. District Court, Western District of Arkansas, Fort Smith Division.

7. Droege first came to the attention of federal authorities in 1981. Along with KKK Grand Wizard Don Black and eight others, Droege helped plot the failed invasion of the Caribbean island of Dominica. He was arrested in April 1981 and was convicted in federal court in Louisiana for violating the Neutrality Act. Droege was a West German by nationality. He served two years of a three-year sentence and was deported with the stipulation that he not return to the United States. While still on probation, Droege was arrested in Alabama as he boarded an aircraft carrying a concealed weapon and a small quantity of cocaine. In February 1985, he was convicted and sentenced to thirteen years in prison on illegal alien, drug, and federal weapons charges. Judgment and Probation/Commitment Order, United States v. Walter Wolfgang Droege (CR–84–C–301–NE), United States District Court, Northern District of Alabama.

8. The Anti-Defamation League of B'nai B'rith, *Extremism on the Right* (New York, NY: The Anti-Defamation League of B'nai B'rith, 1988), p. 130.

9. Thomas Martinez, *Brotherhood of Murder* (New York: McGraw-Hill, 1988), p. 23.

10. "Group Weighed Cyanide Assault, Witness Testifies," *Birmingham News,* 23 February 1988, p. 6b.

11. Jury's verdict in United States v. Robert E. Miles et al. (CR–87–20008), United States District Court, Western District of Arkansas, Fort Smith Division.

12. Government's Pre-trial Memorandum at 2–4, United States v. Robert E. Miles et al (CR–87–20008), United States District Court, Western District of Arkansas, Fort Smith Division.

13. Louis Beam, *Common Sense*, p. 14. Presented as evidence in United States v. Robert E. Miles et al. (CR–87–20008), United States District Court, Western District of Arkansas, Fort Smith Division.

14. "Acquittal of the Haters," *Time*, 18 April 1988, p. 33.

15. Connie Cass, "Town Decks Out to Oppose Aryan Visit," *Birmingham News,* 3 October 1989, p. 1f.

16. Thomas Martinez, *Brotherhood of Murder* (New York: McGraw-Hill, 1988), p. 235.

17. Internal Revenue Service document introduced as evidence at 2, United States v. Miles et al. (CR–87–200008), U.S. District Court, Western District of Arkansas, Fort Smith Division.

18. Latin for "power of the county."

19. Internal Revenue Service document introduced as evidence at 2, United States v. Miles et al. (CR–87–200008), U.S. District Court, Western District of Arkansas, Fort Smith Division.

20. Ibid.

21. Internal Revenue Service document introduced as evidence at 4, United States v. Miles et al. (CR–87–200008), U.S. District Court, Western District of Arkansas, Fort Smith Division.

22. The Anti-Defamation League of B'nai B'rith, *Extremism on the Right* (New York, NY: The Anti-Defamation League of B'nai B'rith, 1988), pp. 106–107.

23. In Response of United States of America to James D. Ellison's Motion for reduction of sentence at 6, United States v. Ellison et al. (CR–85–20006), and United States v. Ellison (CR–85–200017), U.S. District Court, Western District of Arkansas, Fort Smith Division.

24. In trial transcripts at sentencing on 27 March 1985 at 46–47, United States v. Wilhelm Schmitt, Roger Roy Luther and Ernest Foust

(CR–6–84–124), and United States v. Wilhelm Schmitt and Harry Mott (CR–6–84–125), U.S. District Court, District of Minnesota.

25. Presented in testimony at request for bail at 3–4, United States v. Wilhelm Schmitt, Roger Roy Luther, and Ernest Foust (CR–6–84–124), U.S. District Court, District of Minnesota.

26. Indictment filed 21 November 1984, United States v. Wilhelm Ernst Schmitt and Harry Leroy Mott (CR–6–84–125), U.S. District Court, District of Minnesota.

27. Indictment filed 21 November 1984 at 3, United States v. Wilhelm Ernst Schmitt, Roger Roy Luther, and Ernest W. Foust (CR–6–84–124), U.S. District Court, District of Minnesota.

28. Presented in testimony at request for bail at 4, United States v. Wilhelm Schmitt, Roger Roy Luther, and Ernest Foust (CR–6–84–124), U.S. District Court, District of Minnesota.

29. Judgment and probation/commitment orders, United States v. Wilhelm Ernst Schmitt, Roger Roy Luther, and Ernest W. Foust, (CR–6–84–124), and United States v. Wilhelm Ernst Schmitt and Harry Leroy Mott (CR–6–84–125), U.S. District Court, District of Minnesota.

30. Robert Imrie, "Posse Comitatus is a Shell of Former Racist Self," *Birmingham News,* 22 November 1990, p. 2b.

31. In January 1988, William Potter Gale, founding father of SPC, was sentenced in federal court in Las Vegas, Nevada. He and four other members of the "Committee of the States" had been found guilty of conspiracy and of threatening the lives of IRS agents and a judge in Nevada. Gale died less than a year later at the age of seventy-one. The Anti-Defamation League of B'nai B'rith, *Extremism on the Right* (New York, NY: The Anti-Defamation League of B'nai B'rith, 1988), p. 97.

32. Robert Imrie, "Posse Comitatus is a Shell of Former Racist Self," *Birmingham News,* 22 November 1990, p. 2b.

33. Internal Revenue Service document introduced as evidence at 12, United States v. Miles et al. (CR–87–200008), U.S. District Court, Western District of Arkansas, Fort Smith Division.

34. L. J. Davis, "Ballad of an American Terrorist," *Harper's Magazine,* July 1986, p. 58.

35. Government's Pre-Trial Memorandum at 2–6, United States v. Miles et al. (CR–87–200008), U.S. District Court, Western District of Arkansas, Fort Smith Division.

36. Second Superseding Indictment at 90, United States v. Pierce et al. (CR–85–001M), U.S. District Court, Western District of Washington, Seattle Division.

37. Ibid. (Other Order members present included David Tate, Gary Yarbrough, and David Lane.)

38. In one of the last Order publications, three Order members, Denver Parmenter, Yarbrough, and Randolph Duey, were pictured with the caption "Federal P.O.W." Also included was a picture of Thomas Martinez, the Order member-turned-informant, who led FBI agents to Mathhews. Under his picture were the comments:

> "Tom Martinez—his name will live in infamy. This man is responsible for the events that led to the death of Robert Mathews. This man is henceforth branded an outlaw to our Race."

Presented as evidence in United States v. Pierce et al. (CR–85–001M), U.S. District Court, Western District of Washington, Seattle Division.

39. Thomas Martinez, *Brotherhood of Murder* (New York: McGraw-Hill, 1988), pp. 201–218.

40. Ibid., p. 216.

41. Presented in testimony in United States v. James Ellison and William Thomas (CR–85–20006), U.S. District Court, Western District of Arkansas, Fort Smith Division.

42. Transcripts of previous grand jury testimony at 13, presented as evidence in United States v. James Ellison and William Thomas (CR–85–20006), U.S. District Court, Western District of Arkansas, Fort Smith Division.

43. Affidavit of FBI Special Agent Jack Knox at 1–5, presented as evidence in United States v. James Wallington (CR–85–20010), United States District Court, Western District of Arkansas, Fort Smith Division.

44. From Ruth Schweizer's *Illegal Tax Protester Information Book* (Washington, DC: Department of the Treasury, Internal Revenue Service, Office of Intelligence, Criminal Investigation Division, 1986), pp. 15–16. Presented as evidence in United States v. Robert E. Miles et al. (CR–85–20008), U.S. District Court, Western District of Arkansas, Fort Smith Division.

45. FBI interview with Kerry Noble presented as evidence in United States v. James Ellison and William Thomas (CR–85–20006), U.S. District Court, Western District of Arkansas, Fort Smith Division.

46. Indictment at 6–7, United States v. Miles et al. (CR–87–20008), U.S. District Court, Western District of Arkansas, Fort Smith Division.

47. In Response of United States of America to James D. Ellison's Motion for Reduction of Sentence at 7, United States v. Ellison et al. (CR–85–20006); and United States v. Ellison (CR–85–200017), U.S. District Court, Western District of Arkansas, Fort Smith Division.

48. Indictment at 3, United States v. James D. Ellison and William Thomas (CR–85–20006), U.S. District Court, Western District of Arkansas, Fort Smith Division.

49. Government's Pre-Trial Memorandum at 5, United States v. Miles et al. (CR–87–20008), U.S. District Court, Western District of Arkansas, Fort Smith Division.

50. Government's Pre-Trial Memorandum, Indictment, and Judgment in United States v. Miles et al. (CR–87–20008), U.S. District Court, Western District of Arkansas, Fort Smith Division.

51. Indictment at 2, United States v. Robert Smalley and William Brugle (CR–85–20007), U.S. District Court, Western District of Arkansas, Fort Smith Division.

52. "FBI Moves in on Compound," *Southwest Times Record,* 23 April 1985, p.5a.

53. Judgment and Probation/Commitment Orders, United States v. James D. Ellison et al. (CR–85–20017), U.S. District Court, Western District of Arkansas, Fort Smith Division.

54. Judgment and Probation/Commitment Orders, United States v. Robert Smalley and William Brugle (CR–85–20007), U.S. District Court, Western District of Arkansas, Fort Smith Division.

55. Judgment and Probation/Commitment Orders, United States v. James D. Ellison and William Thomas (CR–85–20006); and United States v. Steve Scott (CR–85–20014), U.S. District Court, Western District of Arkansas, Fort Smith Division.

56. Judgment and Probation/Commitment Order, United States v. James Ellison and Kent Yates aka Lonnie Robinson (CR–85–20016), U.S. District Court, Western District of Arkansas, Fort Smith Division.

57. His closest friend was Kenneth Loff, an older farmer who became one of the original members of The Order. L. J. Davis, "Ballad of an American Terrorist," *Harper's Magazine,* July 1986 (Vol. 273), p. 53.

58. Thomas Martinez, *Brotherhood of Murder* (New York: McGraw-Hill, 1988), p. 41.

59. Indictment at 6, United States v. Miles et al. (CR–87–20008), U.S. District Court, Western District of Arkansas, Fort Smith Division.

60. Second Superseding Indictment at 9, United States v. Bruce Carroll Pierce et al., (CR–85–001M), U.S. District Court, Western District of Washington, Seattle Division.

61. Second Superseding Indictment at 9–13, United States v. Bruce Carroll Pierce et al. (CR–85–001M), U.S. District Court, Western District

of Washington, Seattle Division. Twenty-three members were eventually indicted, but evidence reveals that others, like "Bud" Cutler, Daniel Ray Bauer, Charles Ostrout, and Richard Scutari's brother, Frank, were members as well.

62. Thomas Martinez, *Brotherhood of Murder* (New York: McGraw-Hill, 1988), p. 26.

63. Although convicted, Pierce jumped bond and returned to the group, remaining a fugitive until his capture in 1985.

64. Second Superseding Indictment at 16, United States v. Bruce Carroll Pierce et al. (CR–85–001M), U.S. District Court, Western District of Washington, Seattle Division.

65. $230,000 was in American currency and coins, another $4,000 was in Canadian money, and $300,000 was in checks. The checks were discarded. Second Superseding Indictment at 92 and 115, United States v. Bruce Carroll Pierce et al. (CR–85–001M), U.S. District Court, Western District of Washington, Seattle Division.

66. Second Superseding Indictment at 17, United States v. Bruce Carroll Pierce et al. (CR–85–001M), U.S. District Court, Western District of Washington, Seattle Division.

67. Thomas Martinez, *Brotherhood of Murder* (New York: McGraw-Hill, 1988), pp. 88–98, 113–115.

68. Second Superseding Indictment at 18 and 93, United States v. Bruce Carroll Pierce et al. (CR–85–001M), U.S. District Court, Western District of Washington, Seattle Division.

69. The name was later changed to White Aryan Resistance (WAR). For more information on Lane, see The Anti-Defamation League of B'nai B'rith, *Extremism on the Right* (New York, NY: The Anti-Defamation League of B'nai B'rith, 1988), pp. 112–113.

70. Although Tom Martinez claimed that four men were involved in the killing, only three were ever indicted: Pierce, Richard Scutari, and Lane. However, Scutari, as well as Jean Craig, were acquitted in October 1987.

71. Superseding Indictment at 5, United States v. Charles Edward Ostrout (CR–85–0102), U.S. District Court, Northern District of California. See also Second Superseding Indictment at 12, United States v. Bruce Carroll Pierce et al. (CR–85–001M), U.S. District Court, Western District of Washington, Seattle Division.

72. Thomas Martinez, *Brotherhood of Murder* (New York: McGraw-Hill, 1988), pp. 106–108.

73. Indictment at 4, United States v. Charles Edward Ostrout (CR–85–0102), U.S. District Court, Northern District of California.

74. Pierce was given $642,000 to distribute to Mathews' idols. On July 27, Dan Gayman, a former high school principal and organizer of the Identity-affiliated "Church of Israel" in Schell City, Missouri, reportedly received $10,000 of the stolen money. Indictment at 14, United States v. Miles et al. (CR–87–20008), U.S. District Court, Western District of Arkansas, Fort Smith Division.

75. In early August, Bob Mathews traveled to Conectah, Michigan to meet with Robert Miles. Two days later he flew to Arlington, Virginia, where he allegedly gave $50,000 to his mentor, William Pierce of the National Alliance. Indictment at 15, United States v. Miles et al (CR–87–20008), U.S. District Court, Western District of Arkansas, Fort Smith Division.

76. According to testimony later given by Pierce and Richard Scutari, Louis Beam received $100,000; $300,000 went to Glenn Miller (although he admitted to only receiving $200,000); and nearly $300,000 was given to Tom Metger and the White Aryan Resistance. In Response of United States of America to James D. Ellison's Motion for Reduction of Sentence at 7–8, United States v. Ellison et al. (CR–85–20006), U.S. District Court, Western District of Arkansas, Fort Smith Division.

77. Complaint at 6, United States v. Mark Frank Jones and Michael Stanley Norris (CR–85–00010), U.S. District Court, District of Utah, Central Division; transferred to U.S. District Court, Northern District of Alabama, Northern Division and renumbered as CR–85–HM–79–S and CR–85–HM–80–S.

78. From "Declaration of War," presented as evidence in United States v. Bruce Carroll Pierce et al. (CR–85–001M), U.S. District Court, Western District of Washington, Seattle Division.

79. From "Open Letter to the U.S. Congress," presented as evidence in United States v. Bruce Carroll Pierce et al. (CR–85–001M), U.S. District Court, Western District of Washington, Seattle Division.

80. Actually, David Tate may have signed the "declaration of war." The only three names on the declaration I have not positively identified are those of Paul Anderson, Steve Brant, and a third party who signed using a symbol that resembles either a "D," a "T," or a combination of both. The third party may have been Tate.

81. Complaint at 4–6, United States v. Mark Frank Jones and Michael Stanley Norris (CR–85–00010), U.S. District Court, District of Utah, Central Division; transferred to U.S. District Court, Northern District of Alabama, Northern Division and renumbered as CR–85–HM–79–S and CR–85–HM–80– S.

82. Thomas Martinez, *Brotherhood of Murder* (New York: McGraw-Hill, 1988), pp. 192–200.

83. Indictment and Judgment and Probation/Commitment Order, United States v. Charles Edward Ostrout (CR–85–0102), U.S. District Court, Northern District of California.

84. Second Superseding Indictment at 12, United States v. Bruce Carroll Pierce et al. (CR–85–001M), U.S. District Court, Western District of Washington, Seattle Division.

85. 18 USC, sect. 1962.

86. A twenty-fourth person, Ian Royal Stewart, was allowed to plead guilty because of his age and limited involvement, and his name was dropped from the final indictment.

87. Although the local district attorney in Denver sent representatives to the Seattle trial, polled jurors after the trial, and found support for a murder conviction based on the evidence presented regarding the Berg killing, the Colorado D.A.'s office refrained from prosecuting.

88. Judgment and Probation/Commitment Orders, United States v. David Lane et al. (87–CR–114), U.S. District Court, District of Colorado.

89. Terrorist Research and Analytical Center, *Terrorism in the United States: 1989* (Washington, DC: U.S. Government Printing Office, 1990), p. 4.

Chapter 5

Right-Wing Terrorists Try a Comeback

1. Thomas Martinez, *Brotherhood of Murder* (New York: McGraw-Hill, 1988), p. 217.

2. Indictment at 12–13, United States v. David Dorr et al. (CR–88–30004), U.S. District Court, District of Idaho.

3. Indictment at 13, United States v. David Dorr et al. (CR–88–30004), U.S. District Court, District of Idaho.

4. Indictment at 7–21, United States v. David Dorr et al. (CR–88–30004), U.S. District Court, District of Idaho.

5. Anti-Defamation League of B'nai B'rith, *Hate Groups in America* (New York: The Anti-Defamation League of B/nai B'rith, 1988), p. 70.

6. Indictment, United States v. David Dorr et al. (CR–88–30004), U.S. District Court, District of Idaho.

7. Judgment in a Criminal Case, United States v. David Dorr et al. (CR–88–30004), U.S. District Court, District of Idaho.

8. The Anti-Defamation League of B'nai B'rith, *Extremism on the Right* (New York, NY: The Anti-Defamation League of B'nai B'rith, 1988), p. 2.

9. Government's Response to Defendant Oliphant's Objection to Pre-sentence Report at 9, United States v. Jack Maxwell Oliphant et al. (CR–86–336–PCT), U.S. District Court, District of Arizona, Prescott Division.

10. Ibid.

11. Government's Response to Defendant Oliphant's Objection to Pre-sentence Report at 8, United States v. Jack Maxwell Oliphant et al. (CR–86–336–PCT), U.S. District Court, District of Arizona, Prescott Division.

12. See Statement of FBI Special Agent Ronald Myers at 1, United States v. Foster Thomas Hoover (CR–86–338–PCT–CLH), U.S. District Court, District of Arizona, Prescott Division.

13. FBI interview presented as evidence in United States v. Foster Thomas Hoover (CR–86–338–PCT–CLH), U.S. District Court, District of Arizona, Prescott Division.

14. See Statement of Probable Cause, United States v. Foster Thomas Hoover (CR–86–338–PCT–CLH), U.S. District Court, District of Arizona, Prescott Division.

15. Although these events are recounted in the indictments against group members, the best summary of this comedy of errors is contained in FBI Special Agent Ronald Myers Affadavit in United States v. Foster Thomas Hoover (CR–86–338–PCT–CLH), U.S. District Court, District of Arizona, Prescott Division.

16. Judgment and Probation/Commitment Orders, United States v. Jack Maxwell Oliphant et al. (CR–86–336–PCT), U.S. District Court, District of Arizona, Prescott Division.

17. Indictment and Criminal Court Docket, United States v. Rita Schlect (CR–86–337–PCT), U.S. District Court, District of Arizona, Prescott Division.

18. Judgment and Probation/Commitment Order and Consent to Transfer of Case for Plea and Sentence, United States v. J. R. Hagen and Tom H. Palmer (CR–86–292–TUC), U.S. District Court, District of Arizona, Tucson Division.

19. Superseding Indictment and Criminal Docket, United States v. Foster Thomas Hoover (CR–86–338–PCT–CLH), U.S. District Court, District of Arizona, Prescott Division.

20. John Turner, *The Ku Klux Klan: A History of Racism and Violence* (Montgomery, AL: Southern Poverty Law Center, 1986), p. 61.

21. Thomas Martinez, *Brotherhood of Murder* (New York: McGraw-Hill, 1988), pp. 72–73.

22. Indictment at 3, United States v. Stephen Samuel Miller et al. (87–2–01 thru 05 CR–3), U.S. District Court, Eastern District of North Carolina, Fayetteville Division.

23. Bobby Person v. Glenn Miller, Jr. and the Carolina Knights of the Ku Klux Klan.

24. Indictment at 8, United States v. Stephen Samuel Miller et al. (87–2–01 thru 05 CR–3), U.S. District Court, Eastern District of North Carolina, Fayetteville Division.

25. Glenn Miller was sentenced to six months in prison and three years probation. See The Anti-Defamation League of B'nai B'rith's *Hate Groups in America* for further discussion. (New York: Anti-Defamation League of B'nai B'rith, 1988), p. 52.

26. Indictment at 11, United States v. Stephen Samuel Miller et al. (87–2–01 thru 05 CR–3), U.S. District Court, Eastern District of North Carolina, Fayetteville Division.

27. Indictment, United States v. Frazier Glenn Miller, Jr. (87–31–01–CR–5), U.S. District Court, Eastern District of North Carolina, Raleigh Division.

28. Indictment at 3–5, United States v. Robert Eugene Jackson, Douglas Lawrence Sheets, and Frazier Glenn Miller, Jr. (87–03247–01 thru 03–CR–S–4), U.S. District Court, Western District of Missouri, Southern Division. Prosecution of Glenn Miller was transferred to U.S. District Court in the Eastern District of North Carolina (87–57–01–CR–5).

29. Judgment and Probation/Commitment Orders, United States v. Stephen Samuel Miller et al. (87–2–01 thru 05 CR–3), U.S. District Court, Eastern District of North Carolina, Fayetteville Division.

30. Although most sources list Wydra as either "not being charged" or "charges were dismissed," they refer to Wydra's capture in Ozark, Missouri on April 30, 1987, with Robert Jackson, Doug Sheets, and Frazier Miller. He was found not guilty in a jury trial on April 13, 1987, in the case in Fayetteville, North Carolina. From there he travelled to Ozark, Missouri and met with Glenn Miller. Because of his acquittal, authorities apparently decided not to charge him again.

31. Judgment in a Criminal Case, United States v. Robert Eugene Jackson, Douglas Lawrence Sheets, and Frazier Glenn Miller, Jr. (87–03247–01 thru 03–CR–S–4), U.S. District Court, Western District of Missouri, Southern Division.

32. Indictment, United States v. Frazier Glenn Miller, Jr. (87–31–

01–CR–5), U.S. District Court, Eastern District of North Carolina, Raleigh Division.

33. In Response of United States of America to James D. Ellison's Motion for Reduction of Sentence at 1–12, United States v. Ellison et al. (CR–85–20006), U.S. District Court, Western District of Arkansas, Fort Smith Division.

34. Indictment, United States v. Robert Edward Miles et al. (CR–87–20008), U.S. District Court, Western District of Arkansas, Fort Smith Division.

35. In Response of United States of America to James D. Ellison's Motion for Reduction of Sentence at 7, United States v. Ellison et al. (CR–85–20006), U.S. District Court, Western District of Arkansas, Fort Smith Division.

36. Statements later recanted by Bruce Carroll Pierce put the figure given to Miller at between $260,000 and $300,000.

37. Personal interview with assistant U.S. attorney involved in the prosecution of right-wing terrorists who wished to remain anonymous, May 14, 1990.

38. L. J. Davis, "Ballad of an American Terrorist," *Harper's Magazine,* July 1986 (Vol. 273), p. 60.

39. "Supremacists to Gather in Harrison," *Arkansas Democrat,* 8 October 1989, P. 3b.

40. Anti-Defamation League of B'nai B'rith, *Hate Groups in America* (New York: The Anti-Defamation League of B/nai B'rith, 1988), pp. 56–57.

41. Steve Miletich, "Frank Silva Seen as the 'New Leader' of The Order," *Seattle Post-Intelligencer,* 31 December 1985.

42. Lisa Schnellinger, "Order will Survive, Jailed Member Vows," *Seattle Post-Intelligencer,* 31 December 1985, p. a 1.

43. See Murphy v. Missouri Department of Corrections, [No. N84–38–C (E.D.Mo. Dec. 19, 1985), aff'd in part, rev'd in part, 814 F.2d 1252 (8th Cir. 1987), and McCabe v. Arave [626 F. Supp. 1199 (D. Idaho 1986), aff'd in part, vac'd in part, rev'd in part, 827 F.2d 634 (9th Cir. 1987).

44. Thomas Martinez, *Brotherhood of Murder* (New York: McGraw-Hill, 1988). pp. 72–73.

45. David Foster, "Aging 'Aryan Warrior' Passes Torch to Young Skinheads," *Birmingham News,* 19 April 1989, p. 6b.

46. U.S. Attorney General Dick Thornburgh, "Four Tulsa Skinheads Plead Guilty to Criminal Charges," press release by the Department of Justice, 24 January 1991.

47. "Scalping the Skinheads," *Time,* 5 November 1990, p. 37.

48. "Tom Metzger Home to Be Sold," *Birmingham News,* 22 February 1991, p. 3a.

49. See Second Superseding Indictment at 41–82 for an extensive listing of property bought or owned by Order members and subject to forfeiture, United States v. Bruce Carroll Pierce et al. (CR–85–001M), U.S. District Court, Western District of Washington, Seattle Division.

50. Thomas Martinez, *Brotherhood of Murder* (New York: McGraw-Hill, 1988), pp. 231–232.

51. Indictment, United States v. J. R. Hagen and Tom H. Palmer (CR–86–292–TUC), U.S. District Court, District of Arizona, Tucson Division.

Chapter 6

Leftist and Single-Issue Terrorism

1. R. W. Fontaine, *Terrorism: The Cuban Connection* (New York: Crane, Russak and Company, 1988).

2. Terrorist Research and Analytical Center, Federal Bureau of Investigation, *Terrorism in the United States: 1988,* (Washington, DC: U.S. Government Printing Office, 1989).

3. Plea Agreement dated 14 November 1990 at 12–13, United States v. Whitehorn et al. (CR–88–0145), U.S. District Court, District of Columbia.

4. Although Edwin Sutherland's theory of 'differential association' has been criticized for its virtually untestable propositions, intuitive evidence abounds for its support. The lives of these young terrorists are reminiscent of the way Sutherland describes the selection and tutelage of young, professional thieves in *The Professional Thief.*

5. Peter Janke, *Guerrilla and Terrorist Organizations: A World Directory and Bibliography* (New York: Macmillan, 1983), pp. 405–407.

6. Actually, eight were tried for conspiracy to incite to riot. They included Abbie Hoffman, Tom Hayden, Jerry Rubin, David Dellinger, Reynard C. Davis, Lee Weiner, and John Froines. Bobby Seale, the Black Panther leader, was later tried separately due to his outbursts during court proceedings.

7. Evans was charged with battery of a police officer, resisting arrest, and mob action. She forfeited bond and fled but was arrested again in

1971 and pled guilty to the charges, receiving three months in jail and three years probation. For her activities during the "Days of Rage," Laura Whitehorn was tried and convicted of mob action and aggravated assault. Plea Agreement dated 14 November 1990 at 13–16, United States v. Whitehorn et al. (CR–88–0145), U.S. District Court, District of Columbia.

8. Derived from a Bob Dylan song, which included the lyrics "you don't have to be a weatherman to know which way the wind is blowing."

9. Ted Robert Gurr, "Political Terrorism in the United States: Historical Antecedents and Contemporary Trends," *The Politics of Terrorism*, 3rd Ed., ed. Michael Stohl (New York: Marcel Dekker, 1988), p. 563.

10. *Prairie Fire* (New York: Communications Co., 1974), p. 1.

11. Mark Rudd was convicted for his part in the "Days of Rage" in Chicago, fined $3,000, and subsequently placed on probation. Two other leading figures in the Weather Underground, Bernadine Dohrn and William Ayres, surrendered in 1980.

12. FBI interview with U.S. Magistrate Michael Dolinger (SDNY) on 11 May 1985. Presented as evidence in United States v. Whitehorn et al. (CR–88–0145), U.S. District Court, District of Columbia.

13. Chesimard remains a fugitive, living in Cuba. Since her escape she has published a book detailing her life and her struggle for the revolution. She remains a popular cult heroine among radical elements of the black community. See for example *Jet* magazine's recent commentary on her "rightful" contestation of her father's will from Cuba to avoid appearing in the United States and facing arrest. *Jet*, 18 February 1991, p. 30.

14. Plea Agreement dated 14 November 1990 at 12–13, United States v. Whitehorn et al. (CR–88–0145), U.S. District Court, District of Columbia.

15. Eugene Methvin, "Terror Network, U.S.A.," *Reader's Digest*, December, 1984, pp. 111–112.

16. Donald Weems, Judy Clark, David Gilbert, and Sam Brown each received seventy-five years-to-life sentences for the robbery and murders in Nyack. Kathy Boudin pled guilty and received a twenty year-to-life sentence. Others, who aided members after the robbery, received lesser sentences. In addition, prosecutors provided sufficient evidence to convict Silvia Baraldini, the legal aide of attorney Susan Tipograph, and she and Nathaniel Burns each were sentenced forty years for their roles in the Chesimard escape. Eugene Methvin, "Terror Network, U.S.A.," *Reader's Digest*, December, 1984, p. 119.

17. Indictment unsealed 5 May 1988 at 4–23, United States v. Whitehorn et al. (CR–88–0145), U.S. District Court, District of Columbia.

18. M19CO member Linda Evans had lived in Austin in the late

1970s and had knowledge of the types of equipment used in her father's industrial construction business, so it was not surprising that the explosives had been stolen from an Austin construction firm in 1980. Elizabeth Duke, Evans' friend and a member of M19CO, was a school teacher in Austin as well. Significant amounts of the explosives stolen in the burglary in Austin remain unaccounted for. Indictment unsealed 5 May 1988 at 15, United States v. Whitehorn et al. (CR–88–0145), U.S. District Court, District of Columbia.

19. Judgment and Probation/Commitment Orders, United States v. Susan Lisa Rosenberg and Timothy Adolph Blunk (CR–84–360), U.S. District Court, District of New Jersey.

20. Opinion filed 11 April 1989 at 2, United States v. Whitehorn et al. (CR–88–0145), U.S. District Court, District of Columbia.

21. Defendant Linda Evans' Memorandum in Aid of Sentencing at 4–5, United States v. Whitehorn et al. (CR–88–0145). U.S. District Court, District of Columbia.

22. Evans' sentence was later reduced on appeal from forty-five to thirty-five years.

23. "Seven Radicals Indicted in Capitol Bombing," *Newsday,* 12 May 1988, p. 3.

24. "Woman Gets 20–year Term for Bombing the U.S. Capitol," *Birmingham Post-Herald,* 7 December 1990, p. a12.

25. Judgment in a Criminal Case, United States v. Whitehorn et al. (CR–88–0145), U.S. District Court, District of Columbia.

26. "Woman Gets 20-year Term for Bombing the U.S. Capitol," *Birmingham Post-Herald,* 7 December 1990, p. a12.

27. John Harris, "Domestic Terrorism in the 1980s," *FBI Law Enforcement Bulletin,* October 1987, p. 10.

28. John Kendall, "Killing Suspect Ordered Returned to New York; Black Liberation Army Demonstrators Support Shakur at Hearing," *Los Angeles Times,* 19 February 1986, Metro section, Part 2, p. 3, col. 1.

29. Indictment, United States v. Coltrane Chimurenga et al. (84–CR–000818), U.S. District Court, Southern District of New York.

30. Ellen Cates, News release by United Press International for distribution to the New York Metro area, 23 October 1984.

31. Arnold H. Lubasch, "A Rehearsal for a Stickup: Tape Linked to Brinks Case," *The New York Times,* p. b1.

32. Arthur Spiegelman, "FBI Seizes Nine Black Radicals: Says They Planned Court Raid," News release by Reuters, Ltd. for distribution to the New York area, 18 October 1984.

33. Arnold H. Lubasch, "7 Black Radicals Acquitted of Robbery Plots but Convicted of Other Charges," *The New York Times*, 6 August 1985, p. a2.

34. Judgment and Probation/Commitment Orders, United States v. Coltrane Chimurenga et al. (84–CR–000818), U.S. District Court, Southern District of New York.

35. John Impemba, "Radicals Charged in Terror Spree," *The Boston Herald*, 8 March 1987, p. 14.

36. "Terrorist Shoot-out with FBI Avoided," *Daily Hampshire Gazette*, 13 November 1984.

37. Christopher King, the only black member of the group, and Karl Laaman joined in 1980. Laaman served as an SDS organizer at the University of New Hampshire in 1970 while attending school as a parolee from Attica prison. Later convicted in the 1972 bombing of a New Hampshire police station, he joined the UFF after his release from prison. Richard Williams joined the group in 1981; Barbara Curzi, in 1982. With the exception of Curzi and Carole Manning, all of the members were in their late thirties when the UFF members were finally arrested in late 1984. The youngest was Curzi, the twenty-seven year old wife of Karl Laaman. See Kevin Cullen, "Search for 'Cop-Killers' Comes to an End," *The Boston Herald*, 5 November 1984, p. 1.

38. Kevin Cullen, "Search for 'Cop-Killers' Comes to an End," *The Boston Herald*, 5 November 1984, p. 1.

39. Indictment, United States v. Raymond Luc Levasseur (CR–86–180), U.S. District Court, District of Massachusetts.

40. Indictment, United States v. Patricia Gros (CR–84–222), U.S. District Court, Northern District of Ohio, Eastern Division.

41. Judgment and Probation/Commitment Order, United States v. Patricia Gros (CR–84–222), U.S. District Court, Northern District of Ohio, Eastern Division.

42. Terrorist Research and Analytical Center, Federal Bureau of Investigation, *Terrorism in the United States: 1987* (Washington, DC: U.S. Government Printing Office, 1988).

43. Terrorist Research and Analytical Center, Federal Bureau of Investigation, *Terrorism in the United States: 1986* (Washington, DC: U.S. Government Printing Office, 1987).

44. Indictment, United States v. Raymond Luc Levasseur (CR–86–180), U.S. District Court, District of Massachusetts.

45. "Black Activist Pleads Guilty to Sedition," *Birmingham News*, 3 December 1987, p. a-2.

46. Manning was convicted of three counts: two counts of five years each and one count for two years. Although the FBI's annual report (1989) indicates she received a twelve-year sentence, actually the sentences on each count were to be served concurrently, rather than consecutively. See Judgment in a Criminal Case, United States v. Carol Ann Manning (CR–86–180–Y), U.S. District Court, District of Massachusetts.

47. "Terror Gang," *The Boston Herald,* 10 March 1987, p. 1.

48. Christopher King's sentencing disposition, for example, reads: "imprisonment. . . . as close as possible to New England. Defendant to be imprisoned at a facility where he may complete his college education." Court Docket, United States v. Raymond Luc Levasseur (CR–86–180–08), U.S. District Court, District of Massachusetts.

49. Terrorist Research and Analytical Center, Federal Bureau of Investigation, *Terrorism in the United States: 1989* (Washington, DC: U.S. Government Printing Office, 1990).

50. Peter Janke, *Guerrilla and Terrorist Organizations: A World Directory and Bibliography* (New York: Macmillan, 1983), p. 400.

51. Affidavit of FBI Special Agent Richard Hahn, United States v. Alejandrina Torres et al. (83–CR–0494), U.S. District Court, Northern District of Illinois.

52. Peter Janke, *Guerrilla and Terrorist Organizations: A World Directory and Bibliography* (New York: Macmillan, 1983), p. 398.

53. Affidavit of FBI Special Agent Richard Hahn, United States v. Alejandrina Torres et al. (83–CR–0494), U.S. District Court, Northern District of Illinois.

54. Terrorist Research and Analytical Center, Federal Bureau of Investigation, *Terrorism in the United States: 1988* (Washington, DC: U.S. Government Printing Office, 1989).

55. Terrorist Research and Analytical Center, Federal Bureau of Investigation, *FBI Analysis of Terrorist Incidents in the United States: 1982* (Washington, DC: U.S. Government Printing Office, 1983), p. 34.

56. Terrorist Research and Analytical Center, Federal Bureau of Investigation, *FBI Analysis of Terrorist Incidents in the United States: 1985* (Washington, DC: U.S. Government Printing Office, 1986), p. 19.

57. Terrorist Research and Analytical Center, Federal Bureau of Investigation, *FBI Analysis of Terrorist Incidents in the United States: 1986* (Washington, DC: U.S. Government Printing Office, 1987), pp. 16–19.

58. Terrorist Research and Analytical Center, Federal Bureau of Investigation, *FBI Analysis of Terrorist Incidents in the United States: 1982* (Washington, DC: U.S. Government Printing Office, 1983), p. 35–36.

59. Ronald Fernandez, *Los Macheteros,* (New York: Prentice Hall, 1987), p. 43. Other than the use of first-hand court documents, Fernandez's account of the robbery is probably the most elaborate description of the surrounding events and the subsequent investigation.

60. Later superseded by indictment filed 21 March 1986, United States v. Victor Manuel Gerena (CR–H–85–50), United States District Court, District of Connecticut.

61. Author's field notes, 18 August 1989, conversation with Assistant U.S. Attorney, Hartford, Connecticut.

62. Terrorist Research and Analytical Center, Federal Bureau of Investigation, *Terrorism in the United States: 1989* (Washington, DC: U.S. Government Printing Office, 1990), p. 17.

63. Ronald Fernandez, *Los Macheteros* (New York: Prentice Hall, 1987), pp. 222–223.

64. Two of the nineteen pled guilty prior to going to trial. Paul Weinberg, the only non-Machetero indicted in the case, pled guilty to one count of aiding and abetting the Macheteros in exchange for the dismissal of other charges. Luz Berrrios pled guilty to one count of conspiracy and was sentenced to five years in prison. Judgment in a Criminal Case, United States v. Victor Manuel Gerena (CR–H–85–50), U.S. District Court, District of Connecticut.

65. Carlos Ayes-Suarez was acquitted of the charges. Judgment in a Criminal Case, defendants Palmer, Ayes-Suarez, Maldonado-Rivera, Talavera, Negron, Berrios, and Weinberg, United States v. Victor Manuel Gerena (CR–H–85–50), U.S. District Court, District of Connecticut.

66. "Man Defiant at Sentencing," *Birmingham News,* 15 June 1989, p. a–2.

67. Government's Pre-Sentence Memorandum at 10–11, United States v. Fort et al. (86–CR–572), U.S. District Court, Northern District of Illinois, Eastern Division.

68. Government's Pre-Sentence Memorandum at 10, United States v. Fort et al. (86–CR–572), U.S. District Court, Northern District of Illinois, Eastern Division.

69. Richard Cloward and Lloyd Ohlin, *Delinquency and Opportunity* (New York: Free Press, 1960).

70. Government's Pre-Sentence Memorandum at 21, United States v. Fort et al. (86–CR–572), U.S. District Court, Northern District of Illinois, Eastern Division.

71. Reico Cranshaw wrote how this was accomplished: "Since our return (from Tripoli)—we immediately put into action our five-man cells

throughout thirty-five cities. . . . Thirty-five cities responded; however, it was not publicized after it became known how well disciplined the entire movement had been carried out." Government's Pre-Sentence Memorandum at 25, United States v. Fort et al. (86–CR–572), U.S. District Court, Northern District of Illinois, Eastern Division.

72. Government's Pre-Sentence Memorandum at 25–26, United States v. Fort et al. (86–CR–572), U.S. District Court, Northern District of Illinois, Eastern Division.

73. Indictment, United States v. Fort et al. (86–CR–572), U.S. District Court, Northern District of Illinois, Eastern Division.

74. "Deadly Street Gang's Members Sentenced for Terrorism Plot; Leader Gets 80 Years," *Birmingham News,* 30 December 1987, p. 1b.

75. Davis was allowed to plea bargain in exchange for his assistance in cracking the cryptic code used by el Rukn members when talking to Jeff Fort from prison in Bastrop, Texas. His fifteen-year sentence was suspended. Cranshaw, 56, was sentenced to sixty-three years and fined $241,000. Knox, 35, received a fifty-four-year sentence and a fine of $229,000, while McAnderson, 37, was given fifty-one years in prison and fined $241,000. The youngest member of the group, twenty-four-year-old Roosevelt Hawkins, received the lightest punishment, a nine-year imprisonment. Judgment and Probation/Commitment Orders, United States v. Fort et al. (86–CR–572), U.S. District Court, Northern District of Illinois, Eastern Division.

76. Tom Fitzpatrick, "Fitz," *New York Times,* 14–20 June 1989, p. 5.

77. David Foreman, *Ecodefense: A Field Guide to Monkeywrenching* (Ned Ludd Books, 1985).

78. Edward Abbey, *The Monkeywrench Gang* (Avon Books, 1976).

79. CBS News, Transcripts of "60 Minutes" broadcast 4 March 1990 (New York: CBS News, 1990).

80. Second Superseding Indictment, United States v. Mark Leslie Davis et al. (CR–89–192–PHX), U.S. District Court, District of Arizona.

81. Trial transcripts, United States v. Mark Leslie Davis et al. (CR–89–192–PHX), U.S. District Court, District of Arizona.

82. Terrorist Research and Analytical Center, Federal Bureau of Investigation, *Terrorism in the United States: 1988* (Washington, DC: U.S. Government Printing Office, 1989), p. 37–38.

83. Superseding Indictment, United States v. Davis et al. (89–CR–192–PHX), District of Arizona.

84. Tom Fitzpatrick, "Fitz," *New York Times,* 14–20 June 1989, p. 5.

85. Ilse Asplund was sentenced to thirty days in jail, five years probation, and a $2,000 fine. Baker received six months in jail, five years probation, and a $5,000 fine. Millet was sentenced to three years confinement and ordered to pay nearly $20,000 in restitution. Davis was sentenced to six years in prison. Judgment in a Criminal Case, United States v. Davis et al. (89–CR–192–PHX), District of Arizona.

86. Foreman has apparently been cooperating with federal authorities in identifying the extremist elements within the environmental movement. Despite a federal court clerk's comments in Phoenix that "it will be a long time before his sentence is formally announced" (Author's Field Notes, 14 November 1991, Phoenix, AZ), the FBI released the information in its 1991 annual report.

87. Jonathan Sidener, "Earth First! Divided by Second Thoughts," *The Arizona Republic,* 26 August 1990, pp. a1–2.

88. Ibid., pp. a1–2.

89. "U.S. Probes Animal-Rights Group for Link to Raids on Laboratories," *Chronicle of Higher Education,* 23 June 1993, p. a19.

90. "Arson fire destroys barn at Oregon State U.," *Chronicle of Higher Education,* 19 June 1991, p. a2.

Chapter 7

International Terrorist Activity in America

1. U.S. Department of State, *Patterns of Global Terrorism: 1985* (Washington, DC: U.S. Government Printing Office, 1986).

2. Ibid., p. 15.

3. Kurt Andersen, "Carnage in Lebanon," *Time,* 23 October, 1983, pp. 14–19.

4. George Church, "Targeting Gaddafi," *Time,* 21 April, 1986, pp. 18–27; See also "Seeking the Smoking Fuse," *Time,* 21 April 1986, p. 22.

5. George Church, "Hitting the Source," *Time,* 28 April 1986, pp. 16–27.

6. Brian Jenkins, *Terrorism in the 1980s* (Santa Monica, California: Rand Corporation, 1980).

7. Claire Sterling, *The Terror Network: The Secret War of International Terrorism* (New York: Holt, Rinehart, Winston, Readers Digest Guide, 1981).

8. Terrorist Research and Analytical Center, Federal Bureau of Investigation, *FBI Analysis of Terrorist Incidents and Terrorist Related Activities in the United States: 1984* (Washington, DC: U.S. Government Printing Office).

9. Terrorist Research and Analytical Center, Federal Bureau of Investigation, *Terrorism in the United States: 1988* (Washington, DC: U.S. Government Printing Office, 1989); see also *Terrorism in the United States: 1989* (Washington, DC: U.S. Government Printing Office, 1990).

10. The Omnibus Diplomatic Security and Antiterrorism Act of 1986; for a good discussion of its first use, see Steven Emersen, "Taking on Terrorists," *U.S. News & World Report,* 12 September 1988, pp. 26–34.

11. Several persons suspected of international terrorist activities have been indicted that are not on our analysis of cases. They were excluded because they were not included on the original list of names provided by the FBI. Most notably, there were several arrests related to Armenian terrorism in the period 1982–1984. Other isolated cases not included appear in the annual reports of the Terrorist Research and Analytical Center.

12. Charles Russell and Bowman Miller, "Profile of a Terrorist," *Terrorism: An International Journal,* 1(1): 17–27. See also National Governor's Association, *Domestic Terrorism* (Washington, DC: U.S. Government Printing Office, 1979); and Richard Rubenstein, *Alchemists of Revolution: Terrorism in the Modern World* (New York: Basic Books, 1987).

13. See Arocena, Direct Examination at 2117–2145, United States v. Arocena et al. (CR–83–00821–01), U.S. District Court, Southern District of New York.

14. See Government Sentencing Memorandum at 3–5, United States v. Lopez (CR–84–00880–01), U.S. District Court, Southern District of New York.

15. See Arocena, Direct Examination at 2143–44; United States v. Arocena (83–CR–821), U.S. District Court, Southern District of New York.

16. Superceding Indictment at 5–14, United States v. Arocena [(S) 83–CR–821], U.S. District Court, Southern District of New York.

17. Government's Sentencing Memorandum at 2, United States v. Remon et al. [85–CR–830 (RJW)], U.S. District Court, Southern District of New York.

18. Indictment, United States v. Remon et al. [85–CR–830 (RJW)], U.S. District Court, Southern District of New York.

19. Government Sentencing Memorandum at 18, United States v.

Remon et al. [85–CR–830 (RJW)], U.S. District Court, Southern District of New York.

20. Superceding Indictment at 20, United States v. Arocena [(S) 83–CR–821], U.S. District Court, Southern District of New York.

21. Judgment and Probation/Commitment Order, United States v. Arocena (83–CR–821), U.S. District Court, Southern District of New York.

22. Judgment and Probation/Commitment Order, United States v. Remon et al. [85–CR–830 (RJW)], U.S. District Court, Southern District of New York.

23. Superceding Indictment at 6–12, United States v. Murray et al. (CR–86–118–T), U.S. District Court, District of Massachusetts.

24. See Superceding Indictment and Statement of Facts in Support Guilty Pleas to Information #1 (The Arms Offenses), United States v. Murray et al. (CR–86–118–T), U.S. District Court, District of Massachusetts.

25. See Information and Judgment and Probation/Commitment Order, United States v. Murray et al. (CR–87–225–T), U.S. District Court, District of Massachusetts.

26. Indictment, United States v. Murphy et al. (CR–86–184–MA), U.S. District Court, District of Massachusetts.

27. Judgment and Probation/Commitment Order, United States v. Murphy et al. (CR–86–186–MA), U.S. District Court, District of Massachusetts.

28. Executive Order #12543, dated 7 January 1986.

29. Executive Order #12544, dated 8 January 1986.

30. Superseding Indictment, United States v. Hawamda et al. (CR–88–00168), U.S. District Court, Eastern District of Virginia, Alexandria Division.

31. "North Reportedly the Target of Libyan Assassination Plot," *Birmingham News,* 20 February 1989, p. 12a.

32. Superseding Indictment at 13–29, United States v. Hawamda et al. (CR–88–00168), U.S. District Court, Eastern District of Virginia, Alexandria Division.

33. Docket, United States v. Hawamda et al. (CR–88–00168), U.S. District Court, Eastern District of Virginia, Alexandria Division.

34. FBI Terrorist Research and Analytical Center, *Terrorism in the United States: 1989* (Washington, DC: U.S. Government Printing Office, 1990).

35. Peter Janke, *Guerrilla and Terrorist Organizations: A World Directory and Bibliography* (New York: Macmillan, 1983), pp. 255–263.

36. Janke, *Guerrilla and Terrorist Organizatons,* p. 258.

37. Indictment, United States v. Kabbani et al. (CR–87–78–1–2–3), U.S. District Court, District of Vermont.

38. Judgment in a Criminal Case, United States v. Kabbani et al. (CR–87–78–1–2–3), U.S. District Court, District of Vermont.

39. Claire Sterling, *The Terror Network: The Secret War of International Terrorism* (New York: Holt, Rinehart, Winston, Readers Digest Guide, 1981).

40. J. Bowyer Bell, *A Time of Terror* (New York: Basic Books, 1978), p. 81.

41. Christopher Dobson and Ronald Payne, *The Never-Ending War* (New York: Facts on File, 1987), pp. 223–224.

42. U.S. Department of State, *Terrorist Group Profiles* (Washington, DC: U.S. Government Printing Office, 1988), p. 119.

43. Ibid., p. 119.

44. Ibid., p. 119.

45. "Terrorist Gets Long Term," *Birmingham News,* 9 February 1989, p.10a.

46. David Ottaway, "U.S. Suspects that Gaddafi backs Resurgence of Terror," *Birmingham News,* 3 June 1988, p. 2a.

47. Indictment, United States v. Kikumura (CR–88–166), U.S. District Court, District of New Jersey.

48. "Terrorist Gets Long Term," *Birmingham News,* 9 February 1989, p. 10a.

49. FBI Terrorist Research and Analytical Center, *Terrorism in the United States: 1988* (Washington, DC: U.S. Government Printing Office, 1989), p. 9.

50. Steven Emerson, "Taking on Terrorists," *U.S. News & World Report,* 12 September 1988, pp. 26–34.

51. The Omnibus Diplomatic Security and Antiterrorism Act of 1986 created Chapter 113A (Extraterritorial Jurisdiction Over Terrorist Acts Abroad Against U.S. Nationals) as well as numerous other changes to 22 USC. It includes 18 USC 2331 (Terrorist Acts Abroad Against U.S. Nationals), which covers homicide, attempted homicide, and actions that cause injury to U.S. nationals.

52. Indictment at 4–5, United States v. Yunis (CR–87–0377), United States District Court, District of Columbia.

53. Steven Emerson, "Taking on Terrorists," p. 28.

54. "Making it Stick," *U.S. News & World Report*, 12 September 1988, p. 34.

55. Judgment in a Criminal Case, United States v. Yunis, (CR–87–0377), United States District Court, District of Columbia.

56. Jill Smowok "A Voice of Holy War," *Time*, 15 March 1993, pp. 31–34.

Chapter 8

Criminalizing Terrorism: Problems Without Easy Solutions

1. See Emile Durkheim's *Suicide* (New York: Free Press, 1951) and Karl Marx and Frederick Engel's *The German Ideology* (New York: International Publishers, 1970) as exemplars of these theorists' models.

2. Austin T. Turk, "Social Dynamics of Terrorism," in *The Annals of the American Academy of Political and Social Science*, Vol. 463, September 1982, ed. Marvin Wolfgang (Beverly Hills: Sage, 1982), pp. 119–128.

3. "Either directly and as a whole, or through the agency of one of its organs, society alone can play this moderating role; for it is the only moral power superior to the individual . . ." Emile Durkheim in *Suicide* (New York: Free Press, 1951), p. 249.

4. From the functionalist (consensus) perspective, Merton's (1938) "rebellion" adaptation is the classic application of revolution to a consensus model. Unfortunately, he fails to address this mode in any detail, probably because of the irony it poses regarding large-scale conflict in a consensus model.

5. Rubenstein's *Alchemists of Revolution* (New York: Basic Books, 1987) is probably the best Marxist rendering of terrorism. Unfortunately, since most left-wing terrorist groups espouse Marxism as their motivation for terror, using the same perspective to explain their actions seems highly tautological.

6. "The normal and the pathological," from *Rules of the Sociological Method* (New York: Macmillan, 1966), pp. 65–73.

7. Actually, rates of deviance that are too "low" are also perceived in the same way. Merton described the polar type he called ritualism as characterized by rates of deviance that are too low—a stagnant, non-changing, pathological social system.

8. Kai T. Erikson, *Wayward Puritans: A Study in the Sociology of Deviance* (New York: John Wiley & Sons, 1966), p. 13.

9. Ibid., p. 25.

10. Ibid., p. 187.

11. Richard Quinney, *Class, State, and Crime,* 2nd Ed. (New York: Longman, 1980), pp. 59–66.

12. Carl B. Klockars, "The Contemporary Crises of Marxist Criminology," *Criminology,* 1979, 16(4):477–515.

13. Austin T. Turk, "Analyzing Official Deviance: For Non-Partisan Conflict Analyses in Criminology," *Criminology,* 1979, 16(4):516–526.

14. Murray Edelman, *Politics as Symbolic Action* (Chicago: Markham, 1971), p. 3.

15. See, for example, Hubert M. Blalock's *Power and Conflict: Toward a General Theory* (Newbury Park, CA: Sage, 1989) and Kenneth Boulding's *Three Faces of Power* (Newbury Park, CA: Sage, 1989).

16. Austin T. Turk, *Political Criminality: The Defiance and Defense of Authority* (Newbury Park, CA: Sage, 1982).

17. Ibid., p. 66.

18. Ibid., p. 55.

19. Ibid., pp. 50–54.

20. The following discussion is derived from two previously published articles by the author: "Antiterrorism Legislation in the United States: Problems and Implications," in *Terrorism: An International Journal,* 1984, 7(2): 213–231; and "State Antiterrorism Legislation in the United States," in *Conflict Quarterly,* 1988, 8(1): 29–47.

21. Model Penal Code 211.3 (Proposed Official Draft, 1962).

22. See Brent L. Smith, "State Antiterrorism Legislation in the United States," *Conflict Quarterly,* 1988, 8(1): 29–47.

23. Jordan Paust, "Terrorism: A Definitional Focus," in *Terrorism: Interdisciplinary Perspectives,* ed. Yonah Alexander and Seymour M. Finger (New York: John Jay Press, 1977), pp. 18–29.

24. Grant Wardlaw, *Political Terrorism: Theory/Tactics and Counter-Measures* (New York: Cambridge University Press, 1982), p. 4.

25. California Penal Code 11.5.422/422.5 (1977).

26. People v. Mirmirani, 636–PZ–d (California, 1982).

27. Second Superseding Indictment at 7, United States v. Bruce Car

roll Pierce et al. (CR–85–001M), U.S. District Court, Western District of Washington, Seattle Division.

28. Judgment and Probation/Commitment Order, United States v. Eduardo Arocena [(S) CR–83–00821], U.S. District Court, Southern District of New York.

29. Minutes of the Court Reporter dated 7 April 1988, United States v. Robert E. Miles et al. (CR–87–20008), U.S. District Court, Western District of Arkansas, Fort Smith Division.

30. Judgment and Probation/Commitment Orders, United States v. Alejandrina Torres et al. (83–CR–0494), U.S. District Court, Northern District of Illinois, Eastern Division.

31. Howard Becker, *Outsiders: Studies in the Sociology of Deviance* (New York: Free Press, 1963).

32. See Tony Poveda's *Lawlessness and Reform: The FBI in Transition* (Pacific Grove, CA: Brooks/Cole, 1990) for an excellent discussion of these issues.

33. Kevin Cullen, "Search for 'Cop-Killers' Comes to an End," *Boston Globe,* 5 November 1984, p. 4.

34. Author's Field Notes, telephone interview with assistant U.S. attorney (name and office withheld by request), 15 December 1990.

35. Indictment, United States v. Miles et al. (CR–87–20008), U.S. District Court, Western District of Arkansas, Fort Smith Division.

36. Indictment, United States v. Raymond Luc Levasseur et al. (CR–86–180), U.S. District Court, District of Massachusetts.

37. Indictment, United States v. Whitehorn et al. (CR–88–0145), U.S. District Court, District of Columbia.

38. Author's Field Notes, telephone interview with assistant U.S. attorney (name and office withheld by request), 10 May 1991.

Chapter 9

Punishing Terrorists

1. United States v. Raymond Luc Levasseur (CR–86–180), U.S. District Court, District of Massachusetts; United States v. Coltrane Chimurenga et al. (84–CR–000818), U.S. District Court, Southern District of New York; United States v. Laura Whitehorn et al. (CR–88–0145), U.S. District Court, District of Columbia.

2. United States v. Wilhelm Schmitt et al. (CR–6–84–124 and 125), U.S. District Court, District of Minnesota, Sixth Division.

3. This particular federal form has been changed to: Judgment in a Criminal Case.

4. United States Sentencing Commission, *United States Sentencing Commission: Annual Report, 1990,* (Washington, DC: U.S. Government Printing Office, 1991).

5. Minutes of the Court Reporter dated 7 April 1988, United States v. Robert E. Miles et al. (CR–87–20008), U.S. District Court, Western District of Arkansas, Fort Smith Division.

6. United States v. Raymond Luc Levasseur (CR–86–180), U.S. District Court, District of Massachusetts.

7. See, for example, Superceding Indictment, United States v. Murray et al. (CR–86–118–T), United States District Court, District of Massachusetts.

8. Judgment in a Criminal Case, United States v. Hawamda et al. (CR–88–00168), United States District Court, Eastern District of Virginia, Alexandria Division.

9. See, for example, Superceding Indictment, United States v. Arocena [(S) 83–CR–821], U.S. District Court, Southern District of New York.

10. Judgment in a Criminal Case, United States v. Kikumura (CR–88–166), U.S. District Court, District of New Jersey.

11. Judgment in a Criminal Case, United States v. Yunis (CR–87–0377), U.S. District Court, District of Columbia.

12. United States Sentencing Commission, *United States Sentencing Commission: Annual Report, 1990,* (Washington, DC: U.S. Government Printing Office, 1991).

13. The "leader" category includes first and second echelon leaders and supervisors. It does not necessarily include those with special skills (e.g., bomb making, document falsification, etc.) unless those persons were in leadership roles within the group.

14. Judgment and Probation/Commitment Order, United States v. Mark Frank Jones (CR–85–HM–80–S), United States District Court, Northern District of Alabama.

15. Thomas Martinez, *Brotherhood of Murder,* (New York: McGraw-Hill, 1988).

16. Response of United States of America to James D. Ellison's Motion for Reduction of Sentence, United States v. James D. Ellison (CR–85–

20006 and CR–85–20017), U.S. District Court, Western District of Arkansas.

17. United States v. Coltrane Chimurenga et al. (SSS 84–CR–000818), U.S. District Court, Southern District of New York.

18. United States Sentencing Commission, *United States Sentencing Commission: Annual Report, 1990* (Washington, DC: U.S. Government Printing Office, 1991), p. 9. Much of the discussion in this section is derived from Chapter Three: "Legal Issues" of this document.

19. Ibid., p. 10.

20. For a list of cases affirming this standard see Note 7, United States Sentencing Commission, *United States Sentencing Commission: Annual Report, 1990* (Washington, DC: U.S. Government Printing Office, 1991), p. 10.

21. See, e.g., McMillan v. Pennsylvania, 477 U.S. 79 (1986); United States v. Romano, 825 F.2d 715 (2d Cir. 1987); United States v. Garcia, 698 F.2nd 31 (1st Cir. 1983).

22. United States v. McCaleb, 908 F.2d 176 (7th Cir. 1990).

23. United States v. White, 903 F.2d 457 (7th Cir. 1990).

24. United States v. Barbontin, 907 F.2d 1494 (5th Cir. 1990).

25. United States Sentencing Commission, *United States Sentencing Commission: Annual Report, 1990,* (Washington, DC: U.S. Government Printing Office, 1991). p. 13.

26. Government's Response to Defendant Oliphant's Objection to Pre-Sentence Report at 2, United States v. Jack Maxwell Oliphant (CR–86–336–PCT), U.S. District Court, District of Arizona.

27. For example, the federal judge in the trial of Harry Mott, associated with Sheriff's Posse Comitatus, directed the prosecution to refrain from "making any statements, directly or indirectly, relating to tax protestation or the tax protest movement, the Posse Comitatus, Gordon Kahl, the Patriot Movement," except as is permissible. Government Response to Defendant Mott's Motions at 3, United States v. Wilhelm Schmitt and Harry Mott (CR–6–84–125), U.S. District Court, District of Minnesota, Third Division.

28. Defendant Linda Evans' Memorandum in Aid of Sentencing at 9–11, United State v. Laura Whitehorn et al. (CR–88–145), U.S. District Court, District of Columbia.

29. Referred to as "A.O. Codes." For further discussion of the codes, see United States District Courts: Sentences Imposed Chart, Twenty-Four Month Period Ended June 30, 1986 (Washington, DC: Administrative Office of the U.S. Courts, 1987).

30. Consequently, the comparisons control the effects of title, section, subsection, and A.O. (offense) codes by comparing the sentences of defendants matching all of these variables.

31. Split sentences, in which the defendant receives a prison term of normally six months or less plus a specified period of probation, were excluded from analysis.

32. Defendant Linda Evans' Memorandum in Aid of Sentencing at 13, United States v. Laura Whitehorn et al. (CR–88–145), U.S. District Court, District of Columbia.

33. Marvin Wolfgang et al., *The National Survey of Crime Severity* (Washington, DC: U.S. Government Printing Office).

34. See United States Sentencing Commission, *United States Sentencing Commission: Annual Report, 1990* (Washington, DC: U.S. Government Printing Office, 1991).

35. Ibid., pp. 10–13.

36. Ibid., p. 13.

Chapter 10

Dream On: Facts and Fantasies about American Terrorism

1. See, for example, Marvin Wolfgang, Robert Figlio, and Thorsten Sellin, *Delinquency in a Birth Cohort* (Chicago: University of Chicago Press, 1982).

2. "Making it Stick," *U.S. News & World Report,* 12 September 1988, p. 34.

3. Prosecutions of FALN members in Chicago and New York during the late 1970s and early 1980s are an exception to this general finding.

4. See Tony Poveda's discussion of the "adequacy of terrorism resources," pp. 129–132 in *Lawlessness and Reform: The FBI in Transition* (Pacific Grove, CA: Brooks/Cole, 1990).

5. See Chapter 8, table 1, first and last columns.

6. See, for example, the federal judge's ruling in United States v. Laura Whitehorn et al. (CR–88–145), U.S. District Court, District of Columbia.

7. Richard Lacayo, "Tower Terror," *Time,* 8 March 1993, pp. 25–35.

8. Ed Schafer, "FBI arrests alleged terrorists in Midwest," *The Birmingham News,* 2 April 1993, p. 5A.

9. *New York Times,* 11 October 1991 (sec. A, p. 1, col. 2).

10. Jonathan Sidener, "Earth First! Divided by Second Thoughts," *The Arizona Republic,* 26 August 1990, p. A-1.

11. Sam Negri, "Earth First! Co-founder Quits," *The Arizona Republic,* 15 August 1990, p. B-1.

12. Jonathan Sidener, "Earth First! Divided by Second Thoughts," *The Arizona Republic,* 26 August 1990, p. A-4.

Name Index

245

Subject Index